HANDBOOK OF HATCHES

Introductory Guide to the Foods Trout Eat and the Most Effective Flies to Match Them

SECOND EDITION

Dave Hughes

STACKPOLE BOOKS

0 11557 03182 9

Published by
STACKPOLE BOOKS
5067 Ritter Road
Mechanicsburg, PA 17055
www.stackpolebooks.com

Printed in China

10 9 8 7 6 5 4 3 2

*Photographs, including cover photograph, by Dave Hughes except for the
hellgrammite on page 267 by Ted Fauceglia
Cover design by Caroline Stover*

Library of Congress Cataloging-in-Publication Data
Hughes, Dave, 1945-
    Handbook of hatches: a basic guide to recognizing trout foods and
selecting flies to match them / Dave Hughes.—2nd ed.
        p. cm.
    Includes bibliographical references and index.
    ISBN 0-8117-3182-0 (alk. paper)
    1. Flies, Artificial. 2. Aquatic insects. 3. Trout—Food. 4. Fishes—Food.
I. Title.
SH451.H779 2004
688.7'9124—dc22
                                                                    2004007298

    ISBN 978-0-8117-3182-9

To Rick Hafele,
who introduced me to the world of aquatic insects,
and with whom I still share it.

Contents

Introduction

I got conned on the Yellowstone River.

Richard Bunse and I arrived at the river on a September midafternoon, in the wake of an early storm. The sun glanced brightly off deep new snow. The air nipped at us painfully. But the sun struck down and warmed the slow currents where the broad river ambled over shallow beds of rooted weeds. We sat in the pickup for a minute, looking down over the flats. Then a fish swirled on the surface, and a few seconds later another came up. Bunse cried, "Those are rises!" Then he bolted.

He had his waders on and rod built and was twenty feet out, stalking a pod of working fish, before I could decide how many pairs of socks to pull on.

"There's a hatch," Bunse yelled up to me while I sat on the tailgate, agonizing into cold waders. He scooped an insect out of the water and looked at it.

"What is it?" I called down to him.

"Don't know. Some sort of mayfly dun. A size sixteen with an olive body and gray wings. See if you can figure out what it is." He tied on a fly and started false-casting.

"Oh . . . okay," I said foolishly, and picked up my insect-collecting net instead of my fly rod. I thrashed through the snow to the river, waded in, and began netting mayfly duns while Bunse cast and caught a trout.

"What did you catch it on?" I asked.

"A size sixteen Blue-Winged Olive," he answered. Then he asked, "What's that insect?"

"I'll have to check it out," I said. I struggled up through the snowbank to the pickup, holding a couple of the mayflies captive in my net. I found the right book and paged through it until I found what I took to be the right insect. I compared its picture with what I held in my hand. They looked reasonably alike. I closed the book and walked back down to the river's edge. It had only taken about half an hour, my literary search sped by continual shouts and splashes as Bunse hooked, landed, and released two more fine trout.

I said to Bunse, "I think it's a *Paraleptophlebia.*"

"A what?" he asked, a bit astonished.

"*Paraleptophlebia.* I don't know what species. Now can I borrow one of those Blue-Winged Olives?"

"Sure."

I waded out to him, this time carrying my fly rod rather than my insect net. He gave me a fly. I looked at it. "Remarkably like the real thing," I mumbled. I waded away and looked around for a rise to cast to. But there weren't any. Either the fish had quit working or Bunse had caught them all.

We reeled up, waded out, and drove away. Bunse had taken three fish, the largest eighteen inches long. I had taken two mayflies, size 16.

I found out a long time later, looking at them under a microscope at home, that they were *Ephemerella.*

It finally became clear to me, after years of diligently studying and matching hatches, that *matching the hatch* always came first, out on the stream or lake, whereas *identifying the insect* always came later, at home, long after the fishing was finished. The success of my fishing was always based on what I observed in the field, and what I did about it right then, while fish rose all around me.

The study of insects is a pleasant adjunct to fishing. You can take it to any level you want. The further you take it, the more you will know about the aquatic world in which trout live and swim and eat. Every added increment of knowledge about that world will give you one more thing to enjoy when you are out fishing. And the more you know, the more trout you will catch, in the long run.

This book is about the study of insects at the simplest level—out in their own world, the world where trout make a living eating them. It is about recognizing that an insect is a mayfly dun, size 16, with an olive body and gray wings. It is about matching that dun with a size 16 Blue-Winged Olive dressing and presenting it the way the natural insect arrives to trout, thereby enticing trout to take it. This book is about reducing the process of matching hatches to its most important elements. It is about letting somebody else worry whether an insect is a *Paraleptophlebia* or an *Ephemerella*.

Our continent is large and has a great diversity of geographies and water types. Our aquatic insects have adapted to this wide range of conditions by evolving into a wide range of species. Professional taxonomists, with doctoral degrees and high-power microscopes, haven't yet penetrated all of their mysteries, nor have they classified and named all of the species. New species are constantly discovered: Old species are constantly reclassified into new genera and subgenera and given new names. Not only is this confusing to the lay angler, but it also abruptly outdates any angling book that identifies all trout foods by species.

Everything you need to know about an insect in order to match it, and to fish its imitation with the proper presentation, you can learn by holding the insect in your hand and observing it closely. A labyrinth of things remains to be learned beyond what you will discover by taking a close look at the natural, but the few things you need to know to catch trout make a good place to start, and they might be as far as you ever want to go.

I hope this book helps you understand the aquatic insects, the fly patterns that match them, and the fish that eat them. I hope it helps you catch more and larger trout.

I insist that it help you have more fun doing it.

Axioms

- It is the first axiom of this book that *within each of the three major orders, adults of all species have the same shape.* They vary in size and color but are true to the shape of the rest of the order (page 4).
- This leads to the second axiom of this book, that *within each important order of aquatic insects, all species can be matched with size and color variations of the same pattern style* (page 8).
- It is the third axiom of this book that *endless study of someone else's work will never tell you what insect hatches are important on your own home waters* (page 27).
- It is a minor axiom of this book that *you choose your pattern style based in part on the type of water on or in which the pattern will be fished* (page 8).
- It is another minor axiom of this book that *if something resembles something else so closely that anglers and trout mistake it for whatever else it looks like, then a pattern that imitates the something else will work fine, and there's no need to create and carry a new one* (page 220).
- A valuable rule for any extended fishing trip is to *see the whole day.* Be on the water from daylight to dark, watching the water, on the first or second day of any trip. After that you'll know the best times to be on the water and the safe times to take your leisure (page 71).
- An important stillwater rule and small-moving-water rule is to *suspect midge pupae whenever trout are rising but you can't see what they're taking.* It's likely to be midges in this almost invisible transitional stage (page 190).

- Most often on stillwaters, the slower the retrieve, the faster the fishing (page 201).
- Anything you can learn about trout will increase your ability to catch them, whether that information is applied immediately, in the form of an imitation tied to your tippet at once, or becomes a part of your body of knowledge about trout and the world in which they live and is applied over time (page 190).

Chapter 1

Trout Don't Speak Latin

Trout eat aquatic insects. They eat other things, too. They eat grass-hoppers and scuds, snails and leeches, and sometimes even each other. But all trout get going in life eating aquatic insects. And most trout, including lunkers that make a lot of their living pursuing big-ger bites, end their lives still eating aquatic insects.

Trout don't speak Latin. They can't identify insects. The most brilliant trout in the stream will spend its entire life gobbling may-flies, caddisflies, and stoneflies in all of their immature and adult stages, without ever pausing to consider what it has just eaten. Trout can be alarmingly selective, however, despite all of their ignorance.

Trout eat insects without identifying them. But they know ex-actly what the insects look like, and exactly how the insects move on or in the water. You can match insects with dressings that will take trout, even highly selective trout, without identifying the in-sects that your dressings imitate. To do that consistently, though, you, like the trout, must know what the insects look like, and how they move on or in the water.

It will help you to be able to recognize insects on the elemental level of *order:* the mayflies, caddisflies, stoneflies, and a few other types of flies. But you do not need to know Latin and taxonomy to do it. Even identification to that level is not entirely necessary. You don't need to separate the aquatic orders to successfully match the insects they contain. It will help, though, and it's not hard.

Let me confess that I know lots about Latin. I find aquatic in-sects to be fascinating beasts. I collect them in nets. I drop them tumbling into tiny aquariums to watch the way they swim. I astonish them by firing flashes to illuminate them for photographs.

Sometimes I pickle aquatic insects in vials of alcohol and key them out as far as I can, or I send them off to a professional taxonomist for exact identification. The insects come back labeled through all the levels: order, family, genus, and species. But all this labor of Latin doesn't always translate into more trout caught. Without an accompanying approach based on observation along the stream, peering at insects through a microscope doesn't help me catch any more trout. Sometimes I get tangled up in matters that don't really make much difference to the trout.

I sat one summer noon on a sagebrush bank above Oregon's Deschutes River, baking in the heat. I was wadered and brogued in my embarrassing best. I wore or carried or was bound up in every item that has ever been declared essential to an angler's success. Had you stumbled upon me, you would have cried, "Now here is a man who looks like he knows what he is doing!" You would not have been entirely right.

A brief hatch had happened that morning. I'd captured a few specimens and tweezered them into a vial of alcohol. They were from a net-spinning family of caddis, size 14, with tannish brown bodies and the same color wings. They were *Hydropsyche*. I didn't know the exact species, but I arrived at a fly and got it close enough to catch a couple of fat trout. The largest was fourteen inches long.

I had released the two fish, then sat down happily in the shade of some sage and busied myself studying the poor pickled insects. I roughed a sketch of them in a notebook and wrote a few observations on their size and color for the preparation of some future exact imitation. Then I leaned back on my elbows, satisfied with what I had accomplished. I would get the insects identified to species later.

I looked downriver and saw an angler working slowly upstream toward me, fishing from the bank. He wriggled into a small indentation in the shoreline brush, where I could no longer see him. His rod tip flicked in the sun above the brush, then stilled. Suddenly it danced, and I knew he'd hooked a fish. The rod tip disappeared, and I knew he'd bent to release his fish.

The fisherman reappeared. I saw now that he wore hiking boots and light pants that looked comfortable in the hot sun. So did his khaki shirt and baseball cap. He wore no vest, carried no creel. Had you stumbled upon him, you might have cried, "Now here is a throwback who looks like he has no idea what he is doing!" You would have been entirely wrong.

He edged into another indentation, closer to me this time. He flicked his rod a few times, then settled his dry fly to the water inches from an overhanging clump of bunchgrass. I didn't see the swirl, but I saw his rod tip bounce. Soon he kneeled to release another trout. He dried his fly and cast it beneath an overhanging alder branch. He hooked and landed another fish. I saw this one as he lowered it back into the water. It was at least sixteen inches long, perhaps longer.

He had already caught and released more and larger trout in the few minutes I'd watched him than I had taken all morning. He caught one more fish before he reeled in. Then he looked up and saw me hiding beneath the sage.

"Hi," he said.

"Hi," I said back.

"Doing any good?" he asked politely.

"Did real fine this morning," I lied.

"Lots of caddis out, aren't there?" he said.

I sat up. "There sure are. Have you identified them yet?" I thought he might know what species they were.

"Yes," he answered. He shook a sage stem that hung out over the water. A cloud of caddis flew out. He swiped a few out of the air in his useful hat, looked at them, and said, "They're a size fourteen tan caddis."

"Oh," I said, disappointed. I had hoped I might be able to learn something from him.

"What fly you using to match those caddis?" I asked him.

He shook the insects out of his hat and put his hat back on his head. "A size fourteen Tan Caddis," he told me.

That made sense, even to a guy cooking in the finery of waders and brogues. I stood up. "Can I see it?" I asked.

"Sure." He walked up to where I stood. He pulled a fly box out of a shirt pocket. It was the only box he carried. He opened it under my nose. "Here, have a couple," he said. He speared two size 14 Tan Caddis out of the box and handed them to me. I took them as greedily as had the trout.

"Nice dressings," I said. It was not a lie. They were nicely tied, with tapered tan fur bodies and brisk ginger hackles wound under flared tan elk-hair wings. I peered into the fly box before he closed it. All it contained was size and color variations of the same simple Elk Hair Caddis dressing.

He flipped the box shut and tucked it back into his shirt pocket. "I'd like to stay and talk," he said, "but the fishing's too good to waste."

"Right!" I said. I glanced back at the place where I'd been idling in the sage. "Far too good."

He started off upstream.

"Thanks for the flies," I called after him.

"You're welcome," he called back.

After half an hour to let the fish settle, I started casting along in his wake, using his Tan Caddis and catching an occasional trout.

NATURALS

The fly box that fellow carried had its limits, but it also had its lesson. The flies in the box matched only one stage of one aquatic insect order, the adult caddis. But they matched it simply and well. On the Deschutes, like most trout rivers, caddis hatches are predominant through the midsummer months. The man must have known that, or he would not have carried just one fly box full of variations of one pattern style.

The Deschutes, again like most rivers, is home to dozens of different caddis species. On the one day you can get out to go fishing, it's not easy to know which species will interest trout. Sometimes the river will toss up two or three species at the same time. Sometimes trout will take any caddis dressing you toss at them. Other times they won't. If they see only one kind of caddis, it's likely they will accept a dressing that is at least a fair match for it and refuse anything that is not.

With the flies in his box, the fellow on the Deschutes could have matched nearly any caddis adult, anywhere on this or any other continent, closely enough to catch his share of trout—and my share, too. Why? Because all caddisfly adults, everywhere, come in a variety of sizes and colors, but all are shaped the same.

Three major orders of aquatic insects are of primary importance to trout fishermen: mayflies, caddisflies, and stoneflies. It is the first axiom of this book that *within each of the three major orders, adults of all species have the same shape.* They vary in size and color but are true to the shape of the rest of the order.

All mayfly duns have the same mayfly shape. They have been described, to the weary point of platitude, as tiny sailboats. Novelist Thornton Wilder once wrote that if we shrink from platitudes, platitudes will shrink from us. Let's be bold enough to be precise and say that mayflies look like little spinnaker-rigged sailboats, because that's exactly what they do.

All mayfly duns share the same sailboat shape, with long tails, slender and tapered bodies, and wings held upright over their bodies.

All caddisfly adults have the same caddisfly shape. In contrast to mayflies, caddis hold their wings propped over their backs, folded like tiny tents. Their bodies are short, bulbous, and lie tucked under the wings. A caddis at rest looks a lot like a person in a mummy bag asleep under a low-pitched, slope-roofed pup tent. Once I thought I heard one snore.

All stonefly adults have the same stonefly shape. They fold their wings flat over their backs. They don't look at all like a mayfly or a caddis, neither to you nor to a trout. With the exception of the needle fly, which has rolled wings, stonefly wings are nearly so level that you could set up and have a picnic party on them, if you and your friends were small enough.

Caddis adults all have roughly the same shape, with wings held tentlike over their bodies.

A trout, looking from beneath the water at a mayfly, caddisfly, and stonefly, would behold three distinctly different images. But every species within each order would show it the same image, though again in distinctly different sizes and colors.

This first axiom holds true for the other orders of aquatic insects as well, though with slight degrees of variation. These are sometimes called the *minor* orders of aquatics. This is true when you consider that as food, they are not important as often as any of the big three. But when fish feed critically on a midge or damselfly, that minor insect is suddenly the most important insect around. It is best to know how to recognize, and how to match, the important stages of each of the aquatic insect orders. When you look at the minor orders, you see that all species stay reasonably true to the shape of the order they are in, true enough that variations of one or two pattern styles will match all species within the order.

Each major insect order has hundreds of species. Some of the minor orders, such as the true flies, which include the midges, have thousands. To look at them singly would be nightmarish. Professional taxonomists don't know them all. An educated entomologist might specialize in a single family, study it for a lifetime, and still not know all the species within that family. An angler sets himself

Stonefly adults, with rare exceptions, have wings that are flat and held back over their bodies when they're at rest.

an impossible task if he desires to identify to species all aquatic insects that trout eat.

In contrast, if aquatic insects are looked at as variations on a few simple themes, then what you know about them, and the flies you carry to match them, can be transferred from coast to coast, and even continent to continent. A mayfly in Maine has the same shape as a mayfly in California. A caddis from a North Carolina mountain stream sleeps as peacefully under its pup-tent wings as a caddis from a British Columbia lake.

Studied on a species-by-species basis, knowledge of the insects is useful for a few blue-blooded hatches on a few blue-ribbon streams for a few blue-sky days. But every lake, pond, river, and stream has its own important hatches. All are different from each other. Most are different from the few famous hatches on famous waters. All are frustrating if trout are selective and you don't carry flies the fish will accept.

If you concern yourself with the shapes of the aquatic insects, rather than their Latin names, you will be able to match them wherever you find them. They are shaped the same in the stream that runs through your home county as their relatives in the clear-water streams of New Zealand's South Island.

IMITATIONS

Insects evolved into certain shapes. Fly patterns evolved into certain styles. Imagine a mayfly dun, our little sailboat. Now place next to it the image of a traditional dry fly. It could be an Adams, Light Cahill, or Quill Gordon. It doesn't matter; they are all shaped the same. And all are shaped a lot like the mayfly dun. The traditional dry fly has long tails, a slender body, and upright wings. It has a collar of hackle that serves to float the fly but also represents the legs of the natural insect. This traditional dry-fly style, when varied in size and color, will imitate any mayfly dun.

This leads to the second axiom of this book, that *within each important order of aquatic insects, all species can be matched with size and color variations of the same pattern style.*

Choosing a pattern style and then selecting size and color variations works for all of the aquatic orders, not just the mayflies. It works for caddisflies, for stoneflies, and just as well for all the other flies.

Another factor, aside from shape, might make it advantageous to consider more than one fly style for certain stages of certain of the insect orders. It is a minor axiom of this book that *you choose your pattern style based in part on the type of water on or in which the pattern will be fished.* Let's look once more at our favorite mayfly dun.

Some mayflies hatch in the tossed water of riffles. Other mayflies emerge on gliding spring-creek currents. A dry fly tied in the traditional style rides high on its hackles and bounces along the surface of a riffle. It is designed to give trout the idea that the deception dancing on the surface has the tails, body, wings, and legs of a mayfly dun, and therefore must be one. It is an *impressionistic* style.

The same style fly cast onto a glassy surface might stand too stiffly on the tiptoes of its hackles, might conceal too much the outline of its body and the shape of its wings. It might not raise the same trout that would take it eagerly in rougher water. When you fish smooth water, it is often necessary to consider a pattern style that offers a more exact silhouette of the natural insect.

Exact imitations reflect the specific body parts of a particular hatching insect and have nothing in the way to obscure their silhouette from trout. A Compara-dun dry fly has split tails, a tapered body, a fan of deer hair for the wing, and no hackles. Its body and

When your imitation must float on a riffle, such as this one on the Elk River in British Columbia, then the added flotation of a traditional hackled tie will help you hook trout. If you were to find your fish feeding selectively in the smoother water, to the inside of the riffle, you might find it beneficial to cast a more imitative dressing.

The traditional Catskill dry-fly style, with its hackle tail and collar, floats well and is an excellent mayfly imitation on water that is at least slightly rough.

The imitative Compara-dun style has nothing to hinder the silhouette of the body and wing, in the view of the trout from below, and is excellent for matching mayfly hatches on smooth currents.

When you must fool trout feeding selectively on water as smooth as many stretches of the Bighorn River in Montana, you need imitative flies such as the Compara-dun when trout are taking mayflies.

wing sit right down on the water, showing trout the unobstructed shape of a natural mayfly rather than an obscured impression of it. It's an *imitative* style.

Finding the proper balance between the impressionistic and imitative approaches depends to a degree on the demands of the water type you're fishing. It also depends on your tying ability. Some imitative styles can be complicated and hard to tie, especially those in the category called *realistic* imitations. I avoid these difficult flies myself, and not just because they're hard to tie. Many of them look real in the vise but look like nothing in nature when they're wet and on water. Few situations call for them. On fast water, an imitative dry that won't float will not catch as many trout as an impressionistic dry that rides up where you and the fish can both see it. On slow water, a fly that captures the essence of an insect, and leaves out its details, makes for an excellent imitation, so long as you show the proper silhouette of the insect to the trout.

It is a good general rule to fish imitative patterns only when the trout and the water type demand it. The chapters on specific orders offer a predominance of impressionistic styles. Imitative styles are added if the habitat of the natural, and the consequent selectivity of the trout, warrant a different level of imitation.

Once you've chosen your pattern style for an insect order, based on the shape of the insect and the water type where you'll fish it, you need only tie or buy size and color variations to match the hatches that you find wherever you fish.

I suggest arranging your flies, at least at first, by reserving one box for each of the major orders and another for the minor orders. Each box will be easier to organize, and you will know exactly which one to reach for when you need it.

Chapter 2

Aspects of Insects

Five aspects of aquatic insects are of absolute importance to anyone tying and fishing flies to imitate them with the hope of fooling trout. These aspects are *size, shape, color, behavior,* and *habitat,* and they are the keys to this book. Each is a critical variable in the formula that tells you how to tie your fly and fish it successfully.

The *size* of the natural insect dictates the size of the fly you tie to match it. The *shape* of the insect dictates the style of the fly you tie. The *color* of the insect leads to the correct selection of materials with which to tie your fly. These three factors—size, shape, and color—are those on which your fly pattern selection should always be based, whether you tie your own flies or buy them tied by professionals.

People often ask me which of the three I consider most important—size, shape, or color. I always answer *behavior.* Why? Because the most exact match ever devised for an insect, if presented in a way that makes it look unnatural to a trout, is more likely to frighten the fish than to catch it.

The *habitat* of the natural tells you where you should fish your fly. You don't want to present an imitation of a lake-dwelling caddisfly larva in the swiftness of a riffle. You can leave your stonefly box home when fishing your favorite hidden pond, because stoneflies, with exceptions not interesting to the angler, live only in flowing water.

Insect size, shape, color, behavior, and habitat are the key elements in matching any hatch. All five aspects of aquatic insects can be observed by the angler right out on the stream or lake.

SIZE

Great size variations exist among species in most of the aquatic orders. Mayflies run from tiny size 24s to great size 4s. Stoneflies vary in size from 16s to 2s. Caddisflies can be too small to imitate all the way up to a fluttering size 4.

The importance of size is relative to the abundance of a specific insect. If so many of a single species are present that it becomes most or all of what fish are feeding on, then they're selective, and your fly should be the correct size or very close to it. If trout are feeding on a variety of insects, they *likely* will take your fly if it's a size or two away from whatever you are matching.

That's a weak likely. It depends on other factors, such as angler pressure, clarity of the water, speed of the current, and roughness or smoothness of the surface. These are the same factors that force you away from an impressionistic style toward an imitative dressing and, not coincidentally, to tying on a longer and finer tippet as well. This should lead you to the correct conclusion that the more selective the trout, the more critical size selection becomes.

The size of the fly is determined by the size of the hook on which it is tied. In fact, the size of an insect is usually defined by anglers not in terms of the length of its body, but in terms of the hook size of the pattern that matches it. I'd like to indulge in a bit of entomological heresy here and declare that it's all right to answer, "It's a number sixteen!" when your fishing partner calls out to you, "What size is that little dun, anyway?"

I defend this with a confession. If I am the fishing partner calling out the request for an insect's size, and you shout back, "Seven millimeters!" I won't really know what size you're trying to tell me that insect is. I'm not a trained scientist, and I don't think in metrics.

Hook size is an adequate way to describe insect size. Keep things simple, but be accurate. Learning to select hook size by observing insect size takes a bit of practice. I know few fishermen who don't start by glancing at a critter and choosing a fly at least a size larger. It's an instinct, but it's worth resisting. A fly that is too large is a lot less likely to catch trout than one that is too small.

To get the right size, and at the same time learn more about the insect you are matching, capture a natural and toss it into your fly box. Let it wander about in there among what it probably does not mistake for its friends. As it clambers among the size 12s, 14s, and 16s, you will quickly discover which size is closest to it. A few sessions of this exercise will greatly increase your ability to judge insect size.

One last note about size: The smaller the insect, the larger the proportion of error if you misjudge it by one hook size. That leads to a conclusion that should surprise nobody: The smaller the insect, the more closely and more carefully you should look at it.

In each order of insects, there is a wide range of sizes, but a few sizes are the most common. This allows you to carry a small range of dressings, in the most suitable sizes, that will catch fish almost anywhere, almost always. Remember the fellow on the Deschutes with his simple caddisfly dressing tied in a few color and size variations? He had almost all the major caddis covered.

SHAPE

The shape of a natural insect dictates the pattern style that will best match it. Nearly enough has been said about shape, and its relationship to styles of flies, to propel this book into its chapters on the specific groups. But a few repetitions and new notes will help hammer home some points.

Shape varies little within each order, but it varies greatly among the orders. That is what sets them apart, what makes them distinct from each other, what allows you to recognize them easily at the level that will be most useful to you.

This consistency of shape is especially true for the adult stages of the aquatic insect orders. It does not hold as true as we would like for the immature stages. Mayfly nymphs divide into four groups— swimmers, crawlers, clingers, and burrowers—based on their behavior. Each group has evolved into a different shape. Within each group, the various species have retained a similar shape. Stonefly nymphs come in slight variations of a single shape. Caddisfly larvae differ dramatically by being either cased or free-living, and your flies need to account for that difference. Dragonfly and damselfly nymphs are in the same order, but they differ substantially in form.

But all dragonfly nymphs are approximately alike, and all damselfly nymphs are also about alike.

The importance of exact imitation of the shape of an insect depends, as it does with size, on the numbers of the insect present and available to trout, the amount of angling pressure, and the water type in which the insect lives, all of which interpret into selectivity of trout. Because of such variables, a single insect shape can lead to the need to carry a couple of pattern styles to be fished in different water types or angling situations.

There is, in the fly-tying world, a peaceful quarrel between those who favor exact imitations tied with shaped materials and those who prefer impressionistic patterns tied with lively materials. Imitative patterns are sometimes dressed with monofilament bodies and plastic peripheral parts, usually by tiers whose hobby is fly tying rather than fly fishing. Impressionistic dressings usually have fur bodies and natural fibers for their appended parts.

Plastic patterns look very much like the real thing when held in your hand. Some of them look as if they are about to stroll over and ask a natural for a date. But if they lack materials that move in the water, they are unlikely to look like the real kicking and struggling thing when presented to trout. If you are ever in doubt, select a pattern with lots of life over an exact but lifeless imitation.

Always consider the impression your fly makes on the fish. With a dry fly, the dimples made in the surface film can be just as important as the exact size and color of the tails, body, wings, and legs. With a nymph, the movement of body furs in the current, and the vibrancy of tail and leg fibers, are more important than rigid parts that look good until the fly hits water.

Some fly patterns can be excellent imitations even though they look very little like the real thing. On a favorite local lake, I once worked out midge dressings that looked exactly like a hatch I attempted to match. All of my refinements were wasted. They caught no more trout than the rough patching together of feathers and fur I had cobbled up when I first started trying to match the small insects.

Then I tried a size 18 Griffith's Gnat. It's a little puff of grizzly hackle wound the full length of a peacock herl body. Sitting still, it looks about as much like a midge as I look like an Oldsmobile. But

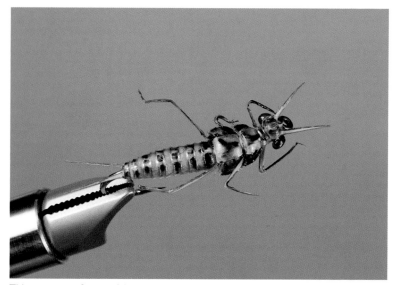

This gorgeous Golden Stonefly Nymph, tied by Chuck Rondeau of Port Angeles, Washington, could be keyed to species by an entomologist.

on the water, it worked. Apparently it gives the impression of a midge struggling in the surface film, trying to escape the skin of its pupal stage. Trout seem to take it eagerly wherever they feed on midges. Trout do not always see things the same way we do.

Pick your pattern style based on the shape of the insect, then vary the size and color to match precisely what's hatching. But also consider the impression the imitation makes on the surface film if it's a dry fly, or the movement of the imitation in the water if it's a wet fly or nymph.

COLOR

A trout might not accept or reject a fly based on the perfection or imperfection of its colors. Then again, a trout might. It depends on selectivity, which in its turn depends on fishing pressure, water type, and abundance of a specific natural. You are never going to hurt your chance to catch a trout by getting the colors of your imitation as close as you can to those of the natural. In many selective situations, the color has to be extremely close in order to interest trout at all.

This rough and ready Golden Montana Stone will be at least as effective as a more exact imitation, and quite often more effective, when golden stonefly nymphs are dominant in the mix of groceries on which trout are feeding.

Colors are deceptive at long range. I spent several seasons during the early instars of my fly-fishing career trying to match a particular mayfly. Everybody told me it was a blue dun. I believed them without ever thinking to observe the insect myself. It looked enough like one at five feet, as I glanced at it while galloping youthfully by on my way to the next pool. But during this blue dun hatch, a Blue Dun dry fly never caught more than a scant few trout.

One day I slowed down long enough to capture one of the duns and look at it closely. My life—my fly-fishing life—has never been the same since. The insect was not blue, or even gray. The closer I looked at it, the darker it got. It was brown on the back. When I flipped it over, it was tannish olive on its underside. That's what the trout saw. That's what I imitated the next time out. It was the first hatch I felt I'd solved. My fishing success increased whenever that insect was around, which was often, and it increased because I'd taken time to look at the natural up close, the way a trout would look at it just before it ate it.

What if there is no hatch, you want to fish a nymph, and you have no specimen on which to base your color selection? A traditional notion is that you should choose your nymph pattern based on the bottom color of the lake or stream you're fishing. It sounds silly, doesn't it? But immature aquatic insects are camouflaged. They reflect the colors of the vegetation or bottom rocks on which they rest, or trout snoop them out and eat them, reducing their success at passing on any progeny. If you have no other clue, follow that old refrain and choose your nymph color based on the color of the habitat over which you intend to fish it.

John Atherton, the artist who wrote *The Fly and the Fish* in 1951, theorized that a trout rejects a fly not because it sees the *wrong* color in the fly, but because it *does not* see the *right* color in the fly. This led him to the conclusion that it's better to mix two or three colors of dubbing to get the correct color than it is to use a single dyed dubbing that is just the right shade. This is the kind of theory that must remain theoretical until trout are taught to talk. Still, it's worth remembering, especially when you consider that the body of an insect is usually a mix of colors.

Just as certain sizes are most common within each order, so are particular colors most common. The result is a pleasantry for the angler: A few size and color variations of a basic pattern style will fish for most species of any order of aquatic insects, all across the continent, all around the world.

What does that mean? It means that not only will your knowledge about insects and fly patterns be transferable from coast to coast, but your fly patterns themselves, when you've tied a small range of sizes and colors of a certain style for a certain order, will fish successfully from coast to coast, on streams from the Catskills to the Rockies and Cascades.

BEHAVIOR

The way an insect moves, whether it's an immature under the water or an adult on the surface, predicts the way you should present your fly to imitate it. How you fish your fly is often more important than what fly you fish. If you float or retrieve the wrong fly through the water in the right way, you might trigger an instinct to strike. If you drag the right fly through the water in the wrong way, you'll more likely trigger an instinct to flee.

Natural insects move in many different ways. Each manner of

moving requires a different type of presentation. When reading the chapters on the individual orders, it is at least as important to note how to fish the flies as it is to select the correct style of imitation.

Some nymphs and larvae cannot swim at all. When cut from their moorings by the current, they simply tumble along with it until they chance back to the bottom, or until a trout chances onto them. This type of movement suggests a dead-drift presentation. Any action added to the progress of your fly will decrease its chances of taking trout. Many nymphs swim feebly, tossed by the currents but making some slight headway toward where they want to go. These can be imitated with a fly presented on a gentle swing, letting the line tease the fly slowly around with the force of the current. A few nymphs swim boldly, striking out across the current or even upstream against it with surprising swiftness. These suggest an animated swing of the fly across the current. If there is no current, a stripping retrieve will capture both their fast swimming movement and the short pauses most of them take between bursts of speed.

Adult insects riding the surface have their own ways of moving. Most ride the surface rather placidly. That's why nearly everything you read about dry-fly fishing insists that to achieve a fooled fish, you've first got to achieve a drag-free float. There is no arguing it, no matter how old it is: A dragless drift will help you catch fish on dry flies most of the time. There are a few times when it won't. Some caddis hop around on the water. When these are active, it can help to give your fly a twitch now and then as it progresses through its float. Other caddis propel themselves like speedboats across the surface, usually on stillwaters. They cruise erratically, sometimes in circles. When this happens, a fly that is left sitting still will be ignored. A fly skidded across the surface will often draw a wake up behind it, followed by a violent take. Large stonefly adults frequently create quite a disturbance on the surface. A big fly fished with a skittering swing across and downstream, like a streamer fished dry, will sometimes urge up a large trout.

Some aspects of insect behavior dictate more than the right way to retrieve a fly. They dictate the level at which to fish it. The mayfly emerger is an example of this. Mayflies often get trapped in or just under the surface film when they attempt the transition from nymph to dun, through the surface of the water. When this happens, you need to fish an emerger pattern, not a nymph or a dun, and you need to notice whether to fish it floating flush in the surface film or sunk just beneath it.

Insect behavior is the wellspring of fly presentation. It can be observed best in the field, while you're out fishing. It can correctly be considered the most important of the five aspects of aquatic insects.

HABITAT

Habitat is one of the simplest of the five aspects of insects. The kind of water in which an insect lives predicts where you will fish its imitation. If you base your studies on your own observations, you will be likely to cast your fly imitating the insect you've captured into the very water from which you captured it. That's one reason your own observations, made during your own fishing trips, are more valuable than what you might read about hatches or hear in rumors and reports.

Insects have adapted to all imaginable aquatic environments. All animals push their capabilities to the absolute limit to live on the extreme edge of available resources. Eventually new species arise to fill new niches. We humans have done and still do this, too.

I once flew from Darwin to Sydney, Australia, high over what's outback of the outback. It was alarmingly abandoned country, without a sign of moisture or vegetation. This went on unbroken for what seemed forever but was probably just around a thousand miles. Then I saw a tree. After many more miles, there were sprinkled trees, one in every few acres. Hundreds of miles before the land looked habitable, out there on the edge with the first few trees, I saw the reflection of a tin roof, probably a ranch outpost or line shack. In another hundred miles, there was a cluster of reflections off roofs, the ranch itself. People had adapted to living out there at the edge of the human environment. The thought occurred to me, "What sort of species might we evolve into, given time, in order to push on and live farther out into the outback?"

Evolution seems out of operation for us, with all of our ability to control our own environment, though we might be in for some sort of surprise. At any rate, it doesn't gallop quite that fast. But the aquatic insects have had more than 250 million years to work things out. They've filled every niche with almost every form you can imagine, and some forms that you can't.

Knowing what kinds of insects have adapted to different water types helps you in a couple of ways. First, it instructs you to avoid casting imitations on water where the natural has never been seen by a trout. Second, it tells you what insects you might expect to find, with a reasonable degree of assurance, in a given water type that you approach for the first time.

Habitat, as it is observed in the chapters on each order, will give you guidelines on where you might successfully fish each given pattern style.

Chapter 3

Making It Meaningful

A few brief notes on the life cycles of aquatic insects will arm you with some very useful information. It is important to understand the life cycle of each order of insect simply because each stage of the life cycle looks different to trout, and each gets in trouble with trout in different ways. An adult stonefly, for example, is an entirely different thing to trout than a stonefly nymph. The adult is taken on the surface, whereas the nymph is grubbed right along the bottom. It's an oversimplified case, but it becomes important when you encounter caddis, with their pupal stage, and mayflies, with that critical emerger stage inserted between the nymph and the dun.

Knowledge of insect life cycles is also useful because it reveals that some stages of some insect orders don't get into trouble with trout at all. The pupal stage of the alderfly, for example, is spent in the soil alongside the stream or lake, where it's remarkably difficult to present imitations. Knowing this about alderflies allows you to completely forget their pupal stage.

HOW INSECTS HAPPEN

Aquatic insects happen in two separate ways. The first is called *incomplete metamorphosis*. Insects with this lifestyle quit the egg and live and grow in the water as nymphs. Then they emerge into the reproductive adult stage.

Stoneflies undergo incomplete metamorphosis. Their life cycle is simple: There is the underwater nymph, then the aerial adult. Dragonflies and damselflies are also examples of such uncluttered

A stonefly nymph, an example of the immature stage of an aquatic insect that undergoes incomplete metamorphosis.

The stonefly adult is an example of the winged stage of an aquatic insect that undergoes incomplete metamorphosis.

lives. The stillwater nymph crawls out of the water, splits along the back, and allows the escape of the adult, which flies off, eats mosquitoes for a few days or weeks, then mates.

Mayflies exhibit a slightly complicated version of incomplete metamorphosis. They start out as aquatic nymphs, then emerge into a preliminary adult stage called a *dun*. A final molt in streamside vegetation produces the reproductive stage, the *spinner*. The mayfly is the only insect, terrestrial or aquatic, with two winged stages.

The second type of life cycle, *complete metamorphosis*, has different life stages with different names. In the first stage of complete metamorphosis, an insect leaves the egg and arrives in life as a larva. It eats and does all of its growing in this stage, going through several instars. Each time it outgrows an old exoskeleton, sheds it, and grows a new and larger one. When it reaches full growth and is ready for transformation, it builds a sheltered cocoon and slowly reforms itself into a pupa. Weeks or even months later, this pupa cuts its way out of the cocoon, makes its way to the water's surface, and emerges as an adult, the final reproductive stage, which will mate and lay the eggs for the next caddisfly generation.

The cased-caddis larva is an example of an aquatic insect that undergoes complete metamorphosis.

In insects that undergo complete metamorphosis, the dramatic physical changes necessary to make the transition from aquatic larva to aerial adult take place in the intermediate pupal stage.

The winged adult caddis bears no resemblance to its aquatic larval stage, true of all insects that undergo complete metamorphosis.

This is the same series of life stages so familiar to us in butter-flies: first the caterpillar, then the pupal chrysalis, finally the beauti-ful fluttering adult. Caddisflies are an aquatic example of an insect with the complete metamorphosis life cycle: larva, pupa, and adult.

Let's take a quick meander back through some of the terminol-ogy I've already been using. It will help you understand the insect stages. First, with incomplete metamorphosis, there are simply *nymphs* and *adults*. That wasn't traumatic. Second, with complete metamorphosis, there is the *larva,* the *pupa,* then the *adult.* Not much fright there, either. Just one more thing, then all this is behind us: The plural of larva is *larvae* ("–vae" pronounced *vee*); the plural of pupa is *pupae* ("–pae" pronounced *pea*).

It seems as though the terminology should be more compli-cated than that. Maybe you should read the last paragraph again before you trot on to the next.

Are you back? Here we go again.

Each stage of each insect can have its moment of greatest importance, but some stages of some orders have no importance to the angler. And each stage of each order has one or two pattern styles, based on its own peculiar shape and the water type in which it lives, that match it best.

OBSERVATION OF INSECTS

It's important to observe insects on your own streams and still-waters, over the fish you are attempting to catch, for several rea-sons. One reason was brought home clearly to me in the earliest days of my curiosity about aquatic insects. I stooped to pick up a rock while fishing a local stream. On its underside were two nymphs. They seemed the same, except for their color. One was dark brown. The other was black with bright gold bands.

I placed both nymphs in a vial of alcohol and gave them to Rick Hafele, the angling entomologist with whom I later coauthored *Western Hatches* (1981) and *Western Mayfly Hatches* (2004). I asked him to identify the nymphs. He keyed them both out to the same species of mayfly.

I was puzzled. "Wait a minute," I said. "They are obviously different."

"They're obviously different colors," Rick answered, "but they're still the same species."

If two individuals of the same species on the same rock in the same stream can vary so violently in color, you will do well to observe the insects in your own streams rather than rely on descriptions in books and magazines. Even if you read numerous articles on the very species you intend to match, yours could very well be a different color from the specimens collected and so lovingly photographed by your favorite author.

That's one reason for observation: Insects of the same species are different colors in different places. Here's another: Different species of aquatic insects are important in different streams, even in different stretches of the same stream. That fact is assured because the species have adapted to different habitats. Each different habitat—riffles, runs, pools, bank water—will have its own abundant hatches.

It is the third axiom of this book that *endless study of someone else's work will never tell you what insect hatches are important on your own home waters.*

Another reason to observe the insects closely is to increase your wonder at the world in which you and the fish and the insects live. It doesn't hurt a bit to be astonished at the brightness of a little yellow mayfly dun, or at the fact that it erupts from an inky black nymph. It won't hurt you to halt your fishing long enough to watch a mayfly dun struggle to accomplish its birth from its nymphal shuck. Some of the things you see while fishing are just as important as the fish that you catch.

The five important aspects of any insect can be observed in the field. You can judge the *size* of the insect accurately against your flies. You can compare the *shape* of the natural with the styles of flies in your fly box. You can see the *colors* in natural light, the way trout see them. You can tip an insect upside down and look at its underside—a necessity but a difficulty when your observation is restricted to color plates in an angling book. You can observe the *behavior* of a nymph or larva by dropping it in the shallows and watching the way it swims or drifts or crawls to cover, and of an adult by watching the way it drifts, flutters, or bounces on or across the surface of the water. Finally, you can observe the insect's *habitat* just by noticing the water type in which you found it.

Collecting an insect to observe is often as easy as swinging your hat through the air or lifting a stone out of the water. But a few small things that are easy to carry will greatly increase your powers of observation.

An aquarium net that costs less than two dollars will enable you to lift floating insects from the surface of a lake or stream. Without one, they will glide mischievously between your fingers. A pair of tweezers is handy to lift the critter out of the net and to hold it so it can't escape while you examine it closely.

To observe underwater stages, I carry a small lid from a pickle jar, brand unspecified, that is white on the inside surface. The features of an aquatic insect placed in the lid, with water, show very clearly against the white background. The stomach contents of a trout, swizzled in water in the lid, slowly separate themselves into

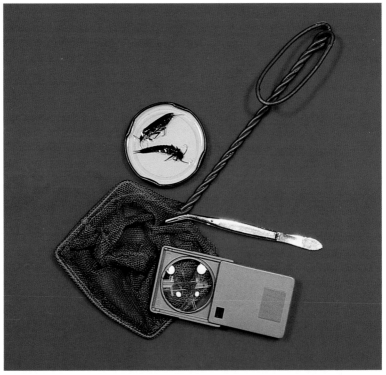

Minimal collecting items include an aquarium net, tweezers, magnifying glass, and jar lid.

things that make sense. A 4X to 6X magnifying glass will give you a close-up look at what you've managed to capture.

An aquarium net, tweezers, jar lid, and magnifying glass—those are all the aids you need to observe insects in the field. They tuck away nicely in a vest pocket or even a shirt pocket. They are worth their negligible weight in proverbial gold when it comes to observing insects.

You should also observe trout. They will tell you important things about themselves, even if you don't catch them and kill them and open them up to examine what they've been eating. By closely observing the way trout rise, you can often tell that, although they appear to be taking mayfly duns during a hatch, they actually are busy intercepting nymphs or emergers just beneath the surface.

An example of learning from trout happened to me late one June evening on the Deschutes River. Adult caddis swerved all around, and trout rose eagerly, sometimes with splashes, to take them. Or so it seemed.

I had a good match for the caddis and could not understand why those trout ignored it ruthlessly. Finally I stopped my futile casting and watched the trout for a while. Some literally ghosted into the air. It was so nearly dark that all I could see was their black silhouettes. The air above the water would be empty, then suddenly a trout would appear and hang a second, then arc over and pierce its way back into the water with a slight splash. It was eerie. Some of the silhouettes looked like they would weigh four pounds.

I recalled that caddis pupae swim to the surface, break through it quickly, and emerge to fly off in a hurry. Trout intercept the pupae on the way to the surface. If a trout angles up to take one just before the pupa breaks out, the momentum of the trout carries it into the air, where it hangs before arcing over and arrowing back into the water.

I switched quickly to a pupal pattern in the fading light. And as quickly, I began catching trout. I kept on catching them until it was too dark to fish. One of the silhouettes that leaped around at the end of my line did weigh four pounds.

Observation, whether of insects or of trout, will help you catch more and larger trout. It will also increase the enjoyment you derive from being in places where trout are found.

THE ANGLER'S NOTEBOOK
Should you keep notes on all of your fishing trips? Absolutely! You
should keep them in detailed form, staying up until two o'clock in
the morning and noting the weather; the hatches; the size, shape,
color, behavior, and habitat of every insect you collected that day; a
full description of the pattern you used to match each stage of each
insect; plus a record of each fish you caught on each fly, the time
you caught it, how long it was, what it weighed, and . . . my pen
ran out of breath.

What you really should do is enjoy your fishing, and make
what notes about it you think will help your future fishing without
interfering with the pleasure of your present fishing. Mental notes
are allowed, but with reservations. Mental notes, at least mine, are
perishable. Some keep longer than others. Most, when I need them,
have deteriorated beyond being useful. When I reach for them, after
a few weeks or, more often, at the same time the following season,
they have degraded into rubbish and confusion. So I keep a written
notebook.

The key to a notebook is making it both useful and used. The
evolution of my own notebooks might show you what I mean. I
started off copying a form from a fishing book. It had blanks and
boxes to fill in or check off about everything from air temperature
to water temperature to my own temperature. These forms were
the best I ever used for recording every aspect of what went on during a day spent astream. The only drawback was that all the detail
drove me crazy, and I quit taking notes.

An approach to fishing as technical as that is not good for me. I
did not enjoy recording my fishing days that way. My fishing days
don't fit in boxes and squares. They aren't that shape at all. So I
modified the forms. I made them with fewer boxes to check and a
lot more blank space to fill in with whatever I would. This suited me
better. Never, for example, did I find a form with boxes labeled
"Trout hanging in air above riffles: [ ] Yes [ ] No." My reformed form
allowed me to stretch out a bit and note such important happenings.

I began to neglect such things as air and water and my own
temperature. With these new forms, I found myself using all the
blank space for notes and leaving all the boxes unchecked. And I
found, again, that I was not as eager as I should have been to sit

Date: _____ Time: _____ Place: _____

Stream/Lake: _____

Section: _____

Who: _____

Weather: _____ Air temp.: _____

Water cond.: _____ Water temp.: _____

Fish: _____

_____

_____

Natural: Time: Imitation:

_____   _____   _____

_____   _____   _____

_____

Notes: _____

_____

_____

_____

_____

_____

_____

_____

_____

Sample page from current form of the author's fishing notebook.

down and record things as they happened, and that my notes were not quite as useful when I did keep them and refer back to them.

The final form—perhaps I should say the most recent mutation—of my notes has become a simple half-page form I made up on my computer and either print out ten to twenty at a time or copy at the local print shop. It has lines for such necessary details as where and when and with whom I fished, the weather, what hatched and what matched it or failed to, and what I might have managed to catch, if anything. Beyond that, most of the remaining room is for free-form notes, which are the kind I most like to keep.

Your own note form and notebook should be a function of your own personality and your own experiences. I have met few anglers just getting into the study of aquatic insects who did not use the most elaborate records imaginable. There's nothing wrong with that.

However you go about it, make your notebook both used and useful. If mental notes are all you care to keep, that's fine. That's the only kind I keep on many of my fishing trips.

THE INSECT COLLECTION
Should you keep a collection of aquatic insects? Yes you should, if you want one and want to do it right. No you shouldn't, if you don't want one or don't want to do it right.

My collecting was very ambitious at first. It helped me learn about aquatic insects, no doubt about it. Collecting got me looking at them, and it will do the same for you.

Here, in brief, is how to do it right. Buy a box of one-dram glass vials from a scientific supply house, or order them from a university bookstore. Be sure they have plastic insert lids. Screw caps restrict the neck space, making it difficult to remove specimens with tweezers later when you'd like to look at them. Cork inserts allow alcohol to slowly evaporate, eventually leaving your specimens dry. Buy a gallon of ethyl alcohol from a scientific supply house. Rubbing alcohol, available from druggists, will preserve the insects but will also make them brittle; the parts you want to study will all fall off, which is inconvenient. When fishing, I always carry a few vials three-quarters filled with alcohol, some blank labels, and the stub of a pencil in a vest pocket.

For labels, cut a white notecard into half-inch-by-one-inch strips. Use these to label your vials. Write on the label with a num-

ber 2 lead pencil—not a pen, because ink leaches out in alcohol—
and put the label inside the vial with the insect when you collect it.
Without labels, you will soon have a collection of small bottles filled
with nothing of any use whatsoever, because you'll never remember where anything was collected, when, or why.

Here's what to write on the label: where you collected the insect, the date, and what it is. If you think it's a *Paraleptophlebia bicornuta* dun, that's fine. But if you write *mayfly dun*, it will be just as
useful to you, a lot easier to fit on the label, and a lot more likely to
be correct, which counts. Write your name on the label, too. If it
turns out to be a rare find, entomologists will know whom to bless.

By correlating the collection to the pages of your notebook, you
will have notes to refer to when you sit down to tie a matching
dressing. A warning here: Colors fade quickly in alcohol, as well as
in any other preservative I've tried, though sometimes more slowly,
so for color records, you'll have to depend on your notes, your
memory, or color photography.

If you do not keep a notebook, then set up a simple card-file
system. Number your vials and reference them on a notecard with
the same number. Keep the kind of information on the card that
you would otherwise keep in a notebook: the five aspects of the insect, plus the dressing you used, how you fished it, where you
fished it, and how happy it made the trout.

Obviously, if you own a computer, you should use it. I now use
a very simple system that orders my small collection by vial number, in the order collected, with a short entry template for each vial.
It takes just moments to enter my notes. If I care to look at a sample
later, in an instant I can have the computer search for the record by
vial number, insect name, or the water where it was collected. Don't
let any collection and record keeping system, on a computer or on
paper, become so complicated that it causes you to neglect it, or to
neglect your fishing, thereby cutting into those on-stream observations that are by far the most important part of any study you
might make of aquatic insects.

A last note on collecting: Don't go out and decimate fragile
streams to collect insects. In some places, it is illegal to disturb the
streambed. On heavily fished or delicate systems, such as spring
creeks, collect only what comes your way in the air, in the water, or
in the stomach of a willing hatchery trout.

THE PORTABLE FLY-TYING KIT

Perhaps the best way to take advantage of your collecting and observation of insects is to tie your matching flies right on the bank of the stream or the shore of the lake where you collected them. It becomes a way of taking notes.

I carry a portable tying kit on every extended fishing trip I take. My late fishing partner, retired army colonel Tony Robnett, encountered my kit in the back of his pickup so often that he once composed a useful sentence about it, and repeated it every time he had to move the kit out of his way to get at something useful. I won't say the sentence. On one trip to the famous lakes in the Kamloops area of British Columbia, the colonel sat me down at a picnic table and absolutely ordered me to use the kit. He waggled a jovial finger at me and said, "I'm not carrying that goddamned thing another mile if you don't tie some flies with it!"

"What do you want me to tie?" I asked.

"I don't care," Tony said. "We've carried that kit thousands of miles and you've never used it. Just tie something."

I tied some flies with the kit on that trip to Canada. We didn't use them. But I'd still hate to go fishing without it. When I want it, I want it bad. It has saved trips. I've condensed it, but I still carry it on any trip after trout where I expect to fish over insect hatches.

With such a poor specimen as me for your example, I suggest you decide for yourself whether you want to construct and carry a portable fly-tying kit.

Chapter 4

Mayflies

The history of fly fishing is wound in tightly with mayflies. The earliest extant angling writings that deal with insects include patterns for mayflies. Early refinements of floating flies, on the limestone rivers of southern England, were attempts to match mayfly duns. The first American dressings were changes worked on these British patterns, adapting them to meet our own eastern mayfly hatches.

The reasoning behind this early emphasis on mayflies is easy to understand. No insects are so dramatically aquatic. Mayflies emerge out in open water where anglers, and trout, can easily see them. In contrast, caddisflies emerge quickly from the water without sitting on its surface for long, making it a transition that is difficult for the angler to observe, though trout don't share that problem. Stonefly nymphs migrate to the streambank and climb out of the water on rocks or logs, usually at dusk or after dark, before the adult emerges. It's another transition that is difficult to observe, even for trout.

Mayflies pop right out and ride the surface currents in plain sight, in bright daylight. Their hatches are concentrated; dozens, sometimes even hundreds, of duns appear on the water and boat the currents at the same time. It's easy to observe them, easy to establish their relationship with the water from which they arise, easy to notice trout feeding on them eagerly and often selectively. That's why anglers, through all trout-fishing history, have looked at mayflies first, imitated them first, considered them first in importance. We know now that caddisflies, stoneflies, and midges are sometimes just as important as mayflies. On some streams and lakes, these or other aquatics are more important. But their importance is not often as easy to observe and convert to trout caught.

Angling books are frequently criticized for placing too much emphasis on mayflies and not enough on other aquatic insects. If it's an error, this book will make it, too. The reason is simple: Mayflies are the most diverse aquatic insects. The things that need to be known about them cannot be so easily compacted as the facts about caddisflies, stoneflies, midges, and other flies.

Mayfly diversity in the adult stages takes the form of size and color variations on the same basic shapes. All mayfly duns are essentially the same shape. All mayfly spinners are approximately the same shape. But in the nymph stage, that doesn't hold true. Mayfly nymphs have adapted so divergently, to so many different aquatic environments, evolving into such different shapes, that they must be treated in four separate categories. But the categories are consistent, and each can be imitated with variations of one or two pattern styles.

MAYFLY LIFE CYCLE

Mayflies undergo incomplete metamorphosis. They forage as nymphs, then emerge as adults. There is no intermediate pupal stage. There is, however, the intermediate winged dun stage before the reproductive spinner stage.

The underwater life of the mayfly, after it leaves the egg, usually lasts just short of a full year. The nymph is tiny at first. It is roughly the shape it will be when mature, but it does not develop wing cases until later in its life. Most mayfly nymphs in streams graze aquatic pastures called rocks. The stuff you slip around on while wading is a thin layer of algae. It is the main food source for mayfly nymphs. In gentle moving waters and in stillwaters, mayfly nymphs clamber around on rooted vegetation or on the bottom, browsing the fine layer of almost invisible growth that thrives on aquatic leaves and the bottom itself wherever sunlight strikes down through the water.

Each time the size of the nymph exceeds the capacity of its skin to contain it, the insect sheds the old one and forms a new one. The period of growth between sheddings is called an *instar*. Mayflies go through as many as twenty instars in the time it takes them to grow to maturity.

As mayfly nymphs near maturity, they develop distinct wing cases. A fully mature nymph is a vehicle to contain and transport the mayfly adult. The body of the dun exists in full form inside the skin of the nymph. The wings are accordioned inside the wing cases.

When ready to emerge, these nymphs get restless. In spring and fall, this usually happens at the time of day when the water is warmest. It occurs at morning and evening, when the water is cooler, during the hottest days of midsummer. Many mayfly nymphs migrate out of fast water before emerging. That is why nymphs you might find all season long in tossed white water suddenly appear in great gatherings on flats above and below riffles just before a hatch.

Some restless mayfly nymphs, eager to emerge but not quite ready, swim around recklessly near the bottom. Others swim up through the water column to the surface, then retreat to the bottom again, sometimes repeating this trip more than once. This restless behavior just before a hatch suggests to the observant angler that good nymph fishing might begin an hour or two before duns start to emerge.

Emergence of mayflies takes place in two ways. Some nymphs crawl out of the water onto protruding rocks or the stems of plants growing out of the water. The nymphal skin splits along the back, and the dun slowly extracts itself with a peristaltic action. The wings unsheathe from the wing cases. They slowly erect, lifted up by fluids pumped through a network of veins. The rest of the body pulls free of the nymphal cuticle, and the tails follow. These duns that emerge on solid objects, out of the water, are not often available to trout, unless wind blows them off their perches and onto the water.

The greater number of mayflies emerge on the surface, out in open water, where trout can get at them. These are the hatches you are most likely to observe, the ones on which trout are most likely to feed actively. These are the mayflies to imitate with dry flies.

Mayflies emerging in open water present more than one target to trout. First, the insect has to get from the bottom to the top, either as the nymph or as a dun after having cast the nymphal shuck along the bottom or a foot or so beneath the surface. Second, many of the insects get caught in the surface film before the fully formed dun pops out on top. Third, the dun must sit on the surface long enough for the veins in its wings to harden before it can fly. These three targets create separate opportunities for the angler. Each allows you to take advantage of trout, which in turn are busy taking advantage of mayflies.

Once the mayfly dun escapes the surface of the water, it flies to the protection of streamside vegetation. There it rests and awaits the time to shed the dun skin and turn into a spinner. The mayfly dun, because of its extra skin, has a slightly cloudy appearance before its final molt. Its colors are often muted and somewhat dulled, though a few are bright yellow.

The molt to the final spinner stage takes place any time from a few minutes to a day or two after emergence. Anglers most often see male spinners. Males dance over the water, flying straight up, then dropping straight back down, repeating the cycle patiently, waiting for a female to emerge from streamside. Sometimes males wait in great clouds. That is how they are most often observed.

When a female appears, a male mates with her in flight. The sperm is transferred quickly, and they separate. The male goes on with his trembling dance, waiting for a chance to mate with another female. Most mated female spinners return to streamside vegetation for a period of anywhere from half an hour to a day and wait for the eggs to become fertilized, then take their chances with trout when they fly back to the water to deposit their eggs.

Some sow their eggs by dropping them in clusters from above the water, bombs away. Most fly to the surface, dip the abdomen to the water to release the eggs, and fly up again, repeating this until they are exhausted of both eggs and energy and fall to the water. A few species deposit their eggs by crawling under water from protruding rocks, limbs, or logs, and attaching the eggs in clusters to the submerged surfaces of the same objects down which they crawled.

A high percentage of female spinners wind up lying spent on the water. Trout are most eager to take them while some eggs are still in them. The body of the female mayfly is an empty shell designed to hold the eggs. When the eggs are gone, so is most of the nutrition her body contained, though trout will feed heavily on exhausted spinners if enough are available.

Male mayflies generally return to streamside vegetation when their dance is done. They are more likely to end their lives in a spiderweb than in the stomach of a trout. In some mayfly species, the male and female are different colors and different sizes. This is another reason to rely on your own observation. Many writers have captured male spinners out of the air, created dressings to imitate them, and written glowingly about them, never realizing that the male in most mayfly species is rarely seen by trout, and that the female is a different color and a different size. Always imitate females collected from the water.

The mayfly life cycle usually lasts one year, egg to egg. There are, however, some that live two or three years as nymphs, and others that have two or even three succeeding generations in a single year, living just weeks or months as nymphs between emergences as adults.

The life cycle of the mayfly occurs in four distinct stages: nymph, emerger, dun, and spinner. Each of these stages presents itself differently to the trout. Each is matched with pattern styles and presentations unique to it.

MAYFLY NYMPHS

Mayfly nymph adaptations to different water types led to the evolution of four distinct body types and four distinct behavior types. This distinction in both shape and movement creates the need to imitate each of the groups with a different fly style, and to fish each of the styles with a different presentation. The four groups are *swimmers, crawlers, clingers,* and *burrowers.*

Before looking at each of the groups separately, let's define a mayfly nymph so you will be able to recognize one when you see it out on the stream. The characteristics that set mayfly nymphs apart from other nymphs and larvae are a single set of wing cases on the thoracic segments, two or three tails, and gills on the abdominal segments.

Only nymphs—immature stages of insects that undergo incomplete metamorphosis—have wing cases. Larvae do not. If you encounter an aquatic insect with wing cases, projections on the back of the thoracic segments, the same segments that anchor the legs, you know that this insect exhibits incomplete metamorphosis. If you encounter an aquatic insect with no wing cases, you know it must develop its wings later in the pupal stage, therefore you know it enjoys complete metamorphosis. Mayfly nymphs have one visible set of wing cases. All other aquatic nymphs have two sets.

Most mayfly nymphs have three tails, making them immediately recognizable, because all stonefly nymphs have two tails. A few mayfly nymphs, however, also have two tails, the same as stonefly nymphs, confusing matters slightly.

The key characteristic is the position of the nymphal gills. All mayfly nymphs have gills on their abdominal segments, and only there. These gills extract oxygen out of the water and transport it into a tracheal system, which in turn transports it directly into the individual cells of the insect. The gills are usually platelike. In one group, they are slender filaments. In another they resemble a showgirl's plumes. But they are always on the abdominal segments in mayfly nymphs. Stonefly nymphs, the only ones you're likely to confuse with mayfly nymphs, either lack gills or have them on the thorax. In a very few cases, stonefly nymphs have tufts of gills on the first one or two abdominal segments as well, but never *just* on the abdomen, as in all mayfly nymphs.

An aquatic insect with one set of wing cases, two or three tails, and gills along the abdominal segments is a mayfly nymph. From there it can be taken into one of the four categories history has declared for mayfly nymphs.

Mayfly Swimmer Nymphs

Natural
It's supposed to be sunny and warm in the desert, but this early-November desert didn't know that. Rick Hafele and I spent most of our time huddled in the tent, set up on a flat next to the river and surrounded by sagebrush hills, out of the wind and rain. The tent door looked out over a long, boulder-broken run in the slowly flowing river, one hundred feet away. Rooted vegetation nearly choked the current in places, but open channels meandered through the run, and we knew these deeper breaks in the weeds sheltered rainbow trout.

Our mournful glances at the river, from the cover of the tent, produced no useful news all morning. I read a novel. Rick, still in his master's program, worked at an aquatic entomology text. We ate lunch. In early afternoon, Rick got restless and wandered down to the river's edge. A few minutes later, he came high-stepping back. "Trout are rising out there!" he cried.

We shrugged into hip boots and slickers, grabbed vests and rods. Who can resist rising trout, even in the most miserable conditions?

The rises were subtle, the reason we had not spotted them from the tent. Trout tipped up and sipped something in the narrow channels, the disturbance of each rise quickly erased by raindrops and wind shivers. Whatever the trout took was invisible to us. We stood looking for quite a while before I finally spotted a small mayfly dun, blown ragged and scudding down the current of a channel. It wound up shipwrecked on a mat of vegetation that broke up through the surface. I was surprised no fish got to it before it got out of their reach.

"It might scare the fish," I told Rick, "but I'd like a look at that insect." I waded out, shipped water over my hip-boot tops, but tweezered the dun into captivity and proudly brought it back.

The dun was grayish, about a size 16. I reckoned it to be remarkably close to a size 16 Adams, which is what I tied to my leader and cast over the trout. They had quickly returned to feeding following the disturbance of my wading.

Rick took a close squint at the dun and made an intuitive leap without whispering a word of it to me. He tied a simple nymph to his leader and presented it with upstream casts, on a floating line and long leader, just as if he fished a dry fly like mine. The difference in our results was conclusive. In the next hour Rick hooked seven rainbows, brought only five to his hand, and lost two in the weed beds. In the same short time, I hooked one nice trout but lost it quickly when it flopped across the top of a floating mat of vegetation, leaving the leader in a frightful snarl, minus the ineffective Adams.

Suddenly a squall dashed down out of the sage hills, chasing tumbleweeds along its front. The mayflies quit hatching and the fish quit rising. Rick and I waded out and ran to the flapping tent.

He had kept two of his trout from this very prolific and underfished stream, one of them for *my* dinner, the ultimate humiliation.

Rick cleaned the trout and opened their stomachs, squeezing the contents into a jar lid filled with water. Great numbers of small mayfly nymphs sorted themselves out. "Just what I suspected," Rick mumbled. "The nymphs were restless, but not many would emerge into that weather. Trout were taking them just under the surface." Only then did he reveal that he'd recognized the dun as a kind that emerges from a swimmer nymph, and that he'd been fishing a nymph all that time.

Where habitat is suitable to mayfly swimmer nymphs, they are usually present in great numbers. As their name indicates, they are very active. Some are strong swimmers, darting boldly about, swimming along the bottom and into and out of undercut banks. Some are more cryptic but still take short darts from place to place. Their favorite areas in flowing water are weed beds. This defines the type of water in which they will be most abundant and therefore most important. Aquatic plants take root only in streams with moderate to slow currents and with no violent spring runoff to uproot them. Spring creeks and tailwaters with extensive weed beds often have astonishing numbers of swimmer nymphs.

Quiet stretches of freestone streams and rivers always support at least modest populations of swimmer mayflies. Swimmer nymphs also live in riffles. But they generally shelter in the spaces between rocks, in fast water, where trout need jackhammers to get at them. Most species that live in riffles are small, and it's rare that trout feed on them selectively in brisk water.

Swimmers are the predominant mayfly form in lakes and ponds, though burrowers can also be abundant in scattered stillwaters with the right kinds of bottoms for burrows. A collecting net swept through a weed bed in spring will often come up wiggling with swimmer nymphs. On warm early-summer afternoons, the air can be clouded with dancing male spinners that emerged a day or two earlier from swimmer nymphs.

Mayfly swimmers are distributed nationwide. The blue-winged olive, often abbreviated BWO, inhabiting spring creeks, tailwaters, and freestone streams almost everywhere, is a swimmer mayfly. The gray drake, scattered in peaceful streams across the West, is also a swimmer. Lake and pond speckle-wings are swimmers.

Rick Hafele on a placid stretch of a tailwater trout stream, the kind of water where aquatic vegetation takes root and where swimmer mayfly nymphs are usually abundant.

Mayfly swimmer nymphs look a lot like little fish with legs. Most have three tails, though some small ones have just two, and on many the center tail is shorter than the outer two. Swimmer nymph tails are usually fringed with hairs. These give the tails a broad surface area and help propel the nymphs rapidly through the water. The body of the nymph is slender toward the tail end, tapering up to a thicker thorax, which contains the developing muscles that will one day motivate the wings of the adult. Gills on swimmer nymphs are platelike. These broad gills serve two purposes: They gather oxygen out of the water, and they provide more surface area, which helps the nymph swim more efficiently.

The most recognizable feature of swimmer nymphs is not a physical trait but a behavioral one. When captured, they try to swim away rather than crawl away. If you collect one, place it in your white jar lid or hold it in the palm of your hand, and add a bit of water, it will flip around and swim just like a miniature minnow.

A typical mayfly swimmer nymph is torpedo shaped, has three tails often fringed with fine hairs, and has gills along the sides of the abdominal segments.

Mayfly swimmer nymphs vary from tiny size 20s up to large size 6s, about an inch long. Their color covers a spectrum from light olive-tan through light to dark gray—colors traditionally referred to in fly styles as blue and slate—to a reddish brown that is almost amber. Recall that nature tosses color variations at us all the time, to such an extent that professional entomologists long ago threw out reference to color as a legitimate way to accurately identify aquatic insects. Such wide variations in both color and size enforce the need for a restricted number of pattern styles on which imitations of the various species can be based.

Imitation

Mayfly swimmer nymphs break down, although somewhat roughly, into two types: those that are small and normally very slender, and those that are larger and usually more robust. Most of the smaller types are nymphs of the ubiquitous blue-winged olive mayfly duns, a stream type that arrives in sizes 16 down to 22, and the mostly western stillwater group known as the speckle-wing duns, in sizes 12 to 16. The larger types are the nymphs of eastern great leadwing drakes, western gray drakes, and some near relatives of both, in sizes 10 and 12.

The most effective fly style for the smaller types is based on the popular Pheasant Tail nymph. The original Frank Sawyer dressing, devised on British chalkstreams, used ring-necked pheasant center tail fibers for the tails, abdomen, thorax, and wing case. It was tied with fine copper wire rather than thread. I prefer the Pheasant Tail Flashback variation and follow famous Montana tier Al Troth's advice to use peacock herl for the thorax, at least in the larger sizes, 16 and up. The brightness on the back of the nymph either catches the attention of trout or reminds them of bubbles of gas trapped under the cuticle of a hatching nymph. For whatever reason, the flashback seems to work best for me when trout are feeding on small swimmer nymphs. The style is far easier to tie with thread than with wire, especially in the smallest sizes.

PHEASANT TAIL FLASHBACK

Pheasant Tail Flashback

Hook	2X long, size 14–22.
Thread	Brown.
Tails	3 to 5 pheasant center tail fibers.
Rib	Fine copper wire, counterwound over abdomen.
Abdomen	Remainder of tail fibers, wrapped as herl.
Wing case	Several Pearl Flashabou strands.
Legs	Pheasant center tail fiber tips (optional on smallest sizes).
Thorax	Peacock herl.

The best fly style I have found for the larger mayfly swimmer nymphs is based on the Near Enough, originated by the late Polly Rosborough and outlined in his book *Tying and Fishing the Fuzzy Nymphs* (Stackpole, 1978). They are tied on 3X long hooks and capture the long, slender shape of the naturals perfectly. The style is easy to tie, with long tails and loosely dubbed bodies that not only look like the naturals, but also work enticingly in the water. The stray fibers of dubbing at the sides of these fuzzy nymphs look a lot like the gills at the sides of the real insects.

Rosborough was a professional tier. He strived to simplify every tying step so he could tie flies faster. The legs of his swimmer-style dressings are tied in at each side; the butts of the leg fibers are bent back and clipped off to form the wing cases. This not only captures the look of the insect, but it also simplifies tying the imitation.

Polly's Near Enough is tied with gray fox fur, using gray-dyed mallard flank for tails, legs, and wing cases, in sizes 10 and 12. It will be just right on many mayfly waters, especially those where the larger species of swimmers are abundant. But be prepared to create size and color variations on this basic swimmer-nymph style.

NEAR ENOUGH STYLE

Near Enough

Hook	3X long, size 10–16.
Thread	Match body color.
Tails	Hackle or flank fibers.
Body	Fur to match natural.
Legs	Hackle or flank fibers.
Wing case	Butts of leg fibers.

The most promising variations would include brownish olive dressings in sizes 12 to 16, with brown tails, legs, and wing cases. Some eastern and western swimmer nymphs have brownish amber bodies and are up to sizes 10 and even 8. A rare western species has a purple body; its imitation is tied on a 3X long size 6 hook. It's a whopper, but don't tie a bunch of flies to match it unless you encounter it.

I recommend that you tie and carry the original Near Enough, but tie variations on it only if you run into naturals that call for them and selectively feeding fish that demand them.

Presentation

The Pheasant Tail Flashback, especially in its tiniest sizes, is an excellent dressing to fish as a dropper in tandem with a larger nymph, on or near the bottom, in spring creeks, tailwaters, and the calmer areas of freestone streams. Trout in such waters, even large ones, are accustomed to making their living on tiny bites. You'll find that the small fly will often outfish the big one.

Rig with the small fly at the point, on a 5X or 6X tippet, and the larger fly about a foot up, on a 4X or 5X tippet. If weight is needed, add small split shot or molded putty weight above another tippet knot eight inches to a foot from the larger fly. Place either a hard strike indicator or a tuft of yarn on your leader approximately twice the depth of the water from the point fly. Adjust the amount of weight and the distance between the flies and the strike indicator to suit the water in which you're fishing. Add weight or move the indicator higher on the leader if the water is fast and your flies are not reaching the bottom. Remove weight or move the indicator closer to the flies if the water is somewhat slow and your flies continually get stuck on the bottom.

Fish this combination setup on short casts, quartering up and across the current. Lift your rod as the indicator drifts toward you, and draw in line to take out slack. Lower the rod and feed slack into the drift after the indicator passes your position, to extend the drift as far as possible. If you see the indicator twitch, dip under, or merely hesitate in the current, set the hook. If no trout accepts the fly, make your next cast a foot or so out into the current from the one before. Continue to show the two flies along all of the bottom in the same manner.

Be sure your flies are on or near the bottom. If you're not setting the hook to false indications at times, adjust the indicator or add more shot. You'll be surprised how often raising the indicator a foot or adding a single small split shot makes the difference between no action at all and a sudden bunch of it.

When many small swimmer nymphs rise to the surface, just before and during an emergence, the appropriate dressing can often be fished best by presenting it to rising trout on upstream casts and downstream drag-free drifts, almost as if it were a dry fly. A dry fly or tiny yarn indicator added to the leader three to five feet above the fly will help you notice takes. Or you can watch your line tip and leader. That's the way Rick Hafele did it that desert day when he supplied my dinner by fishing a nymph with dry-fly tactics.

Larger swimmer nymphs propel themselves with rapid up-and-down flips of the body. These come in bursts, moving the insect from a few inches to a few feet, after which it either comes to rest on some submerged object or else suspends itself to rest in the water in preparation for its next burst.

In lakes, your fly should be allowed to sink a foot or so after the

When fishing a nymph and indicator rig on the kinds of calm water where swimmer nymphs are plentiful, keep the rig light—small flies, tiny shot, and yarn indicators—and make your casts as delicately as you would with dry flies.

cast, more if fish are feeding over and around deep weed beds. Then the fly should be retrieved in short strips alternated with brief pauses. Another way to achieve the darting motion is to lower the rod tip nearly to the water, then draw line in slowly while constantly twitching the rod tip. Even when retrieving this way, give your fly an occasional rest, because fish often pick up a natural when it pauses just after a burst of speed.

Presentation in streams is dictated by the current. Because swimmer nymph populations are greatest in slow to moderate currents, it's usually best to cast across and slightly downstream. Allow the current to swing the fly across without added action, or give it teasing pulses with the rod tip. In faster water, you will want to use mends of the line to slow the drift of the fly to a reasonable speed. In fast water, no added action is required from the rod.

Never overlook undercut banks. Swimmer nymphs are not the

only aquatic animals that prefer them. Large trout tuck in there, too. A large swimmer-style dressing tossed close to the bank, allowed to sink a foot or two, then teased along the very edge, might draw out the largest trout you'll hook this season.

Mayfly Crawler Nymphs

Natural

Mayfly crawlers are among the most important insects in moderate to fast freestone trout streams, which most of us must confess is our own favorite habitat. Some, such as pale morning duns, are adapted to living in weed beds and are also very abundant in spring creeks and tailwaters. Crawlers are distributed widely from East to West and are found in moving water worldwide. They are perhaps best known for producing such hatches as eastern olives and sulfurs and western pale morning duns and green drakes.

With exceptions that few fishermen will ever encounter, mayfly crawler nymphs live in moving water and are not important in lakes and ponds. They have, however, adapted to all habitats in flowing water. Some will be found in weed beds of spring creek and tailwater currents, others in all habitats—riffles, runs, and pools—in freestone rivers and streams.

Their favored habitat might be described as a moderate to brisk current over a clean stone bottom that has lots of what scientists call *interstitial space.* These spaces are the nooks and crannies and gaps between rocks, down in and even under the streambed, which form living rooms for insects. The insects are protected from currents there, and from such evil creatures as hungry trout. They can feed on trapped detritus and also have easy access to the photosynthetic plant growth on the top and sides of the rocks under which they hide.

Most crawler nymphs have stout bodies, and though a minor number are somewhat slender, all are a lot less streamlined than swimmer nymphs. Their legs are thicker and stronger for clambering around on rocks in moderate to fast currents. Crawler mayfly nymphs can swim, but not remarkably well.

Crawlers can be recognized by a few simple features: They always have three tails, which lack the thick fringes of hair found on most swimmer nymph tails. Their gills are small plates, usually

Crawler nymphs are usually more robust than swimmer nymphs. They have three tails, gills along the abdominal segments, and stout, muscular legs.

held over the abdominal segments rather than extending out to the sides. When you lift a crawler out of the water, depriving it of a constant flow of fresh water over its gills, it will start working them up and down at a rapid rate. This movement is an attempt to get oxygen.

The eyes of crawler nymphs are always at the sides of the head, like those of a trout, not inset into the top of it, peering upward like those of a flounder. This bit of information separates them from clinger nymphs, the only insects with which you are likely to get them confused.

The size range of mayfly crawlers is more extreme than that of swimmers. They run from tiny size 24s up to blocky size 8s. The smallest sizes are not important to nymph fishermen, because trout seldom feed selectively on crawler nymphs, and anything that small would not make a very effective searching pattern. The important size range is at the medium and large end of the scale, with sizes 12, 14, and 16 most useful to the angler, because those are the sizes of crawler nymphs trout feed on most often.

Colors of crawler nymphs are not so wide ranging as swimmers. They must blend with bottom rocks and are generally dark brown or dark olive-brown. There are exceptions, most often based on adaptations to bottoms of different colors. And there is variation within species on various waters, even in the same water. It was a pair of contrasting crawler nymphs that I captured on the same rock and sent to Rick Hafele, early in my fly-fishing career, and that he identified as members of a single species.

Imitation

The best dressing style I have found for crawler nymphs is the old, drab Gold-Ribbed Hare's Ear, though I use it most often with the addition of a bright gold or brass bead at its head. It's anything but imitative and makes an excellent searching fly. Trout feeding on the bottom in moderate to fast currents seldom feed on a single food type and are seldom selective. A tumbled Hare's Ear, especially with a beadhead, looks like a lot of the insects that live in riffles and runs. Remember, your goal is to trigger fish to feed, not to produce a carbon copy of a natural insect. A beadhead Gold-Ribbed Hare's Ear pulls a lot of triggers, for a lot of different reasons, when fished along the bottom of a riffle or run.

The Hare's Ear should be tied on a standard length or 1X-long hook to capture the blockiness of the natural. It should be weighted at least slightly, though the bead serves as weight as well as flash. Lead wire fattens the fly a bit and ensures that it gets down to the bottom where it belongs. The Hare's Ear has a tuft of hare's-poll fur, from between the rabbit's ears, for the tail. The rear half of the body is tan hare's-mask fur, ribbed with narrow gold tinsel. This darkens when wet and is close to the color of most crawler nymphs. The front half of the body is darker hare's-mask fur, dubbed roughly with the guard hairs left in to represent the legs of the insect. This thorax is tucked firmly behind the bead.

In larger sizes, 14 and up, a brown turkey-quill segment tied over the thorax forms the wing case. In almost all respects, this style of fly is perfect for the crawler mayflies. You could certainly get more exact if you wanted, but I doubt your exactness would catch you any more fish in the kind of water where most crawler nymphs live.

It's difficult to tell exactly why the bead makes the fly more effective, though we know it does. Perhaps it's because the winking bead catches the notice of more trout, or because the bead looks like a bubble of air trapped under the cuticle of a nymph about to rise up for emergence, or just because the bead delivers the fly down deeper and gives it a jigging motion. The increased effectiveness of beadheads might stem from some reason that only trout know about.

GOLD-RIBBED HARE'S EAR

Hook	Standard or 1X long, size 8–18.
Head	Gold or brass bead.
Weight	8 to 12 turns lead wire the diameter of the hook shank, or one size finer.
Thread	Black.
Tail	Tuft of hare's-poll fur.
Rib	Oval gold tinsel.
Abdomen	Tan hare's-mask fur.
Wing case	Turkey quill section on size 14 and larger.
Thorax	Dark hare's-mask fur, with guard hairs.

Beadhead Gold-Ribbed Hare's Ear

Promising variations for this dressing include creamish tan flies in sizes 14 and 16, and olive-brown dressings in sizes 12 up to 8. I have also encountered brick red crawler nymphs, but not in situations where trout turned up their noses at a properly tumbled Hare's Ear.

Presentation

Crawler nymphs are feeble swimmers. When knocked loose in the currents, they do their best to get back to the bottom. But their best isn't very impressive. Most of the time they just tumble along to wherever fate takes them: either back to the bottom or delivered up to a waiting trout.

The most effective presentation is keyed to this helpless nature of the natural. Your fly should drift downstream with the current. Rig with indictor and split shot. A Gold-Ribbed Hare's Ear makes an excellent lead fly above a tiny Pheasant Tail Flashback when you desire to offer trout a choice between two nymphs. Present the fly or flies with an upstream cast, seldom fishing more than thirty- to forty-foot casts. Allow the fly to sink, then tumble it right along the bottom, with as little influence from the line and leader as possible.

It is difficult to determine takes when fishing this way. Trout usually intercept an insect, or an imitation, as it drifts past them. There is seldom a sudden wallop. You don't feel a thing. Your line slowly tightens in the current as it drifts down below the stopped fly. But by the time you notice this, the fish will likely have rejected the fly as a fake.

A strike indicator can increase your hooking percentage five or six times when tumbling nymphs along the bottom. When the fly is intercepted, the indicator will twitch forward a bit, or just hesitate a second while the current keeps going. These are subtle signs you must learn to notice. Without the indicator, you fish almost blind. With one, and with a properly presented Gold-Ribbed Hare's Ear, you will often take trout after hungry trout from riffles and runs.

Rig crawler nymphs with indicators and split shot, and fish them on upstream casts, allowing them to bounce along the bottom in fairly brisk water.

Mayfly Clinger Nymphs

Natural

It was a big river. Trout rose to take mayfly duns in the center of the broad tailout of a pool, where the water welled up before breaking over into the wide and rushing riffle below. I waded out to the tops of my waders, until a sixty-foot cast just reached the fish. But my dry fly would drift a foot or two, then the line would catch the current and race the fly around, leaving a V wake that would have pleased me had I been fishing for summer steelhead. I wasn't.

The dry fly sank on one cast. Before it swam ten feet, I felt a sharp rap. The fish came away quickly, but it gave me a hint about what might be going on out there. Clinger nymphs live in that kind of water. They emerge into the kinds of duns I could see boating the surface. Many clinger duns leave the nymphal shuck behind on the bottom and rise up through the water column with their wings pulled out of the nymph wing cases and furled above the thorax. Other clinger nymphs swim awkwardly to the surface, or to a point just beneath it, before casting the nymphal shuck for emergence. Trout often take more nymphs than duns during a clinger mayfly hatch.

I switched to a March Brown wet fly, cast, and mended the swing of the sunk fly to slow it down. It worked. Trout didn't suddenly get greedy for my fly, but I got a hit every few casts and caught half a dozen fish before I put the rest of them down. I moved downstream to the next tailout, saw the same thing happening, and caught another half dozen trout on the same wet fly.

Clinger nymphs have taken the swift-water adaptations of mayfly crawlers a final step forward. They live almost exclusively in the fastest water of rapids and riffles. Even in the most brutal current, there is always a thin layer of slow water, caused by friction, flowing right along the face of a bottom rock. This layer of livable water is only about a sixteenth of an inch thick. An insect that adapts to surviving in this kind of water, without getting swept away, is forced to develop a low profile. Clinger nymphs are flat as Frisbees.

The most famous clinger hatches are eastern. The natural imitated by the Quill Gordon is a clinger. So is that imitated by the Light Cahill. The western march brown over which I fished a wet

Mayfly clinger nymphs have two or three tails, gills along the sides of the abdomen, and heads that are at least as broad as the thorax. Note that the eyes are inset into the top of the head.

fly, out in the center currents of that large river, is an important early-season clinger hatch.

The flattened head and body is the simple key to recognition of clinger mayfly nymphs. The head is usually as wide as or wider than the thorax behind it. The eyes have migrated, through eons of evolution, to the top of the nymphal head. They gaze up like a flounder, rather than out like a trout.

Clinger nymphs have either two or three tails, without fringes of hairs. Clinger gills are on the abdominal segments, most often platelike. In one clinger group, the gills overlap front and back and spread to the sides, limpetlike, to form a suction cup on the underside of the insect. A few clinger nymphs have tufts of gills that look a bit like cheerleaders' pom-poms.

The size range of mayfly clingers is narrow. Few at maturity are smaller than size 16, and few are larger than size 12. The color range is just as compact. Clingers are generally dark brown to dark slate gray, with a few species running to tans, and some so dark they are nearly black. They reflect the drab colors of the bottom rocks on which they live.

Imitation

I'm going to be a heretic and suggest that you don't need to tie imitations for clinger nymphs at all. They cling so efficiently to bottom stones that they are seldom available to feeding trout in great numbers. There is a phenomenon called biologic drift, in which aquatic insects redistribute themselves by letting go their grip on the bottom and drifting with the current. When this happens, clingers are indeed available to trout. But it usually happens at night.

The same Gold-Ribbed Hare's Ear that worked for crawlers, with or without the beadhead, will work as well for clingers. When fish forage on the bottom, they seldom do it selectively. A Hare's Ear will be taken readily if a substantial number of crawlers and clingers are available, and the average trout will have no idea which one you pretend your fly to be.

You can't bolt on to the next section yet, however. Clingers display an important aspect of behavior, brought out clearly when I fished the tailout of that broad pool. Most clinger nymphs, when mature, migrate out of brutal water to tailouts and edge curents before emerging. Then they split open the nymphal shuck and emerge as duns *under the water*. This behavior leads us straight back to the old wet fly as the most effective imitation.

When an insect emerges underwater, it rises to the surface with its wings emerged from the nymphal shuck but furled above the thorax. The dun is unable to swim with any efficiency. It is generally tossed at random by the currents. But recall that it prepared for this, while still the nymph, by migrating out of the worst currents. Fish clinger nymph imitations along the edges of fast water, or in the flats of smooth water above and below a riffle.

The traditional wet fly works out to be about the best pattern style to fish for mayfly clingers. It is most effective during the hatch. It can often be more effective than a floating dry fly, even when duns are visible on the water. A wet fly fished to imitate a clinger mayfly asks you a few favors. It wants to be tied with a loosely dubbed body, hen or soft rooster hackles, and wing material that will vibrate in the current rather than cleave it like a blade. Mallard and wood-duck flank fibers are better than mallard wing quill sections. These softer fibers look and act more like the tossed wings of the natural dun.

When you fish a sunk fly during a clinger hatch, you want to imitate the emerged dun as often as you want to imitate the pre-emerged nymph. Trout take one or the other or both, and it's difficult to tell which they prefer without killing a trout and doing an autopsy.

It's often a good idea to fish two wets on the same cast, one the color of the nymph, the other the color of the dun. For some trout, the color of the nymph is your model. For others, the color of the dun is your model. It's a drab nymph that produces the Quill Gordon, the Light Cahill, the bright little yellow may, all of which arise from clinger nymphs. The most common dun colors are pale tans, creams, and light browns.

The most common sizes are 12s, 14s, and 16s. I have always found that a small wet-fly box containing a few traditional Light Cahills, Dark Cahills, and March Browns, in the given sizes, takes a lot of fish for me. They arm me well for most clinger mayfly hatches.

TRADITIONAL WET FLY

Hook	Standard length, size 12–16.
Thread	Match nymph or dun body color.
Tail	Wood-duck or mallard flank fibers.
Body	Loosely dubbed fur to match natural.
Hackle	Hen or soft rooster to match insect leg color.
Wing	Hackle or feather fibers to match emerging wing of natural dun.

Traditional wet
Light Cahill

A few traditional wet flies will cover almost all emergences of clinger mayflies. They will also fish well in a lot of other situations, and I use them often as searching patterns, when I have no idea what trout might be taking.

Wet flies are out of favor today. They've been replaced in our affections by more imitative nymph styles. But I still like to fish old-fashioned wets. They're fun, they're pretty, and they catch fish, especially when clinger mayflies are active.

Presentation

The wet fly fished as a rising clinger nymph or dun emerging beneath the surface should be cast either slightly up or slightly down from straight across the stream. Then it should be allowed to drift freely with the current. Tend the drift with mends, tosses of extra line, or whatever it takes to extend the free drift of the fly. But do not lift it off the water when the free drift ends.

Allow the current to pick up the line and swing the fly around until it is straight below you. A surprising number of trout will take it on the swing, or even after it comes to rest straight downstream. It is a mistake to assume that once the fly has drifted out of the

When clinger mayflies are active, a wet fly cast into a fast current, and allowed to cross the seam into slow water, will often prod trout into taking.

main current the reasons for fishing that cast are over. Recall that these nymphs migrate to gentle water before emergence. Fish the fly over into the slower water, at the edges of a run or a riffle. Many strikes will come when the fly crosses the seam from fast water to slow.

It takes patience to let the fly drift into that edge water. But it has its rewards when clingers are hatching.

Mayfly Burrower Nymphs

Naturals

Burrower nymphs are the big characters in the mayfly cast. They can be important, because they are such large bites that fishing gets hectic whenever they are available to trout. But their hidden and nocturnal habits limit their availability to the period just before and during emergence.

Burrowers live in either placid moving waters or stillwaters. They enjoy pools and slow runs in rivers and streams with bottoms of clay, firm mud, or silt. They do well in lakes with bottoms of the right composition. When found in either moving or still waters, they require a bottom soft enough to dig a tunnel into, yet firm enough that the tunnel will not collapse.

Burrower nymphs dig U-shaped tunnels with two entrances. They live inside, safe from trout, and come out at night to feed along the bottom. Some nymphs don't dig a burrow, but protect themselves from fish predation by working their bodies into gravel or silt until they're out of sight. They remain cryptic on the bottom during daylight and come out to feed across the bottom in the night.

Burrower nymphs have rows of plumelike gills along both sides of the abdomen. These pulsate in a rippling sequence, causing a constant exchange of fresh water through the burrow, bringing oxygen to the wavering gills.

Because they protect themselves so well from trout, burrowers are not of great importance until they are mature and ready to emerge. Then they suddenly arise in great numbers, swim to the surface, and emerge slowly into the aerial dun stage. No trout, no matter how large, will ignore such an operation when it is per-

Burrower nymphs have fringed tails, plumelike gills, and mandibular tusks for digging their burrows.

formed by such large insects. Burrowers include the largest mayflies, some with nutritious bodies more than an inch and a quarter long, excluding tails.

Most important burrower hatches happen in the East and Midwest. The range of a couple of species extends to the Rockies, and one is found as far as the West Coast. The most famous burrower is the eastern green drake. It emerges on May and June evenings from gentle stretches of Pennsylvania, New York, and New England streams. The Michigan caddis, a misnamed burrowing mayfly species, has a wider distribution and the largest following. Its imitations are fished at night, when big trout can be heard walloping out in the darkness, mostly in marl-bottom rivers of the Midwest.

Another burrower, the brown drake, hatches in many midwestern waters and also extends into a few of the famous rivers in the West Yellowstone, Montana, area. The Henrys Fork of the Snake River in Idaho has good, though elusive, hatches of brown drakes. It is this elusiveness of some of the largest hatches that makes observation, and an ability to match the hatches you find where and when you find them, so important to the success of your fishing.

Recognizing these large mayfly nymphs is relatively easy. They have mandibular tusks, some of which are shaped like elephant tusks, others like horns on a bull. These tusks are used by the insect for digging its burrow. The long and feathery gills of burrower nymphs are another key characteristic. They undulate constantly. The rhythmic, wavelike movement is impossible to miss, and is a beautiful thing to see, when you capture a specimen and place it in water.

Burrower nymphs always have three tails. Some are fringed with hairs, but many are not noticeably fringed. The bodies of burrowers are slightly flattened, not as much as the bodies of clingers, but oval rather than round.

The size range of burrowing mayflies is all stacked at the large end of the scale. A small one is a size 10, 3X long. A large one would be as big as size 4. Colors range from tannish yellow to dark brown.

Imitation

Burrower nymphs are large and distinct. Their hatches seldom overlap. It is best to be aware of a pattern style that will match them, then tie one that suits the species you collect when you need it.

The best imitation style I have seen was described by Poul Jorgensen in his book *Modern Fly Dressings for the Practical Angler* (Winchester Press, 1976). His burrower dressing is tied on a 3X long hook. The tails are mini ostrich-herl tips. The body is a soft fur or synthetic, dubbed loosely, trimmed top and bottom, then teased out on the sides to represent the gills of the natural nymph. The wing case is a patch of fur darker than the color used for the body, cut short and tied over the back to represent the wing cases of the natural. The naturals are good swimmers and hold their legs tucked against their sides when they do so. This indicates the need for a fast retrieve and negates any need to imitate the legs on your imitation.

You can achieve a realistic flattened body by weighting the fly with wraps of lead wire, then flattening it with a pair of pliers before dubbing the body over the lead wraps. This weight also helps get the fly right down to the bottom, where the natural starts its swift ascent to the surface.

BURROWER NYMPH

Burrower Nymph

Hook	3X long, size 4–12.
Thread	Color of body fur.
Weight	10 to 20 turns of leader wire, wrapped and flattened.
Tails	Mini ostrich-herl tips.
Body	Loosely dubbed fur over flattened lead wire; trim fur top and bottom, then tease out at sides.
Wing case	Darker fur, tied on as tuft over body.

The most common colors of burrower nymphs are dark brownish olive, tannish yellow, and dark brown. Common sizes are 10s and 8s, but some are much larger.

It is best in these large sizes not to deal with *commons,* as you might with mayfly crawler nymphs—tying flies in advance that average what you might encounter. Trout are usually selective when they take insects this large. It's best to capture a specimen and match its size and color as closely as you can.

Presentation

When a burrower nymph emerges, usually late in the evening or after dark, it leaves its tunnel and swims boldly to the surface. This suggests that their imitations be fished by casting them across stream, giving them time to sink at least a foot or two—or even better, down to the bottom. Then swim them around on the current with a staccato pulsing of the rod tip. This is like streamer fishing. The flies are the size of streamers. The trout that come out to work on these hatches are the kind you would expect to catch on streamers—the largest in any river or lake.

In lakes, it is important to remember that trout take burrower nymphs as they swim toward the surface, and that this will almost always happen at dusk or even later, except on days darkened by overcast skies. The best bet is to use a floating line and a weighted dressing. Cast long, let the fly sink a few feet, then sweep it up toward the surface, swimming the fly smoothly and steadily. Repeat this raising of the fly, alternated with time to let it sink again, until you feel a whack. That's a fish.

MAYFLY EMERGERS

The Henrys Fork of the Snake River, in Idaho, is a formidable bit of trout water. Its fish have master's degrees in selectivity. Its currents are broad, its surface is smooth, its anglers are many. Its mayfly hatches are always astonishing, often bewildering.

The first time I fished the Henrys Fork, many years ago, I didn't try to tackle it without advice. I stopped at Osborne's Bridge, looked down at the glassy water, and immediately saw trout rising. I fought all my instincts that prodded me to rush down there and fish for them, and instead leaped back into my rig and drove straight to the nearest fly shop—there are several along its banks— and asked the clerk, "What's happening out there, and what do I do about it?"

Silt- and marl-bottomed midwestern rivers produce the best hatches of burrower nymphs. Present their imitations on the swing in and near tangled trees along the bank, usually at night.

He told me, "There's a daily hatch of blue-winged olive mayflies. It looks like the fish are taking duns, but they're actually feeding on nymphs in the surface film. You have to use emerger patterns." He handed me a size 18 olive-bodied dressing that looked exactly like a nymph with a knot of gray synthetic yarn hunched on its back.

"You dress the knot with floatant," he said in answer to my puzzled look, "and it suspends the rest of the fly just under the surface."

I'm amazingly cheap when it comes to buying flies, which I recognize is a mistake. I tie my own—as a minor point of pride, I like to catch my trout on flies I've tied myself—and I also dislike parting with the money good flies cost, which back then was one dollar. I know the price for flies was not then, and is not now, out of line. I wouldn't sell my own flies for a buck apiece then or two bucks now. But I had nothing in my fly boxes that looked anything like the little emerger the clerk showed me, and trout were rising as we spoke. "I'll take a couple," I said grudgingly, and then I raced back out to park by the bridge.

I entered the water wadered and vested and rodded and so forthed. The trout still rose. The rises looked like those of small fish. I saw immediately that the clerk was right about the hatch. It was a blue-winged olive, size 18. I wasn't sure he was right about the rest. It looked to me like the trout rose to take duns. But I tied on one of his flies; I was too cheap to buy them and then not use them.

On the third cast, I nicked a fish. The leader came back without a fly at the end of its tippet. I raised my estimation of the size of the fish and replaced my tippet with one a full size heavier.

I cast again and hooked a trout. After a splashy fight, I brought it to hand. It was sixteen inches long and portly; it must have weighed two pounds. I patted its tail, and it swam away. "Nice work, Davie," I congratulated myself, completely forgetting to give the fly shop clerk any credit. I dried and dressed the fly and cast it again. Half a dozen casts later, water welled up where my fly drifted almost invisibly in the surface film. I set the hook, and a trout took off leaping into the distance, dancing away with my last emerger.

"No problem," I consoled myself after a couple dollars' worth of mild cursing. "I've got lots of flies to match the dun." I tied on a floating Blue-Winged Olive imitation. After an hour of futile fishing, in which I rose but missed just one trout, I wished I'd bought a dozen of those damned dollar emerger patterns.

It's difficult to determine just when trout take emergers in preference to either nymphs or duns. One clue is a lot of rising fish, with the rises apparently right at the surface, while at the same time all of the visible duns on the surface ride the currents without disappearing in swirls. This happens more often than you would think, once you take time to notice it. You'll never see it until you follow the floats of a few duns through the midst of rising trout and see if any are taken.

Recognition of the stage of the insect causing the problem becomes quite easy once you realize what is happening. If you suspend a small aquarium net or hand screen net in the water for a few minutes, you will likely come up with a few emergers that are stuck in their shucks. They will look just like nymphs, but with little knots of forming wings sticking out of their backs.

Natural
Mayflies that emerge in open water must break through the surface tension. This isn't much hindrance to insects size 14 or larger. But it would be a formidable barrier to you, too, if you were size 16 or smaller. Once the surface film is broken, the nymph forces the top of its thorax through. The skin of the nymph splits along the back, and the dun works its way out, head and wings emerging first, body and tails pulled along last.

There is a moment when the nymph hangs at the surface, before the dun emerges and flies away. If surface tension impedes the insect at this point, or if something misfires in the emergence process and the insect gets stuck in its shuck—becoming what is called a *cripple*—the transitional moment can last from several seconds to the end in a trout's mouth. Even when emergence goes smoothly, each insect is suspended for at least a moment with its wings partially erected above its body and, at the same time, its nymphal shuck still attached to its after end. Mayflies as large as sizes 10 and 12 are vulnerable at this instant. It is the easiest time for a trout to take a mayfly.

Certain water types give emergers more importance than other water types. Emergers are not important in fast water. Riffles and

This is a bad photo of a big mayfly emerging in the shallows, but it shows the head and thorax of the dun free of the nymphal shuck. It's usually a small mayfly hatching out in the open on smooth water that you must match in order to fool trout with emerger patterns.

runs constantly break the surface tension; insects can get through it easily. On smooth, unbroken currents, surface tension becomes a factor. The glassier the surface, the greater the chance it will retard the progress of an emerging mayfly. Stillwater is the worst, but most lake species are large enough to penetrate the film without trouble, especially as many of them arrive at the surface with a head of steam built up. Therefore, the importance of mayfly emergers is greatest on the smooth flows of spring-creek and tailwater currents, and on slick tailouts and flats in freestone streams.

Imitation

Imitation of the mayfly emerger stage is not as difficult as recognizing situations in which it will be beneficial. Imitation can be as simple as adding a knot of polypro yarn or synthetic dubbing to the back of an unweighted nymph dressing. This is done by tying a loop of yarn over the nymph body, or by affixing a bit of dubbing to your thread and sliding it down to form a loose lump where the wing case would normally go on a nymph. The knot should be the color of the wings of duns that you see on the water.

Emerger dressings should be tied on light-wire hooks to keep them afloat, though in my own fishing, I've had too many disasters, in the form of hooks straightened by big trout, to use hooks lighter than 1X fine. Dress only the wing knot with floatant, and dress the leader to within six inches or so of the fly. You don't want the leader to tug your emerger under. At best, it will float poorly, though it will often take trout just as effectively when submerged as it does when floating suspended by its knot from the surface film.

The common size and color range of effective emerger patterns is restricted. Most mayflies that get into emergence trouble are matched by flies tied on size 16 to 22 hooks, standard length. Body colors range commonly in the browns and olives, usually with gray or whitish gray wings. When tying an emerger of this sort, it's important to imitate the body color of the *nymph,* not the dun.

WING KNOT EMERGER

Wing Knot Emerger

Hook	1X to 3X fine, size 16–22.
Thread	Match body color.
Tails	Hen hackle fibers.
Body	Fur or synthetic dubbing to match natural.
Legs	2 to 3 turns hen hackle, trimmed from top and bottom.
Wing knot	Gray or grayish white polypro yarn or synthetic dubbing.

Though there are exceptions, a single dressing in the above sizes dressed with medium blue dun tails, a body of mixed tan and olive fur, and a pale gray knot will take enough trout to get you going until you can collect a specimen and match it more closely. You will seldom find that necessary. Imitating the posture of the emerger rather than the dun usually solves the problem, even if the color of your fly is not quite correct. That's not always true, however; if you get refusals, try capturing a natural, notice its exact colors, and copy it as accurately as you can.

An alternate dressing uses a tiny ball of closed-cell foam rolled in nylon stocking material for the wing knot. This is a little harder to tie, but it floats the fly a lot better and is easier to fish.

A second style, the CDC Emerger, floats a bit higher than the Wing Knot Emerger, is more visible, and at times is more effective, even on smooth water. It can also be excellent to fish in tandem with the lower-floating fly, serving as a marker to the less visible fly, as well as giving you a chance to see which fly style trout might prefer during a given hatch. Their tastes can be notoriously fickle. They can also change from moment to moment, or even from fish to fish in a rising pod. Separate the two flies with two to three feet of fine tippet, 5X to 7X, depending on the size of the flies and the heft of the trout you're hoping to catch.

CDC floats high and lightly on the water, making this fly easy to see and to follow through its drift. The style also suspends the body in or even beneath the water. The tail represents the trailing cast shuck of the natural nymph, still attached to the back end of the emerging insect. It's an excellent style, originated by famous professional tier René Harrop for his home Henrys Fork, where trout study mayfly hatches a lot more closely than even the most experienced angler ever will.

CDC EMERGER

CDC Emerger

Hook	1X to 3X fine, size 16–22.
Thread	Match body color.
Tail/shuck	Light gray or amber Z-Lon or Antron fibers.
Body	Olive or pale yellowish olive fur or synthetic dubbing.
Wing	White or light gray CDC.
Legs	Light blue dun or ginger hackle fibers.

The two color variations listed cover the most common mayfly hatches that get into trouble as emergers: BWOs in the East and West, and pale morning duns in the West or sulfurs in the Midwest

You'll find mayfly emergers important most often in small sizes and on smooth waters such as the Henrys Fork of the Snake River.

and East. In this style, the tail represents the cast nymphal shuck. It should be approximately the color of the nymph, while the body of the fly should be the color of the emerged dun.

Presentation

Presentation is based on the helpless state of the natural emerger. It is simply stuck there. Your fly should come on a dead-drift float to the trout. It's important to pick a specific rising fish and present the fly right down its feeding lane. Selective trout on smooth water, which are most susceptible to emerger dressings, will not move far to take your fly.

Because trout working in these kinds of currents are notoriously spooky, you will have quite a bit of difficulty if you cast from downstream right up over them. The line and leader passing overhead will send them sailing. Either work into position straight across from the fish and present your emerger with a cross-stream reach cast, or take a position at an angle upstream from them and present your emerger with a downstream wiggle cast. These presentations will cause your fly to arrive at the fish first, ahead of the line and leader. Both methods are discussed in more detail in the section on mayfly duns.

Mayfly emergers are normally important only in a narrow set of circumstances, usually defined by small insects hatching in smooth water. It's often difficult to notice when emergers are important, because duns will be much more visible on the water. But trout feeding on emergers are almost impossible to take on any other imitations. They snub the best nymph and turn up a cold, wet nose at the most likely dun dressing. If you fish silken currents over small mayfly hatches, always keep emergers in mind, and be prepared to match them when you must.

MAYFLY DUNS

In this educated age, any writer who insists that mayfly duns are the most important stage of the most important insect to the trout fisherman must be prepared to defend his logic. Everybody knows that trout eat more caddisflies, more stoneflies, more midges, depending on who is arguing. That might make these other groups more important to the trout at times. But the mayfly dun has the greatest historical importance, in fly-fishing terms, and I believe it maintains that elevated importance to this day.

Why do I think that? For two reasons. First, mayfly duns tend to boat the water in moderate to great numbers within a limited time period. A hatch of mayflies is well defined, and it causes trout to feed selectively on the surface. You and trout rarely fail to notice a hatch of mayfly duns when it happens. Second, most mayflies emerge in open water, with enough difficulty getting it done to make them available to trout for an enrapturing amount of time. In contrast, most stoneflies crawl out of the water to emerge, most caddis shoot out like missiles flung from subs, and most midges hang in the surface film with a damnable invisibility so that the angler seldom knows for sure what is happening when midges are happening until they are finished happening. Or so it seems in comparison with mayfly duns.

Mayfly duns stand right out there on the water where you can see them and where trout can take them. They are delicate and splendidly beautiful. Their grace and charm, if nothing else, nominate them for the top spot in my affections. None of this diminishes the importance of other insects, or even of other stages of the same insect. It just pushes them all into the running for second place.

Natural

Mayfly duns hatch in all habitats where trout are found. It's rare water that contains trout without holding several species of mayflies. Some productive rivers have enough different mayfly species to produce fishable hatches year-round. Although there are at least scant mayfly hatches at all seasons except the dead of winter in the coldest climates, spring and early summer are their seasons of greatest importance. The earliest hatches start in February and March, in many areas before trout season opens. April hatches are persistent, even when the weather would seem to deny such fragile insects any chance of life. May and June hatches can be heavy, especially on days when clouds obscure the sun and drizzle dampens the air.

Early-season hatches occur during the warmest hours of the day, usually starting between eleven and one o'clock, lasting until things start to cool off again around three or four in the afternoon. These early hatches can be short, lasting only an hour or two, especially if the sun is out and bright. On overcast days, duns can trickle off for hours in sufficient numbers to keep trout feeding on the surface and susceptible to dry flies.

Some warm-weather hatches of midsummer remain in the middle of the day. Others wander toward hours when the water is coolest, in morning or evening. Often a hatch will be over before an angler who fishes from nine to five reaches the stream or lake. Other times the hatch will happen after he has retreated to camp for a martini. A valuable rule for any extended fishing trip is to *see the whole day*. Be on the water from daylight to dark, watching the water, on the first or second day of any trip. After that you'll know the best times to be on the water and the safe times to take your leisure.

I've seen an entire fishing club camp on a lake for a week and never know that the best fishing ended each day just before they launched their boats at nine in the morning. They missed it entirely. I slipped out at dawn every morning, rowed back in for a late breakfast, waving to them on their way out. I had a hatch and lots of good fishing already behind me. I went to bed early at night, got up and rowed out at first light. I never did tell them what they were missing. I should have felt guilty, but I belonged to a different club.

Fall hatches tend toward the center of the day, again when the water is warmest, as in spring. These hatches, and even a few mid-summer hatches, are often sporadic and sparse, especially when compared with the heavy and consistent hatches of spring and early summer. But never overlook the fact that sparse and spread hatches keep trout interested in the surface a lot longer than brief but abundant ones. Both types of hatches have their own importance.

Recognition of mayfly duns is second nature to most fly fishermen. To return to the cliché, they look like tiny sailboats. They address themselves to the water, and therefore present themselves to trout, in much the way a fleet of bitty boats would look upon a lake or stream.

Mayfly duns have either two or three long tails. Their bodies are slender, tapered from narrow at the back to a slightly wider thorax, which supports both the wings and the legs. Dun wings are held

All mayfly duns have approximately the same sailboat shape, though they vary widely in size and color.

The blue-winged olive dun is one of the most common, and widespread, mayfly hatches.

upright and are triangular. The forewings are large; they are what we see when we see mayfly wings. The hindwings are smaller, varying from about a third the size of the forewings down to no hindwings at all. Those of some species have evolved out of existence.

Mayfly duns have six legs, as do all insects. The legs are long and slender. A mayfly on the water, where it earns our most intense interest, is supported by its tails, body, and legs. It is able, by its lightness, to float on the same surface film that caused it so much trouble just seconds earlier, when it struggled through to emerge from the nymphal shuck.

Mayfly duns vary in size from tiny white-winged curses, imitated with dressings tied on size 22 and 24 hooks, to the giant Michigan caddis, the misnamed burrower mayfly, which requires a size 4 hook. The average run of mayfly duns, however, falls in the size 12, 14, 16, and 18 range. Outside of these sizes, you are looking at specialty situations—unique hatches that call for specific imitations.

Colors of mayfly duns range from drab grays to bold yellows, covering a lot of the known color spectrum in between. The most

The western pale morning dun, similar to the eastern sulfur, is common and widespread.

common colors are olives, sulfurs, browns, and grays. A great number of them, so many that it will surprise you when you begin to examine them closely, have a touch of olive as an undercolor on their undersides. Since this is the part a trout observes in the instant before it takes a dun, you will be wise to make it a habit to capture a specimen and tip it upside down before selecting a color for your imitation.

Imitation
Because mayfly duns hatch in such a wide array of water types, it's wise to look at three pattern styles to imitate them. One is for moving water that is broken, where flotation and visibility can both be problems. Another is for smooth currents in moving water and the most demanding surface of all, the tabletop of stillwaters. The third is a compromise that works well on both kinds of waters.

For flowing waters with broken surfaces, no dressings have been designed that beat traditional dry flies, sometimes called Catskill dressings, for the types of water where they originated. These patterns have sturdy hackle-fiber tails, slender bodies of fur or synthetic dubbing, and upright wings of flank fibers, flight feather quill sections, or hen hackle tips. The most characteristic feature is a cocky collar of hackle wound fore and aft of the upright wings.

Traditional dry flies got started in the late 1800s on British chalkstreams, when stiffer hackles were first applied to wet flies in an effort to float them for a bit before they sank. These flies were refined over time to fit the rigid dry-fly code constructed for the day, when it suddenly became sinful to take fish on sunk flies. They crossed the ocean from Frederick Halford to our own Theodore Gordon in the years surrounding the turn of the last century.

Gordon and his confreres fished Catskill Mountain streams. These were more tumbled and turbulent than the waters of South England. Hatches were not as clearly defined, nor as well understood. The British were willing to sit and wait, eat lunch, smoke pipes, talk theory when trout did not rise. Our fishing forefathers were less patient. They wanted to keep fishing, search the water when trout were not working, partly because they noticed trout were quite willing to rise to the surface even when no insects were hatching, partly because hatches on our freestone waters were not so well defined and predictable as those on British chalkstreams. It's easier to be patient if you know a hatch will appear, know approximately what time it will begin, and know that trout will feed on it when it does. It's less easy to be patient when you're not sure a hatch will ever come off and are not certain it will be so abundant that trout will feed on it if it does.

The dry flies our early Catskill anglers used were cast a lot more, onto a lot rougher water, than their predecessors from Britain. There was a distinct need for better flotation. This was achieved by seeking out ever stiffer hackles. The traditional Catskill tie, as it evolved, took the shape of the mayfly dun more and more accurately. As it is tied today, its tails, slender body, and upright wings catch the silhouette of the natural perfectly. The only thing to disturb it is the hackle collar. But this represents both the legs and the wings of the natural. In broken water, it does a good job of representing the *impression* of a mayfly dun dimpling the water, the pinpoints of light gathered where its feet, body, and tails dimple the surface, or else its evolution would have taken a different turn.

Effectiveness of Catskill dry flies is not limited to broken water. They work on stillwaters as well. They also work on spring creeks and tailwaters if angling pressure is not so heavy that trout apply for jobs as instructors in fly-fishing schools, offering lectures on hatches. The traditional dry-fly style is the first to consider if you intend to match mayflies on a wide geographic basis, fishing over all water types. Only when you start fishing specific hatches, over more demanding trout, will you need to tie more imitative dressings.

A common size and color range of traditional ties is easy to select and will be effective from coast to coast. It includes a few patterns that have long years of success behind them. The Blue-Winged Olive in sizes 12 to 20 is the fly with which to start your selection. Small olive mayflies hatch in most running

Blue-Winged Olive

Light Cahill

Adams

waters, almost all year long. They are the earliest important hatches in many waters and continue on through summer and into late fall, often coming off in two or three separate generations per year. In larger sizes, the same fly will fish for many of the lesser and larger green drake hatches from coast to coast.

The Light Cahill in sizes 12 to 16 matches a wide variety of mayfly species. It's a traditional pattern that originated in the East but works as well in the Midwest and West. Its pale colors cover a great chunk of the mayfly dun color spectrum. The muskrat-bodied Adams in sizes 12, 14, and 16 imitates a vast array of grayish-bodied duns. It also represents motion, with its variegated grizzly hackles, and works well as a searching pattern when nothing is hatching. The Adams is irresistibly buggy. It represents a lot more than just mayfly duns. It was originally tied as a flying caddis dressing.

That small selection covers the most common mayfly colors and sizes. It averages a lot of them, and it leaves a lot of them out. I can hear anglers with favorite patterns crying stridently at me now. But most will admit that in almost all mayfly dun situations, on all but smooth water, one of these three flies will take trout most of the time.

TRADITIONAL CATSKILL DRY FLY

Hook	1X fine, size 12–20.
Thread	Match body color.
Wings	Flight-feather quill sections, flank fibers, or hen hackle tips.
Tails	Hackle fibers.
Body	Fur to match natural.
Hackle	Match the mayfly wing.

For calm-water situations that require a more imitative dry fly, a range of Compara-duns will do what you need done. The Compara-dun style is based on Fran Betters's Haystack series, detailed in Fran Betters' Fly Fishing, Fly Tying and Pattern Guide (AuSable Wulff Products, 2nd ed., 1986) and modified and popularized by Al Caucci and Bob Nastasi in Hatches (Comparahatch Press, 1975).

The Compara-dun is a simple style to tie, perhaps even easier than the traditional dry. It consists of split-fiber tails, a slender dubbed body, and a deer-hair wing flared in an arc over the body. That's all there is to it. The split tails and the lower fibers of the wings help support and balance the fly so that it floats upright. The body and wing silhouettes are not interrupted, from the view of a trout beneath the water.

Compara-duns are extremely durable. They get my nod over quill-winged no-hackle dressings simply because quills get tattered after a fish or two. A Compara-dun can be dried off, dressed with floatant, reshaped, and fished for hours. It will take many fish before it becomes ragged, and it will continue to catch trout even after it does. If you use stout nutria or beaver guard-hair fibers for tails, rather than brittle hackle fibers, the fly will last at least as long as a traditional dry. Many times it will last longer; it has no hackle to come undone.

Compara-duns work best in sizes 12 down to 20 or 22. They do not work well larger than size 12, because the proper deer hair is too soft in lengths that will tie such large flies. Finding good Compara-dun hair is a task at times. If you order deer hair through a tackle-house catalog, it will be too long unless it is specified as Compara-dun hair. Sometimes even then it won't be right.

I've had good luck using coastal deer hair, available in natural brown, bleached, and gray-dyed colors, except in the smallest sizes. Calf elk, usually labeled yearling elk, is fine hair and comes in useful natural and dyed colors. It works for all but the smallest Compara-duns.

The best Compara-dun hair comes from the legs of the deer, sometimes from the mask. It is short and solid, not hollow like body hair. It does not have long black tips. If you search fly-shop bins persistently enough, you will eventually find good patches of this fine hair in shades of light and dark brown, tan, and a natural grayish dun. All are extremely valuable. When you find them, buy them and hoard them.

A range of Compara-dun ties for the most common mayfly hatches would approximate the colors of the most useful Catskill dressings, without the intervening hackle. A size 12 to 20 dressing with medium dun tails, tannish olive body, and natural or dyed grayish dun wings is a good start. It imitates the blue-winged olives at the small end of the scale, lesser green drakes at the large end of things. The largest green drakes, east and west, are too large to imitate well with flies tied in the Compara-dun style.

A dressing in sizes 14 to 18, with ginger or white tails, pale yellowish olive body, and a light tan flared wing would cover eastern sulfurs and western pale morning duns, or PMDs. A size 12 and 14 dressing with ginger tails, tan body, and tan wings would cover hatches that are a bit darker. Keep in mind that materials in flies become darker when wet.

A size 12 to 18 tie with blue dun tails, muskrat fur body, and natural dun gray wing matches gray-bodied mayfly species such as the western gray drake, and most blue quills as well.

These four ties cover the common size and color spectrums of the mayfly hatches, but they only average it. There will be times when your observation points to the need for other patterns. But olive, sulfur, tan, and gray Compara-duns will provide the mayfly dun dressing you need most of the time, all across the country, during all seasons of the year, for hatches on both smooth currents and stillwaters.

COMPARA-DUN DRY FLY

Hook	1X to 3X fine, size 12–22.
Thread	Match body color.
Wing	Natural or dyed deer or yearling elk hair flared in arc.
Tails	Guard hair or hackle fibers.
Body	Fur to match natural.

Blue-Winged Olive
Compara-dun

If a tail of Antron or Z-lon is added to replace the split fiber tails, the Compara-dun becomes a Sparkle Dun, a Craig Mathews adaptation that converts the dun dressing into a combination of a dun and an

Pale Morning Dun
Compara-dun

emerger, in essence imitating both stages with one dressing. It's difficult to say which is better. I carry the standard Compara-dun for all the major mayfly hatches I might encounter, but in addition, I carry it in the Sparkle Dun modification for the very abundant BWOs and PMDs. If the original dressing fails, I try the modification. Sometimes it works. Sometimes it fails as well. But it does give an added option, and that is never a bad thing.

The final dun dressing is the parachute style. It's a compromise fly that fishes well enough on fast and somewhat rough water and also gives a realistic silhouette of a natural mayfly dun on smooth water. For some reason, during certain hatches such as the western march brown, the parachute dressing seems more effective than a Compara-dun. Since the natural is most abundant on the smoother waters of freeestone streams—tailouts and the edges of riffles and runs—the traditional Catskill style is not nearly as effective.

The parachute style is also important to carry as an option for such hatches as all the olives, large and small, and both sulfurs and pale morning duns. I carry it in olive in sizes

March Brown Compara-dun

Slate Compara-dun

Blue-Winged Olive Sparkle Dun

Pale Morning Dun Sparkle Dun

12 though 20, pale yellowish olive in sizes 14 to 18, and brown in sizes 12 to 16. Add the Parachute Adams, a very valuable muskrat-bodied dressing, in sizes 12 to 18, and you've got the most important gray naturals covered. The Parachute Adams is also an excellent searching pattern. It takes many trout for me when no insects are hatching and no trout are rising, but conditions on the stream seem to indicate that trout would be willing to rise to insects if any were around.

PARACHUTE DUN

Hook	1X to 3X fine, size 12–20.
Thread	Match body color.
Wingpost	White or pale-gray dyed calf body hair or turkey flat feather section.
Tail	Blue dun, ginger, or grizzly hackle fibers, splayed slightly.
Body	Olive, yellowish olive, or gray fur or synthetic dubbing.
Hackle	Blue dun, ginger, or grizzly, wound around the wingpost.

Blue-Winged Olive Parachute

Pale Morning Dun Parachute

Parachute Adams

Splay the tail by adding a bump of dubbing or using a few extra turns of thread to form a slight bump at the beginning of the hook bend. Tie the tails back against it, and they'll spread just a bit, which helps stabilize the fly on the water. Keep the wingpost short or the fly will tend to be top-heavy and tip over. Use a hackle feather that is one size oversize for the hook you're tying on, to give a wider spread of hackle and help stabilize the fly.

When you begin to tie this style, drop the first few onto water in a dish on your tying bench, before you tie a season's supply. Get the right proportions worked out. It's the tendency of both amateur and commercial tiers to get the wing too long and the hackle too short, so that it becomes common for parachute ties to tip over rather than ride upright on the water. Make sure yours ride right.

Add a drop of head cement to the wingpost base after the fly is finished. When it soaks into the parachute hackle turns, it will keep them from coming unbound after a few trout.

Presentation

Mayfly duns generally ride placidly on the currents, dictating the kind of presentation that works best for their imitations. This cryptic behavior leads to the need for the classic drag-free drift. It is just as important today as it was when British writers began working it out more than a hundred years ago. Now we've got better tools and techniques to execute it.

In choppy water, where you will usually use traditional hackled dressings, a presentation with upstream casts works fine. Trout do not see well through a broken surface. They'll rarely notice the line and leader working in the air over their heads. Nor will the line and leader, drifting downstream on the rough surface ahead of the fly, leading it like a dog on a loose leash, often alarm the fish.

In any riffle or run, and especially on heavily fished water, it's still a good rule to present your fly so it shows itself to trout ahead of the line and leader, rather than trailing behind them, if the shape of the water allows it. This can usually be accomplished by wading into a position that allows a cast quartering up and across the stream, or even straight across the curents, rather than straight upstream.

On smooth runs, glides, and flats, it is always critical to deliver your fly to the fish before anything else goes over it. Trout can see well out of such glassy surfaces. They will be amazed at any sign of your line or leader passing over their heads; it will remind them of kingfishers and osprey and other unfriendly predators. If your line and leader land on the surface, then drift downstream over trout, ahead of the fly, they'll be well aware that something is not right about the fly long before they ever see it. They're not likely to take it. If your cast is straight upstream on smooth water, by the time your fly gets to the trout, they'll at best be wary, at worst be gone.

There have been great advances in the quality of fly-fishing tackle in recent years: graceful and powerful rods, high-floating and delicate lines, leaders that are thin but still very strong. But the greatest advances have been made in presentation techniques. The cross-stream reach cast and the downstream wiggle cast are the cornerstones of dry-fly presentation on all but the roughest of riffles and runs. They're critical when you desire to fool trout with mayfly dun imitations on the typical water where they hatch. They are just as important for fishing mayfly emerger patterns.

The reach cast requires a position off to the side of rising trout, either straight across from them or at a slight angle either upstream or downstream from them. The closer you can get to the working trout, within reason, the more accurately and delicately you'll be able to place your fly. A casting distance of thirty to forty feet is desirable, though you can get closer if you don't spook the fish, and you can use the reach cast at longer distances, though your ability to control the drift will be lessened.

It's important to take a position that, as much as possible, places an even sheet of currents between you and the trout. If you must cast over a seething set of currents, they'll tug your line and leader in all directions, quickly straighten them, and cause drag. Put as many conflicting currents behind you as you can.

To execute the reach cast, make a normal cast aimed to place the fly from two to four or five feet upstream from the rising trout. While the loop of the delivery stroke rolls out toward the trout, lay your rod over in the upstream direction until it is almost parallel to the water. Reach as far as you can with the rod tip. Extend your arm. When the fly lands, the line, rather than lying straight across the currents between you and the fish, will lie at an angle from the rod tip downstream to the fish.

As the fly drifts toward the position of the trout, follow its drift with the tip of your rod. If you're fishing the fly through a pod of rising trout, when the fly passes directly in front of your position, continue following it by reaching downstream with the rod tip and finally by extending your arm.

The reach cast accomplishes two things. First, as the rod fol-

After the fly is delivered cross-stream, in the reach cast, the drift of the fly is followed with the rod tip, greatly extending the free drift.

lows the fly, the fly is given a free drift, sometimes several feet of it. Second, because the line and leader lie at a downstream angle toward the fly, the imitation arrives in the trout's view ahead of the line and leader, rather than trailing along behind them. They see the fly first, floating along as if it's not attached to anything lethal.

If you're not able to place all conflicting currents behind you and still encounter drag after a short drift, then add an element of the wiggle cast to your reach cast. Wiggle your rod tip briskly at the same time you lay it over upstream, and the line not only will land on the water at an angle downstream toward the fly, but it also will have some slack installed into it. As this feeds out, the fly drifts freely toward the trout.

You'll need to carry some extra line in the air, in order to make up for the curves with which the line lands on the water, if you add wiggle to your cast. There is no formula for this; only experience will tell you how much to extend your measuring forecasts and backcasts to compensate for a serpentine delivery. You'll need some practice, as well, to learn to deliver the fly accurately into the feeding lane of a fussy trout while leaning, reaching, and wiggling all at once. It's not as difficult as it sounds, but you'll have to get out more often, fish hatches of mayflies and insert yourself into the midst of rising trout, in order to get the required practice. Go fishing more often; that's not a bad assignment.

Your second assignment, and perhaps the most important one, is to learn the downstream wiggle cast. I cannot count the times that I've floated a river, seen working trout, brought my boat to shore just below them, worked eagerly upstream through them without catching more than one or two, sometimes none, then turned back downstream to return to the boat, only to get detained by hooking many more on the way back downstream than I did while casting upstream. The unfortunate thing is that I usually spend half an hour or so frantically changing flies, to no avail, before I remember that working into position for a downstream presentation is far more important than the pattern I'm casting.

The downstream wiggle cast calls for a casting position anywhere in an arc from 30 to 60 degrees upstream from the trout, on either side of it. Don't take a position that places you directly upstream. Casting straight downstream to working trout will be fine, but for just one cast. There's no way to get your fly off the water for a second cast without frightening the fish it's just gone over. If the first cast fails, that's all you're going to get, if you're casting straight downstream. That's why it's so important to take a position upstream from the trout but at least slightly off to the side.

Your measuring forecasts should be made well off to the side, out of sight of the trout so that the line and leader do not fly over the head of working fish. As with the reach cast when it's made with wiggle added, in the downstream wiggle cast you'll need to calculate an added increment of line in the air to compensate for the curves on the water. Aim your final delivery stroke two to five feet upstream from the trout, and wiggle your rod tip briskly while the line loop unfolds.

The line will land on the water in a series of S-curves. As your fly drifts downstream toward the trout, these curves will slowly straighten, and your fly will get a drag-free drift until all the slack is used up. The fly should have gone over the trout before that happens.

On smooth currents such as these, the single most important thing you can do to hook trout on floating flies is to use a presentation from upstream, not down.

To pick the fly up for the next cast, simply lay your rod over downstream and let the current slide the line and leader away from the trout, off to the side. When they have drifted far enough away that a pickup will not disturb the trout, lift the fly and present it again. Sometimes you'll have to present it again and again and again, up to ten or even twenty times, before the fly arrives in front of the trout at the moment the trout is ready to tip up and take it. That ability to make repeated presentations without spooking the fish you're after is one of the remarkable advantages of the downstream wiggle cast.

Its greatest advantages are the same as those for the cross-stream reach cast: The fly is shown to the trout on a drift free of drag, and it arrives in sight of the trout ahead of the line and leader.

You can extend the downstream drift of a dry fly by wiggling more slack line out of the rod tip and dropping it onto the water right in front of you, right under the rod tip. As this line feeds out, the fly will continue to drift freely downstream. But this has limits; once the wiggles, and therefore the slack, are gone from the leader, you'll likely have microdrag that you're unable to see from your distant casting position. Trout are right up close; they'll notice the slightest unnatural drag on your fly. If currents flow in an even sheet down a long stretch of a smooth run or flat, however, you can sometimes extend your effective float ten to twenty feet or even more by feeding line into the back end of the drift.

You can use some line control techniques to make your wiggle casts more likely to fool trout. These tricks work equally well for the reach cast and downstream wiggle cast, and you should learn to apply them to both. You can practice them either on the lawn or while casting to working trout.

If you wiggle your rod tip in short arcs, almost by shivering your wrist, you'll lay a series of many tight S-turns on the water. This is good for a short drift on currents that approach briskness or that have lots of conflicts. If you wobble your rod tip back and forth in broad arcs, you'll lay a few wide, lazy S-curves on the water. This is more effective for a long drift down a single set of currents with very few conflicts in them.

By beginning to wiggle your rod tip as soon as the line loop starts to unfurl in the delivery stroke, then ceasing to wiggle it before the loop is entirely unfurled, you can lay your S-curves far out, at the end of the line and in the leader itself, while leaving the line closer to the rod lying straight on the water. This works well if the conflicting currents are out in or near the feeding lane of the trout, or if the trout lie in faster currents than those nearer to you.

If you let your line loop unfurl for a few feet before beginning to wiggle the rod tip, you'll leave the line and leader somewhat straight out at the end and lay your S-curves on the water closer to your casting position. This is effective when the trout rises in an even set of currents but you've got a faster current or a set of conflicting currents nearer to your position, between you and the trout. Lay your S-curves onto that swifter or more confused water, and your fly will get a good drift while the curves straighten out.

Learning to add wiggle to your emerger and dry-fly presentations will do more to increase your catch than any other single thing you can do, when you're fishing over rising trout. Wiggle is important in the cross-stream reach cast. It is critical in the downstream wiggle cast. It can even help you take a few more trout on up-and-across-stream presentations. A little wiggle added to almost any cast will increase the likelihood that your fly will get a free drift.

That will always catch you more trout, whether you're fishing a mayfly emerger, dun, spinner, or any other insect imitation on the surface.

MAYFLY SPINNERS

Natural

Mayfly spinners dance in clouds above streams and lakes. This can happen any time of day but is most common in late afternoon, evening, and sometimes early morning. Knowing that the insects in the air are males complicates the task of finding out just what trout might be taking when they feed during a spinner fall. Males seldom fall. They wind up in streamside spiderwebs. Many times male and female spinners are different colors and slightly different sizes. Matching the male will seldom solve a spinner problem. Instead, it might only add to your frustration.

A spent female spinner on the water, seen from underneath, just as a trout might see it when rising up to take it.

Mayfly spinners have the same sailboat shape as mayfly duns, when at rest, but their wings are glossy.

Egg-depositing females, not flying males, get taken by trout. They lie so flat in the surface film that at times they're close to invisible—to us, not to trout—and it seems that the trout rise merely to take sips of water. That's never true of trout.

Fish sip the insects quietly when feeding on spinners. This is an indication that the dying mayflies are caught hopelessly in the water and cannot escape. Trout are in no hurry to take them. In order to collect a specimen of what the trout are truly taking, you will have to look right down into the surface film, practically getting water on the end of your nose. Even then, it can be difficult to detect spent females.

The easiest way to collect a specimen is to hold a small pocket screen net half in and half out of the water and wait awhile. It will collect things that are almost invisible to you from above the surface. But they are very visible to trout from below the surface.

Spinner falls, as a general rule, take place over the quieter stretches of a stream. Most eggs are deposited in gentle riffles or moderate runs, or over pools and flats and tailouts, rather than in rapids, cascades, or swift riffles. Trout can be quite selective when feeding on spinners, because of both the calm water types and the inability of the insects to escape. These factors can force you to use an accurate imitation, necessitating collection of a natural specimen.

Recognizing mayfly spinners is easy. They are shaped a lot like duns, at least until they lie spent on the water. The tails are usually longer, the bodies thinner, and the wings, having cast the fine skin of the dun, are both bright and brittle.

Spinners are not always close in color to the duns from which they molt. Duns come in many colors, but spinners tend toward grays and reddish browns. The wings of the natural, like glass, do not impede much light. The veins in the wings are most visible to fish. The best way to imitate these diaphanous veined wings is with a few fibers of hackle splayed out to the sides. If you tie the same fly with sparse polypro or Antron yarn in place of hackle for the wings, it's just as effective.

Imitation

One of the best and simplest spinner styles is the Compara-spinner, from Caucci and Nastasi's book *Hatches*. These dressings have split-fiber or guard-hair tails, thin dubbed bodies, and hackle wound on as a collar, then clipped top and bottom. That's all there is to tying them. The clipped hackle allows the fly to lie spent in the water. If it is clipped sparse, the wings of the natural will be perfectly reflected by it.

If you'd like to make a more complicated tie, you can add spent hen hackle tip wings, in either light blue dun or white, before winding and clipping the hackle. Such dressings look more imitative, though I can't confirm that they catch any more trout than the simpler tie.

A very narrow size and color selection of spinner patterns will cover many, if not most, common hatches. It would include sizes 12 to 20 dressings with reddish brown bodies and brown hackle-fiber wings, and sizes 12 to 20 dressings with gray bodies and blue dun hackle wings. You might discover need for colors and sizes outside this range. If you do, they can be tied as variations on the same simple theme.

COMPARA-SPINNER

Hook	1X to 3X fine, size 12–20.
Thread	Match body color.
Tails	Brown or blue dun hackle fibers, split.
Body	Rusty brown or gray fur or synthetic dubbing, slender.
Wings	White or light blue dun hen hackle tips, optional.
Hackle	Brown or blue dun, wound and then clipped on top and bottom (substitute sparse polypro or Antron yarn).

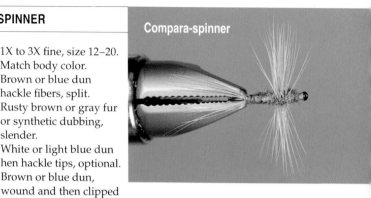

Compara-spinner

For a more imitative spinner dressing, use dyed hackle feather stems, usually called *quill*, for bodies. Stripped and dyed hackle stems can be purchased in an array of colors, the most popular and useful being blue quill and red quill. Refrain from simply stripping the hackle fibers off blue dun and brown hackle feathers. This exposes the core of the stem, which is white, and you'll end up with white-bodied flies rather than the color you're after. Tie quill spinners in the same two colors as in the Compara-spinner style: blue and red.

QUILL SPINNER

Hook	1X to 3X fine, size 12–20.
Thread	Match body color.
Tails	Brown or blue dun hackle fibers, split.
Body	Red or blue dyed hackle stem.
Wings	White or light blue dun hen hackle tips, optional.
Hackle	Brown or blue dun, wound and then clipped on top and bottom (substitute sparse polypro or Antron yarn).

Quill Spinner

Many times during a spinner fall, the dressing that worked for the dun will still take trout. This won't always be true, but it's always worth a try, at least until you can get to the tying bench and arm yourself with an appropriate spinner dressing. Sometimes cutting the hackles off the bottom of a traditional Catskill-style dun dressing will convert it to a spinner pattern that will fool trout. Parachute dressings used during dun hatches can be the best bet during spinner falls; the outspread hackles look a lot like the veined wings of the natural spinner trapped in the surface film.

Presentation

Spinner dressings should be presented much like dun patterns. The reach cast and downstream wiggle cast work best where the water is calmest, the most likely kind of water to find spinners falling. Because you will not be able to see your fly well, it will help if you work as close as you can to your fish before launching your cast.

Spinner falls generally take place on gentle currents, and spinner patterns will float well enough in this type of water if dressed

A traditional Hare's Ear wet fly can work wonders when trout are feeding on Red Quill spinners and you're having trouble following the float of a dry fly that matches them.

with floatant. But they will be very difficult to see on the water, especially at evening. You will have to follow their approximate progress by watching your line tip and setting the hook at any sign of a take in the area of the fly. If it helps, add a small yarn indicator or a bright-winged dry fly four to five feet up the leader from the spinner.

Mayfly spinners often sink and are taken by trout beneath the surface. This is especially true for species that deposit their eggs over runs and gentle riffles. When this happens, a very sparse traditional wet fly, in the appropriate size and color to match the natural spinner, might take more trout than a dry fly. Try a sparse Hare's Ear or Blue Dun wet for starters. These wets should be fished with the traditional down-and-across swing.

Chapter 5

Caddisflies

Much-deserved fuss has been made about caddisflies in the last twenty-five years. Before that they were treated lightly by angling literature. Caddis were usually lumped together with all the other aquatic insects, after the dominant mayflies, which made up the main part of every trout-fishing or fly-tying book, and dealt with in a few leftover pages toward the end. These aren't leftover pages.

Early literature gave caddis such scant attention because of their elusiveness. Mayfly hatches tend to be concentrated, out in open water, where they're easy to notice. Caddisflies, in contrast, are often very difficult to observe, making it hard to assess their importance. A few species emerge en masse, in daylight, in midstream, but not many. More of them emerge at dusk or after dark. When caddis do emerge in daylight, they often trickle off, a few now, a few then. And most come off the water like cannon shots, taking wing almost instantly and shooting off into streamside brush.

A great number of caddisflies get eaten by trout, as many as mayflies. In streams suited to them, where they are therefore more abundant, more caddis get eaten than mayflies. They are grubbed in the larval stage, down on the bottom. They are intercepted as pupae, in transition from the bottom to the top. And they are taken as adults, if not when they emerge, then when they return to the water to lay their eggs.

Average caddis hatches, with some prolific exceptions, are less concentrated, more spread out over time, than mayfly hatches. Trout tend to take them at random more often, to feed on them selectively a bit less often. This gives caddis a different kind of importance to the angler. Sporadic feeding on a specific food form increases the willingness of trout to feed whenever they get a chance at an individual insect, over a long period during any day. That's why caddis dressings often work better than mayfly dressings for drumming up trout when the fish are not feeding selectively, which in real life, on most trout waters, is more than half the time. Patterns such as the Elk Hair Caddis make the best searching flies on average trout streams and rivers.

If trout could be caught only when major hatches were happening, angling opportunities would be greatly diminished. Because caddisflies are responsible for much of the consistent fishing we are able to enjoy between hatches, we anglers owe them a lot.

Caddisflies are extremely diverse, with more than a thousand species in North America, which has such a vast and varied geography overflowing with different kinds of aquatic habitats. This diversity of caddis is likely an advantage to the angler rather than a disadvantage. The wide array of caddis assures that trout see several different kinds of them, sometimes in a single day. This keeps trout from keying in on a specific size and color with narrowminded selectivity, except during concentrated hatches, and allows imitation by average. The flies you use to average caddis and fish in searching situations will work as well when trout focus on a particular species during the few heavy hatches.

Despite their wide diversity, caddis are a lot simpler to work with than mayflies, in both fly-tying and fly-fishing terms. Larvae have only two basic shapes, one of major importance to anglers, the other minor, though obviously of great importance to the continuation of caddis. Pupae have one consistent shape throughout all the species. All adults have the same tentlike caddisfly shape.

CADDISFLY LIFE CYCLE

Caddisflies undergo complete metamorphosis. They live underwater as larvae, pass through the transitional pupal stage, then emerge as adults. The caddis life cycle is one year long, with the exception of a few large species with two-year life cycles and an abundance of very tiny microcaddis with more than one generation per year. Eggs hatch a few days to a few weeks after they are deposited. The larval stage sticks around the longest, in most cases a few weeks to a few months short of a full year, eats all the groceries, and does all the growing.

Larvae are divided into two distinct groups. *Case-building* larvae are more common and more often observed, but less important to anglers. Their cases are held together with silk and secretions.

If they are fast-water dwellers, cased-caddis larvae build their cases of sand or pebbles. This gives them the ballast they need to keep themselves firmly on the bottom. Slow-water cased larvae select lighter materials. Some use pine needles; others cut sections from leaves. A few make their cases by hollowing the centers of twigs or plant stems and crawling inside. Such materials are easily obtained and also offer the larvae perfect camouflage in their natural habitat.

Many case-building caddis leave their old cases when they outgrow them and exist without cases until they can construct new ones. They are naked, vulnerable, and often get caught in the currents and therefore get delivered to trout. Other cased caddis simply abandon satisfactory homes, at times in great numbers, and

Most pebble-cased caddis larvae are too well guarded for trout to eat in all but starvation circumstances. When they're free of the case in the drift, they're great juicy morsels.

enter the biologic drift, delivered downstream helplessly, probably nature's way of making sure all suitable habitat is colonized. Such drift usually takes place at evening or after dark, limiting its importance to trout fishermen, though not to trout.

Free-living caddis larvae build no cases and are far more important to fishermen. Some are predaceous, roaming and hunting across, under, and in and out of the spaces between bottom rocks in riffles and fast runs, feeding on smaller insects.

Other free-living larvae carry no cases but use silk to cobble together crude retreats on rocks on the bottom in riffles and runs, and also in slower currents, sometimes in rooted vegetation and other times in woody bottom debris. These larvae weave silk nets at the entrances of their retreats to seine fine particles of food from the current. These caddis worms do not need to leave their shelters to browse on material collected in their nets.

Caddis larvae grow through five instars and attain full size before preparing for the pupal phase of the life cycle. When ready for pupation, case builders attach their cases to the bottom and pupate inside. Free-living larvae seal themselves inside their crude retreats. If they are completely free living and have no retreats, they construct hardened retreats of sand or stones, weave pupal cocoons inside, and remain cryptic there for the pupal transformation.

Pupation is a thorough transition from larva to adult winged insect. It takes from one to several weeks to accomplish. The larval skin is cast inside the case or retreat. Wings, antennae, legs, and reproductive structures of the adult are all formed and finished before emergence. When transformation is complete, the caddis adult is contained inside the thin pupal cuticle, or outer skin.

When ready to emerge, the pupa cuts its way out of its chamber, and with the assistance of gases trapped between the outside pupal skin and inside adult skin, it swims and floats to the surface. Often this is a swift arising. Less often, it is slow and struggling. Many caddis pupae drift along the bottom for some distance before heading for the surface. Others reach the surface and drift, suspended just beneath it, for a few feet to many yards before popping through, emerging from the pupal skin, and escaping as adults.

This transitory pupal movement, from the bottom of the stream or lake to the top, is the caddisfly's moment of greatest vulnerability to trout. Though able to swim, the insect is in most cases simply

Anglers see mostly caddis adults during a hatch, but trout eat mostly pupae.

at the whim of the current. It has little power to avoid a trout if the fish takes a notion to intercept its trajectory to the surface.

Final escape through the surface film is usually swift. The wings of the adult pop out of the pupal skin quickly, and the adult is able to fly away almost instantly. The winged caddis emerges and is gone.

During any hatch, this risen adult is what you most often observe, but the pupa is what the trout most often eats. There are exceptions, such as the small, early-spring, dark Mother's Day caddis that hatch throughout the West and the small, early-summer, dark blue sedges of the East, both of which ride the currents in great numbers, if not for long distances, as adults before taking wing.

After escaping the surface, caddis adults fly to streamside vegetation. Mating takes place there rather than in the air. Though unable to consume solid foods, caddis can take in moisture and live for a week to about a month, another reason why more of them hang around the stream and show themselves to trout: They don't die off as quickly as mayflies. As we've discovered with our own species, longer life spans result in greater population densities.

Adult caddis bounce and swerve and seem to fly at random over the water, but it's common for their overall direction of travel to be upstream. Sometimes they head toward the headwaters in a constant stream, usually at evening, flowing through the air above the downstream current from which they've earlier emerged. This is nature's way to restock waters out of which the caddis, in their larval stage, have gradually been pushed by the current. The general drift of larvae is downstream. The general flight pattern of adults is back upstream. Nature abhors water that lacks caddis.

Caddis eggs are deposited in several ways. Some are dropped in clusters from above the stream. Some are attached to vegetation hanging over the water. Some are dipped to the water, the female touching down to the surface to wash away the eggs. Many very abundant and therefore important trout-stream caddis crawl or dive beneath the water to deposit their eggs on the bottom. This is risky business; most casualties wind up in the digestive tracts of feeding trout.

Because emergence is so often at dusk or after dark, anglers fishing during daylight hours frequently observe caddis flying out of streamside vegetation rather than emerging out of the water, though at times they're everywhere in the air and it's difficult to tell from whence they came. Caddis hatches often have the term *brush hatches* applied to them, sometimes as a sort of insult. It's really not an incorrect appellation, and it doesn't demean them. Trout likely eat more caddis adults returning to the water from the brush to lay their eggs than they do adults cannonballing off the water during an emergence.

To increase your understanding of both caddis and brush hatches, imagine a time when there is no major hatch. Walk to a streamside willow, sage, or clump of bunchgrass, and surprise it by giving it a good shake. Watch what flies out. Often, throughout those summer and early-fall months, when caddis are most abundant, it will be a minor cloud of them.

Even if only a few caddis adults mill out into the air, you will then be able to capture in your handy hat, or in your aquarium net if you carry one, the very insect that trout have likely been seeing and eating most often in recent days. Match these streamside caddis adults by approximation, and you are very likely to choose a fly to which trout will willingly respond.

Remember that fellow I encountered doing so well along the banks of my home Deschutes River? He wasn't dressed in the latest fly-fishing finery, but he did know exactly what he was doing. He was matching caddis the way they should be matched: with a few size and color variations of the same simple fly pattern style.

CADDISFLY LARVAE

When trout take cased caddis larvae, they ingest them pebbles or plant stems and all. When the case is made of vegetation, there is no sign that trout regret it. They take the caddis happily, digest the nutritious parts, poop out the rest with no problems. Trout, at least in my local streams, feed on pebble-cased caddis only in late summer and early fall, when supplies of other insects dwindle. When caught and held in the hand, the bellies of these trout feel hard, lumpy, uncomfortable to me and probably to the trout. Their anal openings are often red and distended. When trout take pebble-cased caddis, an impressionistic nymph such as the Gold-Ribbed Hare's Ear will usually be taken more eagerly.

Free-living caddis larvae are much more important than any kind of cased caddis. They live in riffles, runs, and any other running water with well-defined currents. They are not found in stillwaters. Net-spinning types need a constant current to deliver their food supply. Predaceous types need brisk flows for oxygen. They also need the myriads of little living rooms between bottom rocks in riffles and runs, where they can prowl around, looking for smaller insects to eat.

Since these two larval types, case builders and free living, have such remarkably different habits and forms, let's look at each separately.

Cased-Caddis Larvae

Natural
There's a lake near my home where big vegetation-cased caddis get their density calculations screwed up. They clamber about in tendrils of rooted weeds. When they lose their grip, they float up to the surface instead of sinking down to the bottom, which I'm sure they would prefer, because then they could crawl back to the base of a

Some vegetation-cased caddis larvae get their ballast wrong and wind up floating at the surface in stillwaters, where trout are happy to find them.

plant stem and begin climbing up it again. When they float up to the surface instead, they get stuck there, hanging from the rafters. They try to claw their way across the underside of the surface but fail to make much progress. When a cruising trout happens upon such a luckless caddis, it makes a bold swirl that can sometimes be seen from two hundred feet away.

These particular lake-dwelling caddis make their cross-hatched cases out of grass stems cut with their mandibles. They are Raggedy Anns. Many other vegetation-cased caddis larvae live in both stillwaters and the slow-flowing backwaters and edge waters of streams. Their cases tend to be a bit more compact, sometimes even incorporating light ballast so they stay on or near the bottom. When such stream caddis lose their grip and drift with a current, they tumble along until they arrive back at the security of the bottom—or get delivered to feeding trout.

Recognizing cased-caddis larvae is easy: They are the only aquatic animals that build substantial cases, with the exception of snails. It's easy to tell a caddis from a snail. A caddis larva has a head and six legs; snails lack legs.

The sizes and colors of cased caddis vary as much as the materials from which their cases can be constructed. Those that are important to trout run in general from about size 16 up to size 8, all imitated with flies tied on long-shank hooks. Colors, though various, will run to natural browns and greens, as most vegetation does.

Stream caddis make their cases from materials that are handy. They always blend with the bottom, and their densities are always in tight relation to the slowness or swiftness of the currents in which they live. Many make light cases that include both mineral and vegetative matter. Most of them make cases of sand or tiny pebbles. Certain larger types actually glue a small stone to each side of the case, in response to the need for added weight to keep them on the bottom. These obviously live in fast water. In my experience, trout avoid eating them. But trout do feed on many smaller mineral-cased caddis.

Imitation

The Brassie, a small, copper-wire-bodied nymph originated by Gene Lynch for boisterous Colorado mountain streams, seems to be an imitation of sand-cased caddis larvae. If it didn't begin that way, it ends up being an excellent fly to fish that way. The bright wire imitates colorful and reflective bits of mineral incorporated into the case of the natural. It is very effective when fished in waters where small cased caddis abound in waters with bright-colored bits of sand on the bottom.

It does not hurt that the heavy body of the fly helps get it to the bottom quickly and then helps keep it there. It will be fished most often in fast water and should be presented in the bottom layer of currents, where trout would find the naturals either clambering around on bottom rocks or tumbling in the flow.

BRASSIE

Brassie

Hook	1X or 2X long, sizes 12–18.
Thread	Black.
Abdomen	Copper wire the diameter of the hook shank.
Thorax	Peacock herl.

The wire body resembles the pebble case of a natural. The darker thorax looks a lot like the head of a natural stretched out the front end of the case. In total, this simple little fly looks like a lot of what trout eat when they're foraging on the bottom in fast water. If it's not an exact imitation of a mineral-cased caddis larva, it's still a very fine fly to use as a searching pattern in fast water when no specific evidence leads to the selection of some other dressing.

For lakes and the slow-flowing parts of streams, I like a style that was originated by the late Gary LaFontaine and written about in his thorough *Caddisflies* (Winchester Press/Nick Lyons Books, 1981). I use it sparingly and take fish with it when they are feeding on those suspended caddis that have their ballast miscalculated. The fly is called simply Cased Caddis. It's tied on a standard dry-fly hook that is bent upward just behind the eye and usually weighted. A forest of four grouse, flank, and hackle feathers of different colors is palmer-wound over the part of the hook behind the upward bend. This ragged material is trimmed into a rough body. Two turns of white chenille or yarn represent the abdomen of the insect reaching out of the case, and a few hackle wisps or partridge fibers make for legs.

This fly, better than any I've seen, represents the struggling of the natural insect. Most lake-dwelling caddis that get stuck in the surface film, and that clamber around in submerged vegetation when they're not hanging helplessly from the top, are large. I tie the fly mostly in sizes 10 and 12, because that's the size of the naturals in my favorite local lake. But it can be tied from size 14 up to size 8.

CASED CADDIS

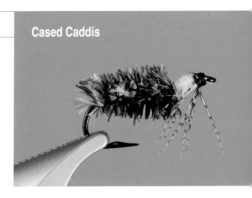

Cased Caddis

Hook	Standard length, sizes 8–14, bent upward behind eye.
Weight	10 to 15 turns of lead wire, optional.
Thread	Brown or olive.
Case	2 to 4 soft feathers, wound and clipped.
Neck	White chenille or yarn.
Legs	Brown or black hackle, or partridge fibers.

The colors of this pattern should be in the range of natural aquatic vegetation in the water where you'll fish it: browns and greens. The optional weight should be used on dressings you intend to fish deep, never on those you'd like to suspend in or near the surface film.

Presentation

The Brassie should be fished with rigging and methods that get it to the bottom and keep it there, usually in fast water. Use a floating line, and add split shot to the leader if they're needed to get the fly down. High-stick the fly on short upstream casts, drawing line in and lifting your rod as the fly tumbles along the bottom toward you, feeding line into the drift and lowering your rod as the fly passes your position and continues to bounce on the bottom below you.

Watch your indicator closely, and set the hook at any hesitation. Adjust your indicator and shot as needed to keep the fly down in waters of different depths and current speeds. Cover all likely water with several casts in the swift riffles, runs, and pockets where this type of fly is most effective. Don't hesitate to cover what looks like unlikely water; trout often find soft spots in bottom currents where it appears that no fish would ever be found.

Vegetation-cased caddis larvae that get stuck in the surface film of stillwaters do a lot of struggling. The best way to imitate them is with a floating line and a long leader dressed with dry-fly floatant to within six inches or so of an unweighted fly. Cast out, let the fly sit a bit, then retrieve it near vegetation with the slowest hand-twist

The edges of lakes and ponds are excellent places to fish cased-caddis patterns, especially if the water is weedy.

retrieve you can accomplish. If you could just let it sit without any retrieve at all, that would probably be better, but I never have the discipline to let anything but a dry fly simply sit.

If you extend a long-handled and fine-mesh net as deep as you can into a lake or pond, or drop your anchor over the side and pull it up covered with weeds, and the net or the weeds are crawling with vegetation-cased caddis, match their size and color as closely as you can, then fish the imitation at the depth where you suspect trout are feeding on naturals. Use a long floating line, long leader, and weighted fly if the water is two to four or five feet deep.

If it's deeper than that, use an appropriate sink-rate line and shorten your leader. Be patient while the fly gets down. Once it's at the level you desire, bring it back with a very patient hand-twist retrieve. The naturals do no more than lumber along; any kind of fast retrieve will not be taken for a cased-caddis larva, which is not to say the trout might not mistake the same fly fished fast in the same water for a dragonfly nymph. But news about them comes later in the book.

Free-Living Caddis Larvae

Natural
The riffle was thin, bright, chattery. No fish rose in the pool that fed into it, nor in the run that swept off below it. But the riffle looked productive. I suspected fish held in sheltered places along its bottom, feeding on stray insects there.

Before taking a cast, I rolled up my sleeves and hoisted a softball-size rock out of the riffle. There were a few clinger mayfly nymphs on it, and some gravel-cased caddis larvae. The most abundant insects, and those that caught my eye, were wormlike, bright green, and looked angry at being removed from the water. There were half a dozen of them on that one rock.

I chose a weighted nymph dressed on a curved scud hook. The body of the fly was green dubbed fur, with a slightly darker thorax and a few partridge wisps between the abdomen and thorax for legs. I started in at the foot of the riffle, casting upstream about twenty feet, letting the fly wash down in front of me just a few feet away. I made sure the nymph got to the bottom, only two feet down. And I made sure it tumbled there freely, without drag from the line or leader. I fished so close in front of my wadered toes that I didn't even bother to use a strike indicator; instead I just watched my line tip.

Trout intercepted the fly every few casts. The takes were subtle. The line tip either halted for just a second or jumped a couple of inches upstream. Each time something looked somehow out of place with my line tip or the leader butt where it entered the water, I would lift the rod. And each time a midsize but portly rainbow trout would come up and toss spray around the surface of the riffle.

Two hours later, I finally fished my way to the head of the riffle. I had taken and released more than thirty trout. They were between ten and fourteen inches long, and all were eager for that same green rock worm imitation.

Free-living caddis larvae are fleshy, wormlike creatures. They are unable to swim. The restless, predaceous kind move a little like terrestrial inchworms, using their front legs and posterior hooks to loop along on, under, and between bottom rocks, often going backward as fast as they go forward. Wherever you find even a few of them, you should give their imitations a try. Trout are always nosing around after them.

The net-spinning variety can exist in tremendous numbers in tailwater currents downstream from dams, often in colonies with their nets spun in the same crevice or on the same rock face. The reason is simple: Planktonic forms are the perfect size to get lodged in their nets, and plankton thrives only in stillwaters. Net-spinning caddis live only in moving water. Wherever plankton is delivered in the currents feeding out of a reservoir, greatly enriching a river with food forms the right size to get filtered out in miniature nets, populations of net-spinning caddis larvae explode to take advantage of the new source of food.

Free-living caddis larvae are distributed in flowing waters from coast to coast. They are present, and therefore important, throughout the entire fishing season in almost all riffles, runs, and gravel-bottom flats.

Recognizing free-living caddis larvae is not difficult, but there are a few other aquatic insects, such as midge and cranefly larvae, with which you could possibly confuse them. The key features of

Free-living caddis larvae have fleshy bodies, jointed legs, and anal hooks where their tails ought to be.

the caddis are fleshy and distinctly segmented bodies, jointed legs, two posterior anal hooks where there ought to be tails but aren't, and gills along the sides that can be fine filaments, brushy tufts, or absent. Midge and cranefly larvae are much more wormlike, with some fleshy stumps for legs but no true jointed legs.

The color range of free-living caddis larvae runs from light tan through muted olive to bright green. A few come in a brilliant, almost fluorescent, green. Most are either tan or green rock worms. Sizes range from a slender size 14 up to a fat size 8, nearly an inch long. The most common kinds can be imitated with flies tied on size 10 to 16 curved scud hooks.

Imitation
The pattern that works best for free-living caddis larvae is a style called simply the Caddis Larva. It is tied with a tightly dubbed body of tan or green fur. Your working thread can be used to rib the body if you'd like to give it a segmented look, though it's not necessary. The fly should be weighted in the thorax region with enough turns of lead wire to get it down to the bottom in fast currents. The

thorax should be of darker fur than the abdomen and dubbed more loosely. Leave the guard hairs in the fur to represent legs, especially on small sizes, or tie in a few grouse or partridge fibers on the underside of the thorax.

This is an extremely easy tie, but it represents the naturals perfectly. It is the dressing I used to take more than thirty trout from a single bright riffle. Since then, the addition of a beadhead seems to make sense, since the fly is as much a searching dressing as an imitative pattern. A bead seems to increase its effectiveness, though I'll confess it does lessen its resemblance to natural larvae. One of my critical searching flies for the faster flows of streams and rivers is an olive beadhead dressing based on the following Caddis Larva formula.

CADDIS LARVA

Hook	Curved scud hook, sizes 10–16.
Head	Gold or brass bead, optional.
Thread	Brown.
Weight	10 to 12 turns lead wire.
Body	Insect green or dirty creamish tan fur or synthetic dubbing.
Legs	Hackle or partridge fibers, or thorax fur picked out.
Thorax	Brown fur.

Green Caddis Larva

Tan Caddis Larva

The creamish tan dressing represents most tan varieties closely enough. Fur turns slightly darker when wet, so your fly when dry should be a bit lighter in color than the natural you're trying to imitate.

Free-living caddis larvae come in all shades of green,

from very dark to alarmingly bright. What is normally labeled *insect green* or *caddis green* fur or synthetic makes a great compromise color. You might have to use different colors on occasion, if you collect an abundance of a particular species that is not matched well enough by an average green tie, but it's doubtful that trout taking green rock worms will very often refuse a properly presented fly tied with insect green fur.

Presentation
The Caddis Larva should be presented dead drift, on the bottom, in water with at least a mild current. Most often you'll fish them in riffles or boulder-broken runs, because that's the kind of water where

Patterns that imitate free-living caddis larvae are perfect for high-sticking through riffles and pocket water.

the naturals are most abundant. Use a strike indicator to detect takes, which are certain to be gentle and difficult to feel. In shallow or slow water, the addition of split shot will not often be necessary, especially if you use the beadhead version of the fly. If the water is more than two feet deep, or moving at more than a patient pace, add shot and make sure your fly is fishing on or very near the bottom.

I have always found that a green Caddis Larva pattern in about size 14 to 16 makes an excellent searching pattern when I want to explore the bottom of any riffle. It will work in water where I've collected at least a modest number of the naturals from streambed stones, when no other insects are either more abundant or actually hatching.

The same green fly, tied with a beadhead and fished with a smaller Pheasant Tail Flashback or Brassie trailed behind it on a foot or less of tippet tied to the hook bend, makes an ideal exploring rig in fast water. No matter how you rig it, make sure to fish it along the bottom, and have some way to gain information about takes. That usually means the addition of a strike indicator on the leader, which is almost always the way I fish caddis larval imitations in moving water.

CADDIS PUPAE

Natural
The pupal stage of the caddis is in large part spent in the cocoon, hidden, armored, and absolutely still, safe from the threat of predation by trout. The moment of most importance, from both the trout's and the angler's point of view, is the pupa's trip from the cocoon to the water's surface.

Caddis hatches are very often sporadic in terms of daily emergence time and the span of days for the hatch. The average caddis species trickles off, a few at a time, over a time period that is at least weeks long, and sometimes lasts for months. The average caddis species also emerges in late evening or even after dark. Two, three, or more caddis hatches often overlap, with more than one species departing the protective cocoon at the same time.

As a result of all of the above, trout feed selectively when caddis are massed, but they get that chance to focus on a single caddis species far less often than they do during mayfly hatches. As a second, and more important, result, the fitful presence of caddis larvae, pupae, and adults keeps trout alert and feeding actively most of the time. They don't just turn on during a hatch and turn right off again once it's over, as they do so often when they're after mayflies.

We have caddis to thank, at least in great part, for the willingness of trout to strike flies when few natural insects are visibly active. That's why it's wise to remember that caddis larva, pupa, and adult imitations all make excellent searching patterns, especially on the average rock-bottomed freestone streams that most of us call our home kinds of waters.

Caddis pupae are, of course, just as widespread in terms of both habitat and geographic distribution as the larvae that lead to them. There are good populations in most lakes, ponds, creeks, streams, rivers, roadside ditches, and stagnant swamps, all across the continent. If water holds trout, it has caddis.

Caddis pupae are taken selectively by trout at times. When this happens, it is important to use a dressing that matches them, and to fish it with the proper presentation. It can be difficult to select the correct dressing, because it's difficult to collect a specimen to match. Caddis pupae are elusive. If you manage to capture one, it's likely to disappear into an adult, leaving a cast skin in the palm of your hand, before you get a chance to have a leisurely look at it.

Sometimes you can corral a few caddis pupae by suspending an aquarium net or hand screen net half in and half out of the water where the current is brisk, and when lots of caddis adults are emerging from the surface. During a very heavy hatch, the net might come up crawling with pupae. During the kind of hatch that prompts trout to feed selectively, you can often look down at the water line of your waders and see several caddis pupae using you as the launching pad for the aerial phase of life.

During anything less than a heavy hatch, capturing a specimen generally requires capturing a trout to see what it has been eating. You don't always have to kill the trout and examine its stomach to see what it has been taking. Once on a narrow, brushed-in spring creek, I spotted a trout rising vigorously and consistently just a rod's length below my position hidden on the bank. I dropped a small soft-hackled wet fly to the water, dapping it off the end of my rod tip, and let it drift downstream over the trout.

The trout rose and smacked the fly and came thrashing across the surface to my hand—it was not large. As I unhooked it, I noticed three or four caddis pupae crawling around on its tongue. The trout was so full it was unable to swallow them, yet it was still unable to pass up my fly. I quickly compared my fly with the naturals so very near it, decided it was an adequate match, unpinned the fish, and released it. In the process, those caddis pupae, so recently eaten, were washed away to safety.

Another way to collect a specimen is to lift rocks off the streambed and examine their cracks and crevices. Cases or sealed retreats affixed to these rocks often conceal pupating caddis. Pick the cocoon apart carefully; it's very easy to destroy the integrity of the fragile caddis pupa you'll find inside.

Recognition of pupal caddis is easy once you finally hold one in your hand. The features that make them recognizable are, first, their aquatic origin; second, their long antennae, usually held back on top of or alongside of their bodies; third, their wing cases, which slope back alongside the fat bulb of a body; fourth, the presence of

Caddis pupae carry their legs, antennae, and forming wings all back alongside their bulbous bodies.

tweezerlike mandibles, which are used to cut free from the pupal cocoon; and fifth, the lack of any posterior hooks or tails.

The size range of pupal caddis is extreme, from microcaddis, which are nearly too small to imitate, up to giant fall caddis, imitated by steelhead fishermen on western rivers with patterns tied on size 4 hooks. The color spectrum of caddis pupae contains some surprises. The expected drab grays, browns, and olives are among them, but there are also bright greens, oranges, and yellows. Nature's primary protection for this transitional stage of the caddis is not camouflage, but a quick trip from the pupal cocoon to the escaping winged adult.

Fortunately there are averages that can be struck in pupal caddis sizes and colors, allowing you to carry a small number of flies but be prepared to fish a large percentage of emergences. Caddis pupae run strongly to sizes 12, 14, and 16. Their colors tend to be tannish browns, olive-greens, and occasional shades of amber to orange. Imitation becomes a matter of choosing a pattern style, then varying the sizes and colors over this narrow range.

Imitation

The starting point in imitation of the common range of caddis pupae is the simple soft-hackled wet fly, originated more than a century and a half ago in Scotland. Soft-hackles were resurrected and revealed to an American readership by Sylvester Nemes in his classic and charming little *Soft-Hackled Fly* (Chatham Press, 1975, reprinted by Stackpole Books, 1993). These patterns are so easy to tie, yet represent so many naturals so well, that many anglers refuse to believe soft-hackles will fool many fish. They spend hours devising more complicated dressings that don't work any better and often don't work as well.

Trout are not often so selective to caddis pupae that they require an exact imitation. But the naturals have so many moving parts that the imitation must be active, must look alive in the water, or it won't capture the current-tossed appearance of the actual insect, in the eyes of the desired trout.

Soft-hackles are constructed with thin floss or fur bodies and a couple turns of hackle from a hen, grouse, partridge, or other soft-fibered feather. They were originally fished in the swift streams in

the border region of England and Scotland. They were not trans-
ported to America with any enthusiasm until Nemes's surprising
book came out in 1975.

The reason these fine wet flies failed to cross the ocean earlier is
easy to understand. The tactics that influenced our American fly-
fishing forefathers mostly were developed on the chalkstreams of
southern England, where the dry-fly-only code shunted all sunk
flies, including soft-hackles, to the side. It's too bad these border-
stream flies, and the tactics used to fish them, were lost to us for so
long, because those streams are shaped much more like most of our
own rivers than the chalkstreams are, and the tactics worked out on
freestone border streams are often more useful here than tactics for
chalkstreams.

Many of our caddis waters are ideally suited to the soft-hackled
style. When cast into moderate to fast currents, soft-hackled wet
flies present trout with the impression of an insect body surrounded
by a constant working of fibers that look like trailing antennae, legs,
and wing cases. That these same flies look like drowned mayflies,
stoneflies, and certain terrestrial insects that also fall to the water
and get eaten by trout doesn't have anything to do with caddis, but
it also doesn't hurt your fishing when you use one.

Nemes lists fourteen dressings in his book. The three that he
lists first, and says that he fishes most often, are the Partridge and
Yellow, Partridge and Green, and Partridge and Orange. He ties
them in sizes 10, 12, and 14. This compares very favorably with
what we have already noticed about caddis pupae: The most common colors are tannish brown, olive-green, and amber to orange.
The most common sizes are 12 to 16.

A tiny fly box containing Mr. Nemes's three favorite patterns, in
a size range from 10 to 16, would cover a lot of caddis pupal emergences. The same flies would also catch a lot of trout for you when
fished as searching patterns. I suggest this from experience, for I
carry just such a combination of flies myself and use it constantly.

Whenever I am faced with an evening situation and can see
trout rising but can't tell what they are taking, I reach for either my
mayfly spinner dressings or, more often, my soft-hackles. It usually
does not take long to find out which one the trout will take, because
I often try them two at a time.

SOFT-HACKLED WET FLY

Hook	Standard sizes 10–16.
Thread	Yellow, orange, or green silk, or match body color.
Hackle	Brown or gray partridge, or hen hackle to match natural.
Body	Yellow, orange, or green silk floss, or fur to match natural.
Thorax	Hare's-mask fur.

It's no secret that soft-hackled wet flies work as well for submerged caddis adults as they do for caddis pupae, for reasons I'll get into in the next section. For now, let me mention that my favorite soft-hackle dressing for summer and fall evenings, when adult caddis flit around in the air and dance around on the surface, is Sylvester Nemes's March Brown Spider. It is tied with a hare's-mask body, gold tinsel rib, brown partridge hackle, and orange tying silk. It fishes for pupae rising to the surface, and for adults submerged in the water as well.

To get more technical about caddis pupae, in terms of imitation, they often make that dash to the surface propelled at least in part by bubbles of gas trapped between the outer skin of the pupa and the inner skin of the encapsu-

Partridge and Yellow

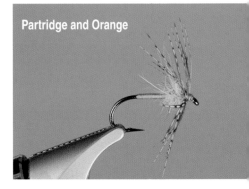

Partridge and Green

Partridge and Orange

March Brown Spider

lated adult. The aspect of the insect that shows itself most brilliantly to trout, the trigger that keys them to strike, is often less the shape of the insect than it is these bright bubbles.

It can be more important to capture this flash than to represent perfectly other aspects of the natural. That's why many early American wet flies had tinsel bodies: It was an attempt to capture the appearance of a bubble of gas in the reflections of light off the tinsel. It didn't work well. Place a fly with a tinsel body underwater, and you'll see why. It looks just like a fly with a tinsel body, not anything like an insect with bubbles of air attached.

The major breakthrough in solving this problem came with the publication of Gary LaFontaine's *Caddisflies* in 1981. In it, he revealed his Sparkle Pupa patterns, using triangular Antron fibers, which, when submerged, reflect light off their flat surfaces. If you're going to imitate caddis pupae with anything more sophisticated than softhackles, these are the flies with which to do it.

LaFontaine tied his sparkle pupae in two versions: the Deep Sparkle Pupa, to imitate those naturals that leave the cocoon and drift for some time right along the bottom, and the Emergent Sparkle Pupa, to represent those pupae that reach the surface, then pause before breaking through it. Those are the two times during which caddis pupae are most vulnerable to trout.

It is speculated that naturals drifting along the bottom, before beginning their combination swim-float toward the surface, might use the drift time to generate the gases, which are then trapped between skins and used to buoy the natural upward. It's very likely to be true. If they emerged from the pupal cocoon with bubbles of gas already trapped, they'd have little choice but to begin the trip toward the top at once. A weighted Deep Sparkle Pupa, presented right along the bottom, is the most imitative pattern you can fish at such a time.

The deep pattern is weighted with lead wire. The body is a mix of chopped Antron fibers and fur, sheathed over with Antron yarn tied in at the back, top, and bottom, then brought forward and tied in again at the front. A few grouse or partridge fibers represent the legs and antennae of the natural. A bit of fur dubbing or peacock herl represents the head. The wing cases are not copied, in the belief that the bubbles, not the wing cases, are the trigger that causes trout to pounce on a natural, and therefore the key characteristic to capture in the fly pattern.

The Emergent Sparkle Pupa is tied without weight, in order to fish shallow, sometimes in the surface film itself. It has the same sheath of Antron over a mixed body. Some of the Antron fibers are picked out to represent bubbles of gas escaping off the back of the natural, as well as the shuck of the pupa being shed in the film. A wing of very sparse deer hair over the back represents the emerging wings of the natural adult. It has the same head of fur or herl.

LaFontaine listed each of the styles in four primary colors and eleven secondary colors. I recommend tying them in the four basic colors, since those will cover almost all hatches. If you encounter caddis pupae that are not within these color themes, and trout refuse those that you try, you can vary the colors to match what you must. The four colors are brown and yellow, brown and bright green, dark gray, and ginger.

The most useful sizes are 12 to 16, just as with the soft-hackled wets when used to imitate the same set of insects.

DEEP SPARKLE PUPA

Brown and Yellow Deep Sparkle Pupa

Hook	Standard wet fly, sizes 12–16.
Weight	Lead wire the diameter of hook shank, affixed to length of underside of hook, then several turns wrapped around shank.
Thread	Match head color.
Overbody	Antron yarn, tied in at back, top, and bottom, then brought forward over underbody, to encapsulate it.
Underbody	Chopped Antron mixed with fur dubbing in appropriate colors.
Legs and antennae	Speckled grouse, partridge, or flank fibers.
Head	Fur or peacock herl.

The weighting wire is over-wrapped with thread so that a length of it is affixed to the underside of the hook shank. The remaining lead wire is then wrapped forward in loose turns over the hook shank and the layer of lead wire, almost to the eye of the hook. The Antron yarn for the outer sheath is combed out before it is tied in, so the fibers are spread. Avoid a thick overbody.

The Emergent Sparkle Pupa should be tied sparsely in all parts. It's an attempt to capture the essence of the insect, not to imitate all of its features exactly. If tied correctly, it can be dressed with floatant and fished in the surface film or left undressed and fished just beneath it. If you're in doubt about which way to fish it, rig with one dangled off the hook bend of the other, on about two feet of fine tippet. Dress the first, leave the second undressed, and one will float while the other sinks. Trout will let you know which they prefer. Most times it will be about 50-50, and you can clip off the dangerous dangler.

Brown and Bright Green Deep Sparkle Pupa

Dark Gray Deep Sparkle Pupa

Ginger Deep Sparkle Pupa

EMERGENT SPARKLE PUPA

Hook	Standard dry fly, sizes 12–16.
Thread	Match head color.
Overbody	Antron yarn anchored back and front, on both top and bottom; tease out a few fibers to trail the fly.
Underbody	Chopped Antron fibers and fur, mixed.
Wing	Sparse deer hair.
Head	Fur dubbing or peacock herl.

Tie this in the same four color schemes as used for the Deep Sparkle Pupa: brown and yellow, brown and bright green, dark gray, and ginger. Choose deer hair that is light or dark, suiting the body colors of the fly tied. If you're imitating a specific caddis hatch, the body, wing, and head colors of your fly should be chosen to match that natural.

Presentation

The natural pupa leaves the pupal chamber, drifts along the bottom for anything from a brief to a somewhat disastrous distance, then rises to the surface, propelled by a combination of gases trapped under its pupal skin and a brisk swimming kick with its fringed legs. Trout see an insect that is drift-

Brown and Yellow Emergent Sparkle Pupa

Brown and Bright Green Emergent Sparkle Pupa

Dark Gray Emergent Sparkle Pupa

Ginger Emergent Sparkle Pupa

ing downstream with the current while at the same time struggling upward toward the surface, sometimes sheathed in bubbles of air that can dominate the actual appearance of the natural.

One of the best ways to present a fly to match this type of behavior is with the traditional wet-fly swing: chuck-and-chance-it. A lot of the success of wet flies and the old manner of fishing them is thought to be accidental, but it can be based on the behavior of caddis pupae. Early anglers imitated it without even knowing much about it. Or perhaps they did know about it and didn't tell us.

Sylvester Nemes's favorite way to fish his soft-hackled wet flies calls for a cast that is slightly downstream from straight across in a moderate to brisk and broken current. He uses a dry line and tosses mends into his drift to keep the fly ambling steadily downstream with as little pull as possible from the line and leader. When the fly comes to the end of this free drift, Nemes leads it across stream, on a slow and constantly mended swing, until it comes to rest down below him.

This is an extremely effective method. It captures almost exactly the movement of natural caddis pupae as they near the surface in streams and rivers. Soft-hackled wets, fished with this simple drift-and-swing method, resemble a lot more than caddis pupae. They'll take trout that are feeding on a wide variety of naturals and will fool the fish a high percentage of the time when you don't know what might be going on, and therefore don't know precisely which fly and what method might work best. It's important to remember this when you're exploring water, trying to figure out how to catch a few trout. A soft-hackle, or brace of them, fished on the swing will catch trout more often than not.

Many stillwater caddis pupae, especially the larger types, make a bold dash from the bottom to the top, getting that trip over as quickly as possible. It's likely they have an instinct that tells them it's their most vulnerable moment, and that they'd better put it behind them before they become groceries for trout.

When fishing lakes and ponds during caddis emergences, it is often helpful to imitate this kind of swift emergence. Use a weighted fly, long leader, and floating line. Cast out and let the fly sink. Then raise the rod tip smoothly and steadily, pulling the fly up toward the line tip. Don't pause, because the naturals don't hesitate. Keep the fly moving, or trout might turn away.

The old-fashioned wet-fly swing can be extremely effective whenever caddisflies are active, especially when the line is mended a few times to slow the speed of the fly.

I once used this method on Oregon's famous Hosmer Lake to take a nice selection of its landlocked Atlantic salmon, which in this lake are twelve to eighteen inches long and behave precisely like trout. Hosmer's water is clear as air. I could see schools of the salmon cruising toward me for two hundred feet and more. A few large caddis adults paddled around on the surface. I'd been using dry flies that matched them, but without success.

Suddenly a school of about twenty torpedo shapes, averaging around sixteen inches long, headed my way. Every few feet, a salmon would bolt out of the school and chase something down in the mid-depths. Several caddis adults paddled right above them. The salmon ignored them.

"Strange," I thought. "What can they be taking?" The salmon continued to ignore the floating adults, but they made those sudden subsurface dashes. "Could they be intercepting caddis pupae on their way to the surface?" I wondered.

I tied on a large weighted dressing. I cast it well ahead of the cruising fish. The fly sank rapidly and thudded on the bottom. I waited patiently while the fish approached it. When they were within ten feet of the fly, I lifted the rod tip and started swimming the fly toward the surface. A twenty-inch salmon homed on it like a shot arrow.

I released the fish, cast again, and waited for another school. This time, when a school approached, I started the rise too soon. No fish saw it until the fly was three feet below the surface. Then one bolted for it. I slacked off on the upward sweep, not wanting to drag the fly through the surface film. The fly slowed. The fish lost its interest, turned away from the fly, and went back to the school.

Through the next hour, while pupae still rose and salmon cruised on the lookout for them, I caught six more salmon. None came when the fly was swept up at anything less than flank speed. None came if the fly slowed in its ascent. None struck if the fly was retrieved horizontally through the water, rather than lifted vertically through the water column. I never did manage to collect, or even observe, one of the pupae.

Perhaps the most interesting note is about the fly. I'd been fishing the nearby Deschutes River and had stopped at Hosmer Lake on my way home. The only weighted flies I had with me were salmon fly nymphs, big, black, and ugly. They might have been about the size but could not have been nearly the shape or color of those caddis pupae. But fish jumped them so long as they were retrieved right.

The correct presentation will often fool fish, even when the fly is absolutely wrong, during any kind of hatch.

Presentation of the Deep Sparkle Pupa in streams should obviously be right along the bottom. Since the naturals at that point drift more or less helplessly along with the current, your fly should tumble as freely as possible, without action imparted by the leader. If the water is shallow enough, and you can get the fly deep enough without split shot, then it is best to fish without the additional weight. Cast upstream, give the fly plenty of time to sink, then high-stick it down toward you, watching your line tip and leader butt carefully for strikes.

It will be easier to detect takes if you add a strike indicator to the back end of the leader. Gauge the length of leader between the fly and the indicator by the depth and speed of the current. If you're not ticking bottom once in every cast or two, you're not getting deep enough. If placing the indicator higher up the leader fails to solve the problem, add shot to the leader ten to twelve inches from the fly, and sacrifice some of the naturalness of your drift. If you don't get the fly down there, trout are not going to take it, when they're feeding on caddis pupae drifting along the bottom.

I'll confess that I often underweight my Deep Pupae, using just a few turns of lead wire a diameter finer than the hook shank, and fish them on the swing through feeding trout. This method is not mentioned in Gary LaFontaine's book, but it's in keeping with what I know of the behavior of the naturals. They swim and are buoyed quite briskly toward the top. A Sparkle Pupa fished a foot or two deep on a mended swing looks a lot like them. It works for me when trout are feeding with splashy rises in fairly fast and broken water, when a few adult caddis are in the air, but the fish refuse floating imitations. Switching to the shallow pupal dressing often brings them to the hook.

The Emergent Sparkle Pupa should be fished most often with the same type of presentation you'd use for a dry fly in the same situation. If you're fishing the fly sunk, cast it upstream or across and give it a free drift, just as if it were a dry fly. When it has finished

Emergent Sparkle Pupa patterns work especially well on heavily fished waters such as the Bighorn River tailwater in Montana.

out its dragless drift, fish it on a gentle swing, down around below you, slowing the swing as much as mends allow you. Trout will soon tell you which part of the drift—free or on the swing—that they prefer, and you can adjust your tactics from there.

When fishing the Emergent Sparkle Pupa in the surface film, present it precisely like a dry fly, which in essence it is. Dress the leader to within a few inches of the fly, if that helps keep it afloat. Fish with up-and-across-stream casts, reach casts, and downstream wiggle casts, depending on the best position the shape of the water and the lie of the feeding trout allow.

If you have trouble detecting takes to the low-floating fly, add a small yarn indicator to the leader four to six feet up from the fly. When you see a rise near your indicator, lift the rod to set the hook gently. Don't set it too hard; if no trout has taken the fly, you'll rip it off the water and frighten the fish you're trying to fool.

CADDISFLY ADULTS

Natural

If caddis hatches were as concentrated and as easily observed as mayfly hatches, traditional Catskill dry-fly dressings might have evolved with down-wings rather than upright wings. Caddisflies are now considered by many American fishing writers to be at least as important as mayflies, in some cases more important. There is little question that they are at least as important to trout.

The diversity of caddisflies makes them important in virtually every American trout river and stream, lake, and pond. Their presence and importance might be difficult to pin down at times, in terms of fly pattern selection and presentation type, but caddis will reward any research made into their hatches.

The season of most importance of caddisflies generally begins during the waning importance of mayflies, which have their own season of most importance in spring and early summer. Caddis hatches become important beginning in late spring, are dominant in summer, and continue into early fall. These are times of peak importance of the orders, as an average. You'll find fishable mayfly hatches almost all year long, and you'll need to match them when they happen. You'll encounter fishable caddis hatches in spring, summer, and fall, with the subsequent need to match them in order to catch many trout. But the largest abundance of mayflies in the early season tapers into the largest abundance of caddisflies in the summer midseason.

Caddis adults live, batting around in streamside brush and making dashes out over the water, for one to four weeks. They build up in great numbers along the edges of streams and rivers. Shake a bankside alder, willow, or sagebush in July or August, and you are likely to launch a cloudlet of them. This swirl will likely contain more than one species.

The same diversity that makes caddis hard to understand on a species-by-species basis makes them easier to understand on a pattern-style basis, because trout are less often selective to a particular species than they are with the mass-emerging mayflies. Three floating pattern styles, one for fast water and two for slow water, are all you really need to know to imitate adult caddis. I'll throw in a wet-fly style because of the habit of many stream types to dive underwater to lay their eggs. It's often speculated, and I fully agree,

The body of the adult caddis, shown here darkly outlined against the wings, has no tails and is shorter than the wingtips.

that far more caddis are taken beneath the surface, as either pupae or both swimming and drowned adults, than are taken from the top. But never ignore the top. Caddis dry flies work well as exploring patterns, during hatches, and during egg-laying flights.

Caddis adults can be recognized by their down-wing shape, long antennae, short portly bodies, and lack of tails. To be sure you've captured a caddis, look closely at its wings. If they have fine hairs on them, it's a caddis. It might take a handheld magnifying glass to help you spot the hairs on smaller specimens, but they are readily visible on caddis within the normal size range that you will want to imitate.

Caddis can be confused with some moths, but all moths have powdery scales on their wings. These scales will leave a residue on your fingers when moth wings brush against them. There are aquatic moths, even abundant ones on rare trout waters. The infrequent moth fall you might encounter can be matched with the correct color and size variation of the adult caddis dressings given in this section.

Caddis can also be confused with alderflies, covered in Chapter 10. These awkward aquatics have the same bulbous bodies and tentlike wings. Unlike hair-winged caddis and scale-winged moths, alderflies have slick, parchmentlike wings without either hairs or scales. Because of their behavior, distinct from caddisflies and revealed in their own chapter, alderflies need to be imitated with specific alderfly dressings.

Adult caddis are characterized by short, fat bodies, a lack of tails, and hairy wings held like pup tents pitched over their bodies. This common shape runs so true to form that adult caddis can be difficult for amateurs to identify to family, let alone genus and species. It's best to view them as an order and to match them with variations on a few pattern styles.

Caddis vary in size from tiny microcaddis that are the pepper on the buttered bread you accidentally left out on your camp table overnight, up to giant size 4 fall caddis that butt against your hat and shoulders while you warm yourself over the campfire on cool autumn evenings. As usual in nature, the center of the size range is the most common, sizes 12 through 16.

Colors of adult caddis can be as exotic as colors of the pupae that preceded them. Their most common themes, however, are

This photo shows both the hairs on the wings of all caddis adults and the darker color phase matched well by the Deer Hair Caddis.

closer to the center of the color range of natural insects, and lend themselves better to camouflaging the insects in streamside vegetation. That center includes tan, olive, and brown bodies beneath tan, gray, and brown wings.

Imitation
The evolution of caddis dressings has overtaken the diversity, complexity, and refinement of mayfly patterns in the last few years. Excellent pattern styles are now available for adult caddis.

Imitation can be kept as simple as that gentleman on the Deschutes River made it. A small range of color variations on the Elk Hair Caddis style, in sizes 12 through 16, will take trout most of the time, during most caddis emergences. They also work very well during searching situations, when no caddis, mayflies, or any other flies are hatching but trout are still able to recall perhaps dimly in their pea-size brains, that they've seen something of the approximate caddis shape, color, and size lately.

Rough-water caddis imitation was given a great boost with the development of the Elk Hair Caddis, originated by Al Troth, the famous Dillon, Montana, guide and professional tier. The Elk Hair Caddis has a dubbed body, hackle palmered the length of the body and tied down with a counterwound wire rib, and a wing of buoyant elk hair flared over the body and hackle. The butts of the wing fibers are left flared but clipped short to form a tidy head with a narrow band of thread wraps behind it. This represents ideally the head and necklike segment just behind it on the natural caddis.

The Elk Hair Caddis floats very well and is excellent for enticing trout to spear up and out of lies along the bottom in riffles, rough runs, and pocket water. It stands on its hackle tips and prances along like a natural caddis. The hackles, from the underwater point of view of a trout, represent a certain amount of motion—perhaps commotion—on the surface. The fly is easy for them to see, and because it is light-colored and rides high, it's easy for the angler to follow as it floats.

Rises to adult caddis are often splashy. Rises to the Elk Hair Caddis are often just as dramatic, tossing spray on the wind. The confident way trout take an Elk Hair Caddis is one of the most convincing testimonials to its effectiveness as an imitation.

Making this rough-water dressing effective for smooth currents can be as easy as trimming the hackle fibers from the bottom of the fly. Snip them off, and you've lowered the body and wing right down to the surface of the water. Many commercially tied Elk Hair Caddis in size 16 and smaller are tied without any hackle at all. Many in larger sizes, when tied for smooth currents, are also tied without hackle. I prefer to tie all of mine with hackle. They will serve on the freestone waters that I fish most often, but can also be trimmed when called for on a frequent trip to a spring creek or tailwater.

The most popular Elk Hair Caddis sizes are 10 through 16. They are useful all the way down to size 22, and I suppose somebody somewhere stretches the limits and ties them on size 28. The larger sizes make excellent support systems for smaller Pheasant Tail Flashbacks, Beadhead Hare's Ears, or Olive Beadhead Nymphs suspended beneath them.

The most common colors of natural caddis—tan, olive, and brown—lead directly to the three color variations that I find most effective in the Elk Hair style. These include Troth's original tan Elk Hair Caddis, the Deer Hair Caddis, and a version tied with a peacock herl body, palmered grizzly hackle, and brown-dyed elk-hair wing.

The Deer Hair Caddis is a modification of the Elk Hair worked out by fishing photographer and writer Jim Schollmeyer of Salem,

Oregon. The Deer Hair version is tied with a dark olive fur or synthetic body, dark blue dun hackle, and a natural dark gray deer-hair wing. It fishes for the prolific olive-bodied, grayish-winged group of caddis, which includes those from the size 16 and 18 early-spring Mother's Day Caddis to the larger and darker adults that emerge in summer from riffle-dwelling green rock worms.

Schollmeyer always cuts the hackle off the bottom of his Deer Hair Caddis when he ties them, while they're still in the vise. It's standard procedure for him. I tie the fly the same but leave the hackle uncut, preferring to do that surgery astream, if I'm fishing water that is less than rough and I decide trimming will improve the fly.

I often tie the Deer Hair Caddis with a wing of light-gray-dyed white-tailed deer hair or yearling elk. The pale color shows up on the water better than the darker natural deer-hair version, making it easier to see the fly. I find that it fishes as well during hatches and makes a better searching pattern because it's easier to see. I fish with Jim all the time; he has better eyes than mine.

The final brown variation is taken as well by trout as the original tan dressing and Jim Schollmeyer's deer-hair variation. But it's much harder to see on the water, and I fish it only when the color of hatching caddis demands it. In truth, that is not often, and I carry just a few. The combination of grizzly hackle and peacock herl is deadly, however. It's likely that somebody, somewhere, has tied a fly with the same body and hackle combination, under a lighter tan wing that is easier to see, and found it deadly. Perhaps you should be the one to make that experiment and name the resulting fly after yourself.

These three colors—tan, olive, and brown—cover a wide range of caddis emergences. They are effective coast to coast, south to north, throughout the entire season. I rely on the Elk Hair Caddis and Deer Hair Caddis as important searching patterns. I reach for one or the other when I want to fish a dry fly and have no clues that lead me to select a specific pattern.

When I'm fishing water that gives me no hint about what might work that day—floating fly or sunk—it's common for me to rig first with one of the two favorite caddis dry dressings and then to dangle a favorite Olive or Hare's Ear Beadhead Nymph off the dry fly's stern.

ELK HAIR CADDIS

Hook	1X fine, sizes 10–20.
Thread	Tan, olive, or brown.
Rib	Fine gold wire, reverse wound over the hackle.
Body	Tan or olive fur or synthetic, or peacock herl.
Hackle	Ginger, dark blue dun, or grizzly, palmered over body.
Wing	Natural tan elk, natural gray deer or gray-dyed elk, or brown-dyed elk hair.

Elk Hair Caddis

Al Troth tied the Elk Hair with fine wire ribbing to reinforce the hackle, and I've listed his version here. It's difficult to counterwind the wire without matting many fibers under its wraps. Most folks, including me, omit the wire on Elk Hair style drys. Tie the hackle in at the bend of the hook, wrap the body, wrap the hackle over the body, then tie it off at the end of the body. Measure the wing to extend just past the bend of the hook, and tie it in behind the hook eye with eight to twelve tight turns of thread. Lift the wing butts, tuck a layer of thread tight up against them to hold them up, then whip-finish the fly before you trim the butts. If you trim the butts first, you'll have a difficult time working your whip-

Deer Hair Caddis

Brown Elk Hair Caddis

finish under the hair head without wrapping over it. Trim the wing butts last by bracing one blade of your scissors against the hook eye and nipping straight across.

My favorite searching dressings for the three levels of the fly-fishing game—top, mid-depths, and bottom—are the Olive Bead-head listed for green rock worms, the March Brown Spider soft-hackle listed for caddis pupae, and the Deer Hair Caddis given here for caddis adults. I often try more than one of them at once.

For flat water I'll mention one of the best dressing styles you will find. Its brief treatment is not based on any problems with its effectiveness over caddis hatches, rather because it's a somewhat abbreviated version of the Elk Hair Caddis style and is tied almost the same.

The X-Caddis, originated by Jon Juracek and Craig Mathews, and written about in their *Fishing Yellowstone Hatches* (Blue Ribbon Flies, 1992), is a fine fly style for smooth water. The little book is a model for the way regional hatch guides should be researched and written. Its only flaw is a lack of photos of the fly patterns listed. Its information about hatches in the Yellowstone region, the excellent photos of the natural insects, and the quiet but precise prose with which it was written all elevate it right to the top of books of its kind.

The X-Caddis is a combination adult and emerger dressing. Its tail of Z-lon fibers represents the cast pupal shuck of the emerging insect. The body and wing represent the emerged adult. The fly is based on the Elk Hair Caddis, but it lacks hackle, so the body floats flush in the surface film. It's a very imitative style, and one you should consider whenever you're sure the caddis you see on the water constitute an actual hatch, not a return flight of egg-depositing adults.

Consider tying the X-Caddis in olive and tan in the central range of sizes, 14 to 18, and in black for very small caddis hatches, sizes 18 to 22. Many small, dark species, the widespread American Grannoms, hatch on smooth waters. They do not lend themselves to hackled dressings that can be used as searching flies, but you should be prepared to match them with low-floating flies when you find them important on your own waters. The X-Caddis is excellent.

X-CADDIS

X-Caddis

Hook	1X fine, sizes 14–22.
Thread	Match body color.
Tail	Amber Z-lon.
Body	Olive, tan, or black fur or synthetic.
Wing	Natural gray or gray-dyed, natural tan, or black-dyed elk or deer hair.

A variation of the X-Caddis style is the first to consider if you get into a demanding caddis hatch and none of the above colors suit the natural that is hatching. Tie size and color variations to imitate any caddis that you find important wherever you fish.

The Quill-Wing Caddis style is more imitative of the adult stage and copies quite closely the shape of the natural caddis body and wings. It is best used when you notice trout clearly feeding on adults, and on water that is flat rather than rumpled. The style is most useful on spring creeks and tailwaters, but every freestone stream has its edge waters and smooth glides, where trout can get as snotty as they do on the smoothest waters of the meccas of fly fishing.

The Quill-Wing style requires feathers that have been sprayed with artist's fixative and then set aside for some time to dry. If your feathers are not hardened, you'll find it very difficult to tie them in as wings without their fibers separating. Of course, even if they're fixed, they're going to come apart as soon as trout start chewing on them. But that's all right; they'll often continue to fish fine. If they get too tattered, however, you'll have to change them out. They're not nearly as durable as Elk Hair and X-Caddis style drys. Use them only when trout demand them.

QUILL-WING CADDIS

Quill-Wing Caddis

Hook	1X fine, sizes 12-20.
Thread	Match body color.
Body	Tan, olive, or black fur or synthetic, or peacock herl.
Wing	Mottled turkey, mallard, or goose wing feather sections.
Hackle	Ginger, blue dun, brown, or grizzly.

Tie the Quill-Wing style in the same set of basic colors as you would the Elk Hair or X-Caddis style. Because you'll use it most frequently on very smooth flows, it's often best to wait until you've collected the predominant natural, and tie to match it with a variation based on what you see. Trim the hackle off the bottom in order to lower the body and wing toward the water. This makes it float as the natural caddis adult does.

Many adult stream caddis lay their eggs by flying right into the water, breaking through the surface film, swimming down to deposit the seeds for the next caddis generation on bottom rocks or submerged logs and limbs. If you're wading during a heavy caddis egg-laying flight, you'll often find clusters of eggs attached to your wadered legs. If you're boating, when you trailer out late in the day, you might drive off with thousands of caddis eggs drying on the hull below the waterline.

Caddis that display this type of egg-laying behavior are generally in the abundant and widespread spotted sedge and gray sedge groups. The best way to imitate them is with wet flies in the right sizes and colors. The two flies that I've found best are standards, the Hare's Ear Wet and Leadwing Coachman. Both dressings are listed here.

HARE'S EAR WET

Hook	2X stout, sizes 12–16.
Thread	Brown.
Tails	Pheasant center tail fibers.
Rib	Oval gold tinsel.
Body	Hare's-mask fur dubbing.
Hackle	Brown hen.
Wing	Hen pheasant wing feather sections.

Hare's Ear Wet

LEADWING COACHMAN

Hook	2X stout, sizes 12–16.
Thread	Black.
Tag and rib	Flat silver tinsel.
Body	Peacock herl.
Hackle	Hen furnace.
Wing	Mallard wing feather sections.

Leadwing Coachman

Never overlook the March Brown Spider soft-hackle when you suspect trout might be feeding on caddis adults beneath the surface. It's the color of many of the naturals that deposit their eggs underwater. It captures the ragged look of an adult trying to make its bedraggled way back to the surface. You probably already have a few tucked into your fly boxes, because they give the impression of so many other insects. If you're having problems during caddisfly activity, give the drab soft-hackle a try. Trout might mistake it for either a pupa or a submerged adult, or for any of a great number of other things.

It's very likely that the success of the traditional wet-fly style, and of the soft-hackled wet style, owes a lot to their resemblance to adult caddis that swim down to lay their eggs on the bottom. After these adults complete their mission, they attempt to swim back to the surface. Some make it. Trout get the rest.

Presentation

Caddis adults are nervous characters. They flit around in the air. They clamber about in streamside vegetation. Because a streambank or lakeshore is the transition line between their two worlds, terrestrial and aquatic, they always hang near that edge, teetering constantly on it, flirting with the dangers in it. One of those dangers is trout that lurk along the same transition line, waiting for the innocent to errantly cross it.

Caddis cross it often. Set your rod aside some afternoon as the day begins to cool. Creep down near an overhanging willow, alder, or clump of bunchgrass that extends over a fairly deep and relatively brisk current. Sit like a heron and watch for a while. It will take some time before you begin to see anything.

Caddis will begin to materialize—small, drab ones flying out in reckless dashes low over the water. Some circle back and land. Some bounce a time or two to the water, laying eggs. Some drop their flaps and land on the water running, as if they were airplanes and the water a runway, laying eggs again. Some rise up into the air a bit and dash themselves right into the water; they're beginning the trip to the bottom to deposit their eggs down there.

Soon you will see rises, almost always intermittent, sometimes scattered, more often repeated in the same place. These are trout holding in sheltered bank lies and gunning down caddis that enter their gunsights. Sometimes the rises will be splashy. Sometimes they will be so quiet you'll not be sure you saw them. A rise can be so close to the grass you'll wonder if a trout caused it. You'll think it might have been some other disturbance to the current. But watch another while. It will happen again. Caddis keep coming and trout keep taking them, all evening long.

This kind of watching, this setting aside of the rod, is almost impossible for the impatient angler—and what other kind of angler is there when trout are rising? But it's important to take time now and then to watch the way insects and trout interact, always to the disadvantage of the insects.

Okay, you've watched long enough. Pick up your rod and drop your Elk Hair Caddis just upstream from that bunchgrass clump, so it will drift tight along the overhanging edge of it, down to the fish rising right there, as that last unfortunate natural caddis just did.

Natural caddis often float on the surface and show themselves to trout with their wings still and their legs at rest. This kind of behavior naturally dictates a dead-drift presentation. You will want to do all you can to put your fly over the fish with no drag and, if possible, ahead of the alarming line and leader.

Presenting flies this way takes different forms in different water types. In riffles and rough runs, when no fish are working visibly, I prefer to position myself at an approximately forty-five-degree angle downstream, below the water I want to fish and off to one side. I make casts upstream and across to the near water first, and let the fly drift as far as it will without drag. Each cast extends a foot or two outward into the next lane of drift. This goes on until all the water that I can reach with comfortable casts and controlled drifts is covered in a disciplined pattern. Then I move upstream and repeat the pattern, covering the next section of water the same way.

In smoother water of slick runs, tailouts, and flats, it is better to work into position, on spotted rising trout, for the cross-stream reach cast or downstream wiggle cast. Which of the two presentations will be best depends on the shape of the currents, the apparent selectivity of the trout, and the depth of the water—many times the reach cast lets you wade knee-deep in water where getting upstream into position for the wiggle cast would require wading over your head. At least for me, that becomes an easy choice.

The reach and wiggle casts are executed the same way for caddis as they are for mayflies, and therefore all that was written about them in the previous chapter applies here. They're methods that are more dependent on water type than on what is hatching. They work with all the orders of aquatic insects, and with terrestrial insects as well. That's why learning these two presentation methods is the most important thing you can do to improve your trout fishing when you begin to take on the challenge of catching trout rising to insects.

When trout work on caddis along the banks, a very common scenario, then you must work your way quietly along the edge and take your shots as the shape of the water presents them. Most of the time, you'll want to move upstream, either on the bank or wading so near it you can reach out and grab bunchgrass, willows, alders, poison oak, or rattlesnakes to help pull yourself along.

When fishing good bank water during caddisfly time, cast only a foot or two from the edge, not ten to fifteen feet out.

Fishing bank water is not casting from the bank to the water you can reach from it; it's tucking your fly—or flies, if you're using the common exploring outfit of dry and dropper—tight against the structures that create good bank water. In order to be good water, it must have a combination of moderate to fast but not brutal current, one to two feet or more of depth within one to two feet of the edge, and obstructions or indentations that break the current, forming lies for trout.

You move along and read bank water for these interruptions to the flow. They might be caused by fallen logs, banks cut under bunchgrass clumps, submerged or even protruding boulders, or indentations in an even bank line. Any tiny spot where a trout can get out of the direct flow of the current, yet be close enough to it to rush out into it and take something drifting along either in it or on top of it, constitutes a good bank lie.

As you move upstream fishing productive bank water, you want to drop your fly or flies a foot or two above prospective lies, usually a foot or two out from the bank, no more than that. Work your way along with short casts and short drifts. Currents at the edges are typically seething, with lots of conflicts; long drifts increase microdrag, which is hard for you to notice but is never overlooked by trout.

If you notice obstructions to the current farther out from the bank, say five to fifteen feet, cover those as well. They'll hold trout, they just aren't bank water. If the lie is formed by a boulder, make your first casts to the drift line downstream from it, but never overlook the upstream side as well. Water wells up there and forms a pocket of almost still water right in front of the boulder. Get close enough to place your fly two to four feet upstream from it—any farther and you risk drag—and hold your rod high while the fly floats down to that welling of water right on top of the boulder. You'll be surprised how often a trout takes it at the last possible second. That's the way they're used to taking natural caddis adults.

Along some banks, edge flows get reversed, turning back upstream, at least briefly. This happens most often just downstream from the kinds of points that form eddies. When you encounter these reversed flows, it's best to treat them as you would any other bank flows: Wade in at the downstream end and fish them upstream. If you come to a very short stretch of the reversed flow, fish it with downstream casts. Add some wiggle to the presentation and give the fly a downstream drift.

In truth, it's difficult to fish bank water downstream, because you aren't often able to get out away from it and cast downstream at a useful angle. Therefore, every cast is straight downstream. The first showing of the fly has a high percentage of success; in fact, very high. But if a trout fails to take on the first cast, you must pick the fly up right over the top of the lie for the next cast. That's why fishing bank water downstream is less than the best way to do it, unless you can wade out away from the bank far enough to get an angle into your cast, and therefore make the pickup for subsequent casts without frightening the fish.

Some caddis adults are so active on the water that a special presentation is worth trying when they're hatching or returning to the water to deposit their eggs. It's called the *sudden inch* in Leonard Wright's book *Fishing the Dry Fly as a Living Insect* (Dutton, 1972). The method is used on flats or other smooth stretches of streams and calls for giving the fly an occasional twitch as it moves through its drift. This represents the failed and fluttering attempts of the natural to launch itself off the water and into the air.

The cast is made from the wiggle cast position, upstream and off to one side from the lie of the rising trout, but no wiggle is added. In Wright's words, "Cast across and a bit downstream with a good upstream curve in the line, landing the fly three feet or so above a noticed rise. Twitch the fly slightly upstream soon after it touches the water—before line and leader can start to sink. Then give it slack to float drag-free as far as possible."

The cast can be made with an upstream reach or an aerial mend. Oversimplifying that mend, you aim the fly where you want it to land on the water, then lay your rod over in a reach as the line loop unfurls in the air, and bring the rod back upright before the loop has finished laying out. The line lands in an upstream curve, just as Wright has stated it. It's not very difficult to execute if you've practiced enough to become at all proficient at the basic forecast and backcast.

The sudden inch is worth a try when you're working over caddis adults that are hopping around on the surface, and you're casting on smooth water to a specific rising trout. It's not an efficient method for fishing rough or broken water, and it's not worthwhile

A caddis imitation alternately skittered, then allowed to rest, will often bring explosive takes on stillwaters where traveling sedges are found.

if you're exploring water without any rising trout, hoping to drum them up.

Another method that imparts movement to the floating fly is used on lakes, for what are called *traveling sedges*. These caddis adults scoot along like motorboats, usually in circles, as if they had madmen at their helms. Trout often ignore all else, including both naturals and imitations that sit still on the water. When trout are taking traveling sedges at the surface, they express no interest in the most exact imitations that are allowed to sit on the surface. But they often take moving caddis, or a fly fished with movement, with great detonations.

Whenever you see this kind of activity on the water, imitate it by skating your fly across the surface. There is no secret to doing this. Simply cast the fly out and let it sit a bit in case a trout is around that prefers it without movement. If nothing happens after a short wait, start retrieving it with long slides across the top. If you see a wake welling up behind the fly, don't stop. That might cause the trout to lose interest and turn away, just as they do when they're taking pupae rising swiftly to the surface.

Wet flies, when fished to match adult caddis, are best presented with the traditional downstream wet-fly swing. Keep the fly swimming along without allowing the current to race it. Constant mends and sometimes feeding slack will help you keep the fly on a controlled drift and swing that is not too fast. When you get it right, trout will give it a good rap. Your best guide to the right speed in the swing is experience. You'll soon get the feel, based on how things felt when you got takes, for how to fish the fly in currents of different speeds.

That feeling for how your fly is swimming when it's fishing right is called *experience.* There is no substitute for it in any kind of fly fishing for trout. I'm sorry, but it's your assignment to go out and get more of it, because the more you fish, the better fisherman you'll become.

Chapter 6

Stoneflies

The historical literature of fly fishing largely ignored stoneflies. With the exception of the giant salmon fly, which causes brief madness on the Madison in Montana, the Deschutes in Oregon, and a few other large western rivers, stoneflies received little notice in angling books, being lumped in those leftover pages with caddisflies and a handful of other flies, after extensive coverage of mayflies.

In the last few years, two books have been written about stoneflies and fly patterns to match them. This recent interest stems from closer examination of all aquatic insects as trout foods and templates for flies.

Three biological factors give stoneflies more importance than casual observation would assign to them. First, some species are active, emerge, and are available to trout as both nymphs and adults in late winter and early spring, on many waters before even the earliest mayflies. Second, the most important stoneflies are very large, up to two inches long at maturity, nearly twice the size of the largest mayflies. Third, the largest and most abundant stoneflies have three-year life cycles. Second-year nymphs of these are fairly large and available to trout the entire year.

Such perpetual availability of good-size bites for trout leads to one of the most important roles of the stonefly nymph: It serves as fallback food when no other food source is quite so readily available. That serves to keep trout fed. It also serves to make imitations of their nymphs work when other flies fail.

Stoneflies are often considered strictly western in importance, and in one way that is true. A few large and often famous western rivers, with habitat that suits them perfectly, have what could be termed *superhatches* of giant salmon flies and golden stones. The East has its own very large species of stoneflies, but they are not found in the same concentrations, on specific rivers, causing the same excitement, as they do in the West. But the majority of western rivers lack those superhatches as well.

The diversity and numbers of smaller but still very important stoneflies, especially the olive and yellow sallies, are the same East and West.

STONEFLY LIFE CYCLE

Stoneflies undergo incomplete metamorphosis: They live as nymphs, and they emerge as adults. There is no intermediate pupal stage and no dun stage.

Stonefly nymphs have gill systems adapted to water that contains lots of oxygen. With few exceptions, they live in moving water. They can be found in nearly all environments in flowing water. The greatest populations exist in freestone rivers with constant aeration in rapids and riffles. But others live in the gentle currents of spring creeks and even in slow flows over the sandy or silty bottoms of meandering streams, as long as the water contains sufficient oxygen for them. Cold water entrains more oxygen than warm water, so stoneflies become less important as you move south and as you move toward the lowland, warm-water reaches of river systems.

The largest stonefly species prefer riffles and fast, bouldery runs. They are, for some reason known only to themselves, most abundant in big rivers. Many smaller stoneflies live in smaller streams and headwater creeks. They're also found in slower currents but always where the water is cool and therefore contains enough oxygen. They are found in riffles and runs, too, but are just as common in the lazy water along the edges of a stream or among leaf packs and vegetation in still pools and backwaters.

Many small stonefly nymphs, and the early and therefore smaller instars of larger species, spend most of their time burrowed deep down among the spaces between bottom rocks and pebbles, below what could be called the *surface of the bottom*. As these early nymphs grow and mature, they work their way upward through the gravel toward the streambed itself. Some of the smallest species do not come out of the gravel, to where trout can get at them, until it's time for them to emerge into the adult stage.

Stonefly nymphs display two primary behavior types. Some are peaceful vegetarians, browsing on algae, detritus, and rooted vegetation. Their primary food source is the layer of growth that coats riffle rocks and makes them slippery. Large salmon fly nymphs, those that cause the most exciting stonefly hatches, are of this pastoral type. In some rivers rich with them, they are called the cattle herds of streams.

Other stonefly nymphs are carnivorous and mean as hell. These include the large golden stones, constituting the second most exciting stonefly hatch. Collect a golden stone nymph sometime and observe its fierce aspect and powerful mandibles; you can almost imagine the havoc it wreaks among smaller stonefly, caddisfly, mayfly, and midge immatures browsing placidly among a riffle's rocks.

I once netted a few mayfly clinger nymphs and a single mature golden stone nymph for photography. I dropped them all together into a miniature glass aquarium to await their turn on stage. While it waited, the stonefly nymph prowled restlessly, probing for a way out of the aquarium. On one swift circuit of the aquarium, it snatched a flat mayfly nymph and ate it like a sandwich while continuing its frantic march.

Small stoneflies have one-year life cycles. Many medium-size species have two-year life cycles. The largest species, the salmon flies and golden stones, live three years in the nymph stage before attaining maturity and emerging as adults.

Stoneflies nearly all react the same when the urgency of emergence approaches. They begin to migrate toward shore, across the bottom, sometimes in great numbers. They gather up along shore, resting under submerged streambank stones, in shallow water. If you wonder whether this migration is happening, stop fishing long enough to hoist a few rocks from the water almost against the banks and look at their undersides. Sometimes you'll surprise two to five or even more big nymphs clinging to the same surface.

These stonefly nymph migrations are not easy to notice, but they are very important to know about if you'd like to enjoy the best fishing during stonefly hatches. Folks who aren't aware of the importance of nymphs always attempt to time their fishing trips when the big and visible stonefly adults are on. They look for the *front of the hatch,* which can move upstream steadily and almost daily, as water temperatures warm to the magic 50-degree F mark, around which they generally happen.

The front is the few miles of river where the adults are just beginning to show. Anglers are sometimes so thick there that they form clubs and elect officers right on the spot. If you're anything like me, you avoid such mass gatherings of anglers, many of them as frantic as that golden stone nymph I plunked into my miniature aquarium to await its portrait.

The most consistent fishing over salmon flies occurs in the week or two before the appearance of adults, and the consequent appearance of all the anglers, when nymphs make their mass movement toward shore. Trout wait to intercept them along the edges of riffles and runs, out of which the nymphs come marching across the bottom, tumbling, relentlessly advancing. Trout line up near shore, on the inside of the fast water, to work on the nymphs gathering there. At times these trout hold in water so shallow you would normally wade through it to fish the good water beyond it.

Nymphal migration and emergence usually continue for a week or so after the big adults begin to show. Anglers tend to hit a river, at the front if they can, collect an adult and match its awesome size with a dry fly just as big, and immediately begin fishing. They'll draw up an explosive rise from time to time. But trout, if given a choice, seem to prefer nymphs to adults, perhaps because they don't have to ingest those crackly wings.

It's always best, during any hatch of large stoneflies, to kick around in the shallows near shore, look at the undersides of some rocks, even if you're able to observe lots of adults in streamside vegetation, before you decide on a fly and a method to fish it. If nymphs are still present in good numbers, trout will continue to key on them, often ignoring adults.

I had this driven home to me dramatically on the Deschutes River once. It was a hot early-June noon. Lots of adult salmon flies clambered around on streamside willows and grasses. I'd been pounding riffle corners and bank water with an Improved Sofa Pillow. Nothing came to the big, bushy fly. I finally gave up, sat down, captured and chewed a sandwich.

An alder tree in front of me threw a half circle of shade out over a very shallow cobble-bottomed flat. The water was no more than a foot deep at the edge, which was not far from my feet. While I ate, I watched idly out over the sunny part of the flat, where the sun struck through the water and illuminated the bottom. Nothing moved on it.

An adult salmon fly crawled too far toward the slender tip of a blade of bunchgrass that extended out over the water just upstream from me. The insect was an overload for the grass blade; it suddenly found itself in a pickle on the water right in front of me. It

When salmon fly adults hang out in the grass at the edges of any large river, trout move into the shallows to feed on those that make mistakes and fall to the water. But trout will ignore adults and continue to take nymphs if sufficient numbers of the immature stage are still migrating toward shore.

floated and fluttered and yelled, "Help!" for several feet down the slightly wrinkled surface of the flat, about two feet out from the bank on which I sat. It floated into the shade, through it, and safely out the other side, struggling to flap back to shore all that time. It eventually made port without getting whacked.

My attention went into the shade with the floating salmon fly but didn't come out with it. A movement in the shadows caught my eye. I crept nearer and looked closely from behind the tree that cast the shadow. A pod of six trout worked there, in water one to two feet deep, feeding with their noses down, rooting among hardball-size stones in the shallow water. Occasionally a tail just broke the surface, making the mildest disturbance.

I thought these were rises at first. But at such close range, it was easy to see that they were tails wagging in satisfaction, making swirls as trout dashed forward to snatch something off the bottom.

I backed out of there, walked upstream, and captured a few salmon fly adults. I dropped them onto the water one at a time. Each fluttered into and out of the shade and on downstream until it could regain the safety of shore. I saw one of them drift *exactly* over a trout, and the trout didn't even look up—it either didn't notice the insect on the surface or didn't care. No wonder my dry fly didn't incite any action. The trout were not even interested in the naturals it represented.

This incident happened in my fly-fishing youth, before I knew anything about stonefly nymph migrations. I trudged a quarter mile to my pickup and got out a collecting net. I hiked back to the flat, waded into the river well downstream from the pod of trout, and held the net firmly on the bottom, then kicked over a few rocks upstream from it. The net came up crawling with big, black salmon fly nymphs.

I swapped the Improved Sofa Pillow for a salmon fly nymph pattern. I waded carefully, crouched down, into a position about thirty feet downstream and thirty feet out into the current from the working trout. The hypotenuse of the equilateral triangle was a short thirty-foot cast upstream and across to the trout.

My first cast plunked the fly down about ten feet upstream from the lead trout. The nymph hit bottom and bounced just a couple of times before the trout shot forward, making a boil with its broad tail. There was a whap, and the trout took off. I let it run upstream without restraint, then pulled it far away from the bank and played it slowly to my hand, well away from the other fish. It was a seventeen-inch rainbow, fat and brightly colored.

I kept it for four reasons: youthful greed, dinner, a stomach sample, and it was okay to do so back then. It confirmed what my collecting net had already told me—the trout contained several freshly killed salmon fly nymphs and nothing else. It had taken no adult salmon flies, though they were thick in the grasses and trees all along the river, and clearly getting onto it as well.

Those trout concentrated so raptly on their bottom feeding that I was able to catch two more before the last one ran the wrong way and spooked the remainders of them across the flat like fleeing bonefish.

After migration to the waters close to shore, all stoneflies, not just large ones, crawl out of the water to emerge on land. Some go as far as a hundred feet from shore, and climb higher up a tree than I ever want to, before emerging. Most leave their cast shucks on rocks or grasses or tree trunks right at the edge of the river, or within five to ten feet of it.

Stonefly emergence takes place away from the water. The nymph gets a grip on a rock, plant stem, blade of grass, or tree trunk; then the nymphal cuticle splits along the back, and the adult slowly emerges.

Emergence usually takes place just at dusk or after dark. This is a simple and effective defense against bird predation, which would take a terrible toll if these insects emerged in daylight. Emergences start in early to late afternoon on some heavily overcast days. If you watch along the edges on such a day, you'll often be able to observe a nymph crawling out of the water on a rock or log.

You'll usually have to follow its progress for a few minutes while it meanders around on the rocks, or off into the vegetation, to find a suitable perch. Then it will stop wandering and get a good grip on a rock face, plant stem, or tree trunk with its tarsal claws. You'll see the nymphal skin split along the back and the adult slowly extract itself from its former life. Wings will unfold slowly from the wing cases, elongate, and harden. It takes quite a few minutes before the insect is able to fly away. Unless disturbed, it will either remain where it hatched or crawl slowly into hiding.

Stonefly adults survive several days to two or three weeks. Smaller species have shorter adult spans, larger species longer. Some species do not feed at all, taking in only moisture. Others nibble at bits of vegetation. Mating takes place in the grasses, willows, and alders alongside the stream, not in the air. When adults are abundant, it's common to see coupled pairs, and even an occasional threesome when two males compete for the same female.

Egg-laying flights usually take place in late afternoon and evening, but many stoneflies are nocturnal. The eggs are sometimes dropped to the water from above. Most stoneflies dip their abdomens to the water to release the eggs. Many smack themselves against the water to loosen the eggs, fluttering on the surface and generally ending their lives there, or else are swept under the water to waiting fish.

Rivers with large concentrations of salmon flies and golden stones sometimes have mass egg-depositing flights over broad riffles. But these are not the average event. Egg laying is more often sporadic than concentrated. Trout will of course be alert and actively awaiting the largest of luckless stoneflies, whether they arrive as singles by accident along the banks or in bunches out over riffles.

The smaller varieties of stonefly species, mostly in the groups called little brown stones, yellow sallies, and lime or green sallies, emerge and oviposit in the same ways the big ones do. Their nymphs, while migrating to shore and gathering up alongside it,

Though they don't cause the same pandemonium as the larger salmon flies and golden stones, smaller stoneflies such as this olive sally prompt selective feeding that will make you go fishless if you fail to notice them, especially on small and medium-size trout streams.

There are exceptions of interest to anglers, but smaller stoneflies are usually most important on small streams.

might cause selective feeding, but I've never noticed it. Flies tied to match them will be effective, but in my opinion, more often as searching dressings than as imitations.

All three of the smaller groups get the attention of trout when they return to the water to lay their eggs. Sometimes they merely prompt trout to focus on the surface and induce a willingness to take dry flies that are not necessarily imitative. Other times these insects are abundant, and trout become selective to them.

Little brown stones almost always emerge and lay their eggs in late winter and early spring, sometimes when snow still lies on streambanks. Yellow and olive sallies can descend out of streamside alders, falling toward riffles and runs as bright descending sparks lit by the spring, summer, or even autumn sun.

The smaller stoneflies are most commonly important on medium to small trout streams but on occasion appear as if by magic over broad flats of big rivers. Whenever trout see enough of these smaller stoneflies on the water, they become susceptible to fly patterns tied to match them.

Stonefly eggs incubate for one to three weeks on the average. But some hatch within hours after contact with the water, whereas others do not hatch for two or three months, releasing the nymphs when water conditions are most suited to their survival. Then the stonefly life cycle begins again.

STONEFLY NYMPHS

Natural
Stonefly nymphs are important to trout during two phases of their life cycle. The first is the long immature time of life, when lots of nymphs are out there in riffles, runs, and all sorts of moving water, eating, growing, and getting eaten. Because of their great numbers and sometimes great size, stonefly nymphs provide a lot of the stray bits of food that trout pick up nonselectively, during that 80 to 90 percent of the time that they feed along the bottom.

Their moment of most importance is during the migration for emergence. This might be the only time in their life cycle that some stoneflies approach the kinds of concentrations mayfly and caddisfly hatches display. The great migrations of the largest nymphs cause trout to feed selectively. Seldom do the smaller groups of nymphs cause trout to close their minds to other types of available food. But they do coax trout into an alertness, putting them on the lookout for a nymph, or a proper fly pattern, to come tumbling to them along the bottom.

Stonefly nymphs are primarily dwellers of the gravel and cobble of heavy main currents. When they migrate toward shore they pass along the bottom and move out of the heavy currents and into the less boisterous waters at the edges of riffles and runs. Trout wait for them along these current lines during the migration. Where the bottom is broken by boulders and trout are able to find suitable lies, they hold on the bottom right in the fastest water and feed on migrating nymphs knocked loose by the current. Eventually the nymphs end up at the very edge of the stream, where they will later crawl out to emerge.

On some rivers, notably big ones with heavy populations of salmon fly and golden stonefly nymphs, the migration of these nymphs toward shore draws trout in with it. The trout remain in lies along the banks until food supplies diminish there, which can be long after the stoneflies are gone, weeks to months later. So the early stonefly hatch signals the beginning of good bank fishing, caddisflies fuel it in the midsummer months, and it might last most of the rest of the season.

Recognizing stonefly nymphs is easy, for they all have the same basic shape, no matter their size. Mayfly nymphs were broken down into four groups—swimmers, crawlers, clingers, and burrowers—and caddisfly larvae into two groups—cased and free living. Stoneflies can all be considered together and imitated with a single pattern style, despite their great range in size.

Stonefly nymphs have two tails. Many lack gills, taking their oxygen directly through the skin, which is why they must live in oxygenated currents. On some large species, notably the salmon flies and golden stones, the gills appear as tufts on the underside of the thorax and first one or two abdominal segments. These tufts look like white pom-poms. One species, a western golden stone, has tufts of gills between its tails.

Stonefly nymphs all have two tarsal claws at the end of each leg, rather than one as in mayfly nymphs and caddisfly larvae. All stonefly nymphs have two distinct sets of wing cases on the back of the thoracic segments, more easily observed as the insects near

The golden stonefly nymph is a fierce predator, hunting among riffle rocks for anything it can subdue and eat, in trout streams of all sizes, from headwaters to big and boisterous rivers.

The salmon fly nymph is a peaceful browser of aquatic vegetative growth on the surfaces and sides of rocks in the riverbed. During their mass migrations, they gather near shore in great numbers, waiting for nightfall and their emergence time.

maturity. Mayfly nymphs have one set of wing cases; caddis larvae have none.

That is all you need to know to separate stonefly nymphs from mayfly nymphs, the only aquatic insects with which you're likely to get them confused. Mayfly nymphs have only one visible set of wing cases and have gills on the sides of the abdominal segments. Most mayfly nymphs have three tails, though a few flattened clingers and some small swimmers have two.

Stonefly nymphs are long and comparatively slender in the abdomen, but not as tapered as mayflies. The thorax is generally about the same width as the abdomen, or a bit broader and thicker, supporting the legs and the wing cases. The wing cases darken as the nymph approaches maturity and should be represented on the imitation with either a shellback or a tuft of dubbing slightly darker than the rest of the fly.

Large golden stone nymphs, and some of their near relations in medium sizes, have very beautifully marked heads and thoracic segments, with striking vermiculations in patterns of dark and light brown, sometimes almost amber. There is no real need to imitate these markings, but they make these insects instantly recognizable.

The size range of stonefly nymphs is broad, from tiny sizes 16 and 18 up to the giant salmon flies in sizes 2 and 4. It would be going out on a limb to say there is a central size range for stoneflies, and that you can average them out. That's unfortunately not true. Whenever you find them important, you must have the right size flies to fish for them according to their kind: sizes 14 to 18 flies for the sally group, sizes 12 and 14 for the midrange insects, and sizes 4 and 6 for the largest salmon flies and golden stones. These sizes are all on 3X long hooks, making the flies larger than those that would be tied on hooks of standard length.

It's true, however, that on rivers where the big hatches domi-nate, you can use a smaller nymph to imitate the second-year-class nymphs that trout feed upon all year long. A size 10 to 14 Gold-Ribbed Hare's Ear, or the beadhead version of the same fly, will usually do as well as any more exact imitation. Trout are not selec-tive when they're feeding on these younger nymphs. They accept opportunities at them along with the run of mayfly clingers and crawlers, caddis larvae, and various other items that fall in harm's way.

Though the adults of the smaller stoneflies are often bright olives and pale yellows, the nymphs are generally drab, as camouflage in their underwater environment.

The most common color range of stonefly nymphs runs from black through light and dark brown to yellowish brown and olivebrown. I collected a bright green olive sally nymph just once, but most nymphs of the sallies are pale shades of yellow- or olivebrown, for better camouflage in their streambed environment.

If you collect aquatic insects from riffles, over time you'll come across an occasional whitish, almost ghostlike stonefly nymph. Such a nymph has just molted, and its new skin hasn't hardened and darkened yet. Surpringly, if you imitate it, you just might do fine with a dressing that is so pale it's almost white. But I'll not list dressings for this rare occurance.

Imitation
I will probably get burned at the stake of some newly constructed fly-fishing dogmas for saying it, but in my experience, selectivity to and therefore the importance of any but the largest stonefly nymphs is rare. For the smaller species, sizes 14 to 18, I recommend using traditional searching nymphs, especially the Gold-Ribbed

Hare's Ear, rather than tying a full range of small stonefly imitations. If you encounter a situation in which fish refuse these in their standard ties and seem to be feeding selectively on small stonefly nymphs, that's the time to collect a natural and construct its imitation. Even then, a slimmed-down Hare's Ear, or color variation of it, will almost always do it.

Until then, keep your stonefly nymph patterns to a minimum, and enjoy your fishing. I have yet to run into a stonefly situation, outside of salmon flies and golden stones, where I needed an imitative nymph dressing. There are certain medium-size stoneflies that are fed on selectively at times, as nymphs, mostly in western tailwaters. They so closely resemble golden stone nymphs, right down to the vermiculations on the head and thorax, that I have trouble telling them from second-year-class golden stones until I put them under a microscope. I've yet to see a trout peering through a microscope and working over an entomology text, and it's my experience that trout feeding on these slightly smaller nymphs will take a slightly smaller golden stone imitation.

It's my belief that if you fish medium to large western rivers, you should carry size 12 to 14 salmon fly and golden stone nymph imitations, in black and brown, for second-year-class nymphs. Add these to the size 6 and 8 dressings you should carry for the mature nymphs, and just a couple of color variations on a single pattern, in a range of sizes from medium to large, will arm you to fish all year round on waters where stonefly nymphs are important.

My favorite dressing for salmon fly nymphs, based on both long experience with the hatch and the desire to keep my tying simple and impressionistic rather than realistic, is the late Charles Brooks's Montana Stone. A brown version of the same dressing is perfect for golden stones. This fly style, detailed in *Nymph Fishing for Larger Trout* (Crown, 1976), is tied in the round, meaning that it has no back and belly and shows trout precisely the same view no matter which way they see it. It also means the fly looks the same to trout no matter how it might tumble and roll in the current.

Brooks arrived at this style of stonefly nymph after underwater observation of naturals in the water being fed on by trout. He noticed that if a fly was tied with a light-colored underside, representing the tufted gills on the thorax and abdomen of the natural, and a darker back, the fly would flash its light underside to trout as it turned over in the water. The trout would back away, not take the fly, presumably because they don't see the naturals doing that.

I haven't gone underwater myself to prove or disprove Brooks's observations, but I have fished his flies, tied in the round, against more realistic imitations, with light undersides and dark backs, and have found his more productive for me. I tie them in black and brown, in sizes 10 and 12 for both medium-size related species and second-year-class salmon fly and golden stone naturals, and in sizes 6 and 8 to represent mature specimens of the biggest kinds.

MONTANA STONE

Montana Stone

Hook	3X long, sizes 6–12.
Weight	12 to 25 turns of lead wire, diameter of the hook shank.
Thread	Black or brown.
Tails	Split dark goose or light turkey biots.
Rib	Dark brown or gold lace (I omit rib on my own flies).
Body	Black or yellowish brown fuzzy yarn, or fur dubbing.
Gills	One or two light gray or white ostrich herl fibers, tied in and wound with hackle.
Hackle	One brown and one grizzly hen or soft rooster hackle, wound together in two turns over thorax.

Golden Montana Stone

Brooks weighted his stonefly nymphs very heavily, for two reasons. First, he fished them on big and fast riffles on his home Madison River and wanted to be sure they got to the bottom. Second, he did not use the indicator and shot method back then, and depended on weight wound around the hook shank, plus a high density wet-tip line, to get his flies down. My guess is that if the great man were fishing today, he would weight his flies with ten to fifteen turns of wire rather than twenty-five, he would fish with a floating line, and he would slip an indicator onto his leader.

The black version of this stonefly nymph is a fly that I depend on in many searching situations, all around the world, from our continent to Chile to New Zealand. For such exploring, I use it in the smaller sizes, 10 and 12, and use the largest sizes only when I'm fishing over migrating salmon fly nymphs. I use the lighter brown version in large sizes during golden stone migrations, and the smaller sizes whenever I find younger golden stone naturals and some of their smaller near cousins dominant in kick-net samples.

I've never tried tying the same style to imitate the much smaller little brown stones and sallies, though I suspect a slimmed-down version might work fine for them. For those smaller stonefly nymphs, and some of the medium-size ones, I use Gold-Ribbed Hare's Ears in appropriate sizes until I encounter a specimen I need to imitate, which in truth is rare.

If you do find an exact imitation of one of the smaller stonefly nymphs necessary, collect a natural and copy it as closely as you can. Use a very slender dressing, wound with yarn or dubbing, in the appropriate size and color.

Presentation

Most stonefly nymphs are poor swimmers. When cast adrift, they spread their appendages like a sky diver spreads his arms and legs, to stabilize themselves. Then they wait until they arrive back at the bottom. If you collect a golden stone nymph, observe its size, shape, and color, and then want to learn how it moves in the water, release it in the side shallows. You'll see that it spread-eagles itself at first, then swims with an awkward back-and-forth movement of the abdomen, which doesn't accomplish much forward progress.

The exception to this posture is found in the biggest stonefly of them all, the salmon fly nymph, which when released into a current curls into a ball. It holds that position until it contacts bottom, then opens up and crawls toward cover.

Because the naturals swim so poorly, presentation of stonefly nymph dressings, whether as specific imitations or generic searching flies, should be dead drift and down on the bottom, where the naturals live, tumble, and crawl. Tackle for fishing the large and heavily weighted nymphs, if you go out in the morning knowing that's what you're going to do, and you want to arm yourself for doing just that, should be stout. A long rod helps control the drift of the fly.

My favorite outfit for this kind of fishing is a 9-foot rod rated for a 6-weight line. I fish it with a 7-weight floating line, because that loads the rod better on short casts and also helps command all the strike indicators and extra split shot I usually add to the leader. The leader is about ten feet long, tapered to a stern 3X tippet. A large, bright, and hard strike indicator, rather than yarn, is attached near the line-to-leader knot. It suspends all that weight and helps detect takes.

Upstream casts allow the fly to plunge straight down. It can then be fished dead drift back toward you, sometimes almost under the rod top. Short casts are mandatory. On any cast much over forty feet, you will not have enough line control to fish the fly right or to react quickly to takes when they happen. Start by casting nearly straight upstream and work the casts out to cover adjacent swaths of bottom until you are casting at an approximately 45-degree angle across the current. Then it's time to wade upstream a few feet and cover a new patch of bottom the same way.

Each cast is fished from the point where the fly first reaches the bottom above you until it drifts down past you and starts to lift toward the surface below you. Anglers often truncate the downstream portion of the drift for the next cast, because it seems silly to fish water that is behind you and that you might have already fished. Don't make that mistake. It takes a significant portion of every drift to get the fly down to the bottom and fishing there the way it should. Let it stay there as long as possible. Feed line into the downstream part of the drift, just as you did with the dry fly and downstream wiggle cast, to extend the float of that indicator below your position.

When you can't extend the drift any longer, stop feeding line and point the rod straight down the line, with the tip held low to the water. The indicator will stop; the current will lift the nymph up

On big water, nymphs imitating larger salmon flies and golden stones should be high-sticked along the bottom. Fish the shallow water before wading through it, because that's where trout line up to wait for migrating naturals.

from the bottom. You'll often get takes in this instant, though in stonefly fishing, not as often as you will when the fly is in its free drift.

Once the fly has lifted to the surface, or almost to it, you can use the grip of the water on the line to *water load* the next cast. Aim it a foot or so out from the line of drift of the first, and place a wide-arced, open-looped cast up there with no fore- and backcasts. The more you swing that big fly and all the trinkets on the leader around, the more likely you'll get them tangled. That's the reason for the open loop: to keep those things from quarreling.

Rick Hafele and I fished a late-May evening on the big and brutal Deschutes River with such tackle once, during salmon fly time. It was nearly dark when we got to the river. Adult salmon flies were crawling around all over the place. But we walked down to a fast side-channel run and tied on weighted salmon fly nymphs. I didn't even bother to add an indicator.

A long slab of an ancient lava flow paralleled the river and broke off into a few feet of mild current braced against white water on its far side. Rick and I stood at opposite ends of this slab, dry shod. We flipped our heavy flies about twenty feet upstream and out to the near edge of the tumbled water. Each time they sank to the bottom and washed downstream out of the fastest water, delivered to the slower water just inside it, they were greeted by thuds.

These were not the light takes of small trout intercepting nymphs as they drifted to them in the current. They were the broad-shouldered attacks of three- and four-pound rainbows outrushing each other to take our flies on the run. The rod would snap down, doubled and surging, long before any thought of setting the hook had time to enter a head.

We took about four fish each in the last few minutes of lingering light. When we quit, it was too dark to stumble up the snake-crossed trail to camp without flashlights. If fishing at night were allowed in Oregon, we might have taken several more big trout from that same spot.

Salmon fly nymphs were migrating that night. The largest trout in the river were lined up near shore, waiting to ambush them.

STONEFLY ADULTS

It was February. The weather was typical for the dam-subdued middle part of the Deschutes River in late winter. Weak sunshine slowly warmed the grasses and willows along the bank, melted patches of frost along the riverbank. No insects hatched, and no trout were working, when we arrived at ten o'clock. Rick Hafele and I fished shallow back channels fruitlessly for an hour, then backed out to warm up, stretched out in the grass, our rods strung and ready. It was good to warm up again after wading. We watched the river and waited for something to happen.

Not long after eleven o'clock, a few small, dark insects began to appear along the flooded edges of the main current, out where the river sent side currents back in among the willows and the shallower channels we'd already fished without success. These insects materialized around the bases of submerged willow stems and grass clumps. They often ventured out on the water a few inches, but always managed to buzz and skitter back to safety. We saw no rises to them.

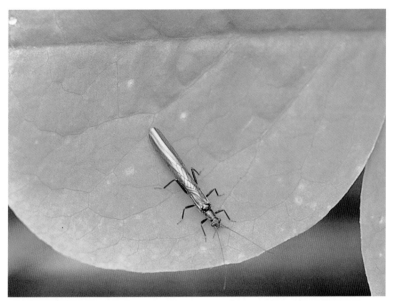

Some small dark stoneflies, such as this needle fly, constitute important emergences in late winter and early spring.

Rick noticed them, stood up, and said, "I think I'll wade out farther and take a few casts." He had fished the same water a week earlier, taking a few nice trout. He waded out into the strong current as far as he dared, all of about five feet, then turned and began casting upstream, placing his dry fly right along the willow edge, with short twenty- and thirty-foot casts. He made no more than ten casts before a barely perceptible swirl arose around his fly. Rick raised his rod to set the hook gently.

There was no relationship between the size of the rise and the fight of the fish. It took off in a strong run that forced Rick to follow it, stumbling downstream a couple hundred feet. Ten minutes later, he led the fish into a shallow sidewater, tried to land it, but it shot out again and fought back into the main current. Finally he brought it in, cradled it gently and held it up. It was a twenty-three-inch brown.

"I think I hooked this same fish last week," Rick said, laughing. "It was in the same spot. I didn't land it then, though."

After Rick released the fish, I looked at his fly. It was a simple creation with no tail, a thin brown body, a woodchuck-hair wing laid flat over the body, and a bristling of grizzly hackle. It was a size 16. It seemed too tiny to interest a trout that size, at that time of year.

"It's my version of a Little Brown Stone," Rick said. "It matches the stoneflies that hatch on the Deschutes, and most other rivers, in February and March."

I waded out and used my aquarium net to scoop up one of the tiny insects drifting near the base of a willow. I compared it with Rick's fly. The natural had a thin brown body and flat wings held over its back. Its little legs worked constantly while I held it. When I dropped it into the water, it took off running across the surface toward the nearest willow stem and didn't stop until it got there. It never did fly, though its wings whirred.

The small stoneflies were active all afternoon. Seldom did we see them in the air. They were always on willows and grasses protruding from the high water or on the surface very near them, bustling around. We saw just a few rises, all very scattered, but were able to bring up and hook almost all of the trout that we saw working. We only took five or six more trout all day. None were as large as Rick's first. But all were browns, and any brown trout taken on a dry fly in February is a beautiful brown indeed.

Natural

The importance of stonefly adults begins in late winter. It quickens as spring tries and fails and tries again to arrive. It reaches a peak in the period when winter gives up to spring. The April opener across much of the country is probably the penultimate moment of the stonefly, especially in the East. The ultimate moment is the May, June, and even early-July—still spring as you go up into the higher elevations—salmon fly hatch on large western rivers.

The warm summer season is a time of drought for most stonefly activity, especially among the large ones, but some of the smaller yellow and olive sallies are present and active all season. Trout are not often selective to them unless they're very abundant, but that happens often enough that you should be prepared for it. Perhaps like adult caddis, one of the primary functions of the scattered smaller stoneflies, from the angler's point of view, is to get gobbled intermittently throughout the day, thereby keeping trout looking up, interested in feeding on the surface.

In late August and through September, even into October on small streams, there are new hatches of small green and pale yellow stoneflies. Though fish seldom rise selectively and exclusively to these, they also seldom will refuse a good impression of them when a few naturals are in the air and on the water.

There are two primary habitats of importance to trout waiting to make meals of stonefly adults. The first is the edge of a fair-size to large river. This is the transition zone between aquatic and terrestrial environments. Adult stoneflies are first available at the edge when they emerge. They continue to be available along the edge as they adventure around there throughout adult life, mating, drowsing in the sun, scrambling with seeming stupidity up and down grass stems that often get overloaded with them and send them plummeting to the water.

The second habitat of importance is the many riffles, large and small, over which most stoneflies prefer to deposit their eggs. This kind of rough water masks the disappearance of stoneflies in rises. Sometimes you'll see detonations, especially to the largest of these insects. Other times you'll not be able to notice the takes without getting right up on top of them, because they are masked by the brisk water.

A lot of female stonefly adults, especially the smaller varieties, get trapped on the surface or even drowned beneath it when they lay their eggs over fast water. Trout take these quietly, often subsurface, almost always without raising the kind of fuss that becomes an easily observed rise.

It is even more difficult to discern the importance of all but the most obvious stonefly egg-laying flights when you consider that they often happen at dusk, in low light. But they happen often enough on cloudy days, and even in bright sunshine in late summer and early fall, to be easily noticed at times. It's always necessary to recognize stonefly situations for what they are when they happen, in order to take advantage of them—or rather, to take advantage of trout taking advantage of stoneflies.

Recognizing stonefly adults, and distinguishing them from mayflies and caddisflies, is just as easy as recognizing their nymphs and distinguishing them from mayfly nymphs and caddisfly larvae.

For one thing, the adults look very much like the nymphs with their wing cases gone and their wings fully formed.

Stonefly adults are sometimes called *flatwings,* in immediate contrast to the upright wings of mayflies and the tent wings of caddis. Stonefly adults have two tails, which in some cases are so short that they are hard to see. They have long antennae. But it is the four wings, all of equal length and all held flat over the body of the insect at rest, that make it easy to recognize stonefly adults.

The size range is the same as that for their mature nymphs: from tiny size 16s and 18s up to 3X long size 2s, nearly two inches long. As with nymphs, it is impossible to average stonefly adults, to give a common size range within which most of the important species will fall. They simply won't. Each important group has its own size that must be matched, not averaged.

The same is true for color. First come the little brown stones of late winter and early spring, February through April. Salmon flies, with their bright orange undersides, hatch next, in late April, May, and early June—as late as July 15 on the Yellowstone Plateau, which is still early spring up there. Then the colorful golden stones emerge, in early June in the lowlands through July at higher elevations. Yellow and olive sallies begin just after the golden stones on some waters, and hatch on various waters all through July, August, September, and into October.

The golden stonefly, sometimes called the willow fly, tends to hatch a bit later and over a far broader geography than the slightly larger and much more famous salmon fly.

The giant salmon fly is justifiably famous, but only on a restricted set of big western rivers such as the Deschutes, Madison, and Yellowstone.

The larger, and also most famous, stoneflies are most important on a few big rivers. When they're around, it's critical to match them, because trout won't fuss with anything less than them. Unfortunately, their size, fame, and restricted distribution can cause rivers to be crowded when the best hatches are happening.

I don't like crowds. I do enjoy the much smaller sallies for their delicate beauty, for their presence on the smaller mountain trout streams that seem to be my own favorite habitat, and for their widespread and stretched-out emergences, which tend to get trout up and working almost everywhere, East and West, and for a lot longer span of each season.

Imitation

It's necessary to work with at least two pattern styles for adult stoneflies, not because their shapes are different, but because there is such a separation between the constantly important small ones and the briefly but abundantly important big ones. What works well for one will not often solve the others. A third pattern style works for the largest of them on waters where the trout are hit heavily and become very selective.

The simplest and best pattern style for the little brown stones, and the yellow and olive sallies, is based on the Sofa Pillow, a fly originally created for golden stones and salmon flies in the 1940s by Pat Barnes of West Yellowstone, Montana. It's not used for those larger insects much anymore, but it forms an ideal basis for imitation of the smaller species of stoneflies.

The Sofa Pillow in its original form has a crimson feather section for a tail, representing the exuded egg sac of the female. It has a red floss body and wings of squirrel tail tied down over the back. The hackle is thick, wide, and tied in front of the wings, representing the whirring wings as well as the busy legs of a natural unhappy to be on water.

The standard Sofa Pillow is tied on 3X long size 4 to 10 hooks. In these large sizes, it can still be fished for medium-size and larger stonefly species, including those for which it was originally tied. But it is most useful when tied as a style, in smaller size and color variations, to match the various smaller stonefly hatches.

The Little Brown Stone dressing that Rick Hafele fished so successfully on the Deschutes River is a change worked on the Sofa Pillow, tied on a small hook with materials chosen to match the dark brown stonefly for which he fished it. Variations of the same style can be tied for the entire size and color range of stonefly adults, with bodies of floss, slender fur, or synthetic dubbing; downwings of squirrel tail, woodchuck body hair, or yearling elk; and bushy hackles in appropriate colors.

SOFA PILLOW STYLE

Hook	3X long, sizes 12–18.
Thread	Brown, olive, or tan.
Body	Brown, olive, or pale yellow floss or dubbing.
Wing	Fox squirrel tail, woodchuck body hair, olive-dyed or natural tan yearling elk body hair.
Hackle	Grizzly, olive-dyed grizzly, or ginger.

Little Brown Stone tied in Sofa Pillow style

These variations of the Sofa Pillow fish as well as any more imitative flies for little brown stones, olive sallies, and yellow sallies. You'll find them most useful in sizes 16 and 18, but sizes 12 and 14, all tied on 3X long hooks, can be useful over a few medium-size stonefly hatches.

For the larger golden stones and salmon flies, it would be foolish to overlook one variation of the Sofa Pillow that has become somewhat the standard for those hatches when they happen on rough water: the Improved Sofa Pillow.

IMPROVED SOFA PILLOW

Improved Sofa Pillow

Hook	3X long, sizes 4–10.
Thread	Brown.
Tail	Orange-dyed elk hair.
Rib	Brown hackle, palmered.
Body	Orange fur or synthetic dubbing.
Wing	Natural tan elk hair.
Hackle	Brown.

If you arm yourself with this single dressing, you'll succeed during hatches of the largest stonefly species in all but the most selective situations, where trout have been hammered. It's an old modification of the original Sofa Pillow, but it's still a standard and still takes many trout.

Randall Kaufmann's Stimulator was originally tied as an imitation of the golden stone but has since been varied so successfully that it can be seen as a style on which you can base variations for all sizes and colors of stoneflies. It's no secret that the same fly, in its smaller sizes, looks a lot like many caddis. That's one reason it works well as a searching pattern. It can also be fished as a hopper.

I don't like to admit that I was once caught out on a windswept Patagonian stream in Chile, with grasshoppers jumping all over the pampas, and had no hopper patterns on me. They were getting blown onto the water and slashed at by brown trout. All I had that looked anything like them were a dozen Stimulators. By the time the wind died, my satisfaction was complete, but my stock of those flies was reduced by about half. I should have known to stouten my tippet, but I was too greedy to get a new fly tied on and get back to casting it.

The following dressing is for the original Stimulator, tied to imitate the golden stone. It's the most useful tie in the style when golden stones are out, and also as a searching dressing. In its largest sizes, it also fishes well over all but the most fussy trout when salmon flies are hatching.

STIMULATOR

Stimulator

Hook	3X long grasshopper hook, sizes 6–12.
Thread	Orange.
Tail	Natural tan elk body hair.
Rib	Grizzly hackle, undersize, palmered over abdomen.
Abdomen	Yellow fur or synthetic.
Wing	Natural tan elk body hair.
Hackle	Grizzly, palmered over thorax.
Thorax	Orange fur or synthetic.

The listed combination of colors imitates golden stones and fishes well enough for salmon flies as well, though a darker version would be more suitable for that famous hatch. The style can be tied with appropriate materials in sizes 16 and 18 to imitate the little brown stones and the olive and yellow sallies. I recommend tying and carrying the original dressing, in sizes 8 through 16, and tying variations in different colors and sizes only when you've collected naturals and need to match them.

A final stonefly style that I'll mention briefly is designed to fish for the largest species, the salmon fly and golden stone, on waters where fishing pressure is heavy and trout often selective. The Henrys Fork style was originated by Mike Lawson, author of *Spring Creeks* (Stackpole, 2003) and long the owner of a fly shop on the banks of the most famous and demanding of all western trout waters, the Henrys Fork of the Snake River in Idaho.

Lawson's big stonefly imitation is designed to lower the body and head of the imitation to the water's surface, to show trout the appropriate silhouette of the real thing. You won't need to fish such an exact imitation on typical salmon fly and golden stone waters, but you'll never go wrong with this fly style so long as you limit its use to waters where you're able to keep it afloat. That can be along the edges of some relatively rough water.

Choose the style in situations where the water is smooth enough that the fly does not drown, and use either a Stimulator or Improved Sofa Pillow where the water is rougher, which will be true in many places where these big hatches happen.

HENRYS FORK SALMON FLY

Hook	3X long, sizes 4–6.
Thread	Fluorescent orange.
Tail	Black moose body hair.
Rib	Brown saddle, trimmed and palmered.
Body	Brownish orange Antron yarn or dubbing.
Wing	Dark natural elk hair.
Head	Black-dyed elk hair, tied bullet style.
Collar	Tips of head hair.

Henrys Fork Salmon Fly

The golden stone version of the style is tied with tan thread; natural light or yellow-dyed elk hair for the wing, tail, and bullet head; and a gold yarn or dubbed body overwrapped with clipped brown saddle hackle. It is tied on hook sizes 6 and 8 for these insects, which are slightly smaller than salmon flies but still very large.

Henrys Fork Golden Stone

It's even been speculated by very keen observers, most of them guides, that trout prefer golden stones over salmon flies when given a choice. On many waters, the hatches overlap, so it's something to keep in mind when you get to the water, notice what insects are out, and select a fly pattern to match what you consider the most important of them. Recall that the presence of salmon fly adults might be the best indication to fish a salmon fly nymph dressing.

The presence of a few adult golden stones, mixed in with a lot of adult salmon flies, might be an indication to fish a golden stone dressing. That is speculation, but it's worth keeping in mind. Your own trout should always be the final arbiters.

Presentation

Presentation of adult stonefly dressings depends to an extent on whether you are imitating the fore or aft end of the hatch. When naturals are crawling out as nymphs to emerge on shore, and freshly emerged naturals are hanging around near and even over the water, or when you see adults clambering about on their daily business right at the edges of the stream or river, your floating imitations should be popped right in next to shore, as Rick Hafele did with his little brown stone imitation on the Deschutes River. Fish your fly tight against the banks, into indentations, sweeping alongside bunchgrass clumps, and beneath the limbs of overhanging willows and alders.

It's always best to try a dead-drift float first, when you're fishing along the banks. But there are times when trout refuse a dead-drifted stonefly dressing or simply fail to notice it floating over their heads if they're concentrating on nymphs at the bottom. When your dry fly is ignored, try giving it an occasional hop or twitch as it floats along. This risks frightening the fish, but it can often entice reluctant trout, because it makes the fly look more alive to them. If you can see them and they continue to ignore it, it's an indication to switch to a nymph.

Fishing dry flies along the banks works best during most stonefly activity. But when females return to the water to lay their eggs, usually at evening or on heavily overcast afternoons, you should turn your attention out to open riffles. Again, a dead-drift presentation is the first tactic to try. But trout will often refuse it, especially when the naturals are of the largest sizes and very active. Then it

When stoneflies are spending their days idly onshore, you should fish your dry-fly imitations along the banks and up beneath overhanging branches.

When female stoneflies return to the water to lay their eggs, you should turn your attention away from the banks, and focus on trout rising to naturals out in open water.

helps to give the fly a bit of action, with hops and twitches inserted into the dead float.

When naturals buzz across the surface of the water, you might have to actually skitter your fly to get trout to take it. Cast down and across the current, as if you were fishing a wet fly or streamer. Set up the line with mends so that a slight downstream belly forms and tugs the fly into a fairly rapid swing. When the fly leaves a V-wake behind it, almost in the manner of waking flies used to take summer steelhead and Atlantic salmon, trout often get excited.

The rise to a big stonefly dressing fished with an active swim across the surface can be swift and brutal. But this method should be no more than a fallback. Many more trout will respond to the dead-drifted dry on riffles or out in any open water where large stoneflies are working the water, depositing their eggs. Most of your trout, during salmon fly and golden stone time, will come to flies floating very near the banks.

When olive and yellow sallies drop like sparks out of canopied trees, and descend to medium- and small-stream riffles to lay their eggs, you'll want to fish your smaller dry-fly imitations on the same waters where the naturals are landing. You'll not always notice rises to them, but trout will usually be aware of them. They get a chance to nip at a natural now and then and will almost always be willing to take an imitation, even when just a few of the smaller stoneflies are in the air.

If you don't have an imitation on you, an Elk Hair Caddis in the right size might be close enough.

It can also be effective to try a Partridge and Green or Partridge and Yellow soft-hackled wet fly, when olive or yellow sallies are in the air. Many of them drop to riffles, lay their eggs, and are swept under by the currents and drowned. Trout, especially in small streams, take many more of them beneath the surface than they do on top. A soft-hackle the same size and color as the naturals, fished upstream on short casts, presented more like a dry fly than a wet, will often work wonders.

You'll have to watch your line tip and leader for the slightest twitch or jump. When trout take wets during descents of small stoneflies, they do it so subtlely that it's easy to miss them.

Chapter 7

Midges, Craneflies, and Mosquitoes

A speckle-wing mayfly hatch started around noon on the small mountain lake. I used an olive Compara-dun dressing to take several trout in the hour or two the hatch lasted. Then the duns were gone and my success abruptly ended. I started to row the pram toward shore for lunch, but a few trout kept on rising, long after the last dun had gone down in a swirl, and naturally I kept on trying to catch them.

They rose all afternoon, and I could not get unstuck from that mayfly hatch, thinking the trout must be taking some sort of leftovers from it that I was not seeing, most likely crippled duns. I tried all sorts of flies but never could catch one. It was frustrating. I forgot about lunch.

The solution eluded me until I finally got mayflies out of my head and set my mind in pursuit of other possibilities. One of the most obvious ones, which quickly grew to a probability, was an emergence of midges. I could not see any of the insects the trout took, and it's a rule to suspect midges whenever you can't see what trout are taking, so midges suddenly seemed most likely. I tied on a size 16 nymph that was no more than some slender dark dubbing wrapped on a hook, segmented by several turns of silver ribbing.

I began casting it out, letting it sink a bit on a floating line and ten-foot leader, inching it back with a hand-twist retrieve. Within minutes the line tip twitched, and soon I had a stomach sample to study.

The little lake has no inlet or outlet streams where trout can spawn. It's stocked with trout or it wouldn't own any. Two weeks before opening day, a tank truck backs up to it and poops out five thousand eight- to ten-inch soft-fleshed rainbow trout. A month later, by the time insect hatches get good, the survivors of those trout have acquired a damnable snobbery. Their flesh has firmed up, and they're as selective as natives might be.

The lake is a clinic for me. It has good insect hatches and reasonably difficult trout. Since the trout are plants, I feel little regret about taking stomach samples and later eating fine fish dinners cooked over a campfire.

I stirred the stomach sample into water in a white jar lid on the seat of the pram, and it proved quite enlightening. There were mayflies, all right, a predominance of them. Most of them were nymphs, fairly decomposed, indicating that they had been taken a long time earlier, and also that I had missed some fair fishing for an hour or two before the speckle-wing hatch started. A few partially digested duns showed that the trout had fed on the surface during the hatch, which was when I had my best fishing.

Among the mayflies was a scattering of midge pupae. They were large for midges; a size 14 fly would have matched them better than the size 16 I'd guessed at. They were so brown they were almost black, with distinct segmentation of their slender bodies. Their thoracic regions and heads gave them the look of hunchbacks. Plumelike tufts of whitish gills extended above their heads. These midge pupae had been taken by the trout so recently, clearly after the end of the mayfly hatch, that some of them were still alive and kicking. They worked their tragic little bodies feebly in the water in the jar lid.

I needed pictures of midge pupae and decided to take this rare opportunity to get them. I rowed back to the launch, got my camera bag out of my rig, and fetched out a tiny aquarium. I filled the aquarium with water from the lake and carefully tweezered the midges into it. Then I turned to the camera and began setting up to take pictures of the midges.

If you think fumbling with an excess of fishing tackle can be frustrating during a blitz of a hatch, try assembling a camera with macro lens and big bellows and double flash setup, all perched precariously on top of a tripod, while the most elusive of all aquatic quarry waits in a glass aquarium half the size of your coffee cup. You would fumble, too. The secret is to ignore the subjects, because if you try to watch what they're doing and what you're doing at the same time, you'll begin scattering expensive trinkets all over the ground.

When finally I had everything approximately assembled, I turned back to the insects and got the finest little surprise. Two of them were gone. Their cast pupal shucks floated empty on the surface of the water in the aquarium. The adults had emerged and flown.

I got my pictures. The remaining midges posed nicely. What else can midge pupae do, if they don't emerge and fly away? When emerging in a lake or pond, not trapped in an aquarium, some float to the surface slowly, others swim to it surprisingly quickly. When they get to the top, they just hang there, heads bumped against the surface film. After a short while, they get impatient and begin to bang their tiny heads against the ceiling. After a long while, they finally manage to poke their heads through, the pupal skin splits along the back, and the adult crawls out to stand on the raft of its abandoned shuck. Then it flies away. It's all one of nature's wonders, and you should watch it happen if you ever get a chance, though about the only way to get that chance is to capture a trout feeding on midge pupae and pump a throat sample, or kill the fish and take a stomach sample.

Imagine for a moment the delight trout must feel when encountering hundreds, even thousands, of something so helpless as midge pupae hanging from the surface film. It's a fairly rare occurrence. Midge pupae are taken most often either a foot or two above the bottom, just before they begin the trip to the surface, or within the same distance of the surface, as they prepare to make their assault on the surface film.

Because of their usual small size, the importance of midges is easy to overlook. But they should never be ignored. Around a thousand species of them have been identified, with perhaps that many more still to be classified by professional taxonomists. Midges live in virtually every aquatic habitat, from sewage lagoons to the purest chalkstream currents. Where trout swim, midges are always around. It's as simple as that. And some midges are far from small.

MIDGE LIFE CYCLE

Midges undergo complete metamorphosis. The larvae grub around down on the bottom, sometimes down *in* the bottom. Or they worm around in the tendrils of aquatic vegetation. Though they are absolutely prolific, trout rarely take them selectively. When trout feed in the type of habitat preferred by midge larvae, they usually find and are happy to feed upon quite a variety of mayfly nymphs, caddisfly larvae, crustaceans, and whatever other creatures come along.

Midge larvae are wormlike tubes. They have no true legs and no appendages that would help them swim. They get around by a random flipping movement of their bodies. Their progress through the water seems directionless, though they might know where they're going and how they're going to get there. The larval stage is the time of growth. The longer the larva has to eat and grow, the larger it will get. This seems a wasted statement, but let's look at another aspect of midge behavior and make it mean something.

Midges sometimes have two, three, or even more generations per year. Their eggs are laid, the larvae hatch and grow, the pupal transformation takes place, and the adults emerge to lay more eggs and die. This whole process can take as little as three or four weeks or as long as a year. Midges with the most generations and the shortest life cycles live in the warmest climates. Because they have such short growth times, they can be disturbingly tiny, down to size 28. Midges with a single generation and the full-year life cycle live in the coldest climates. They can be alarmingly large for something carrying the diminutive name *midge*. The farther north you go, the larger they get. Some Canadian midge larvae are nearly an inch long, their imitations tied on 3X long size 8 hooks.

A midge larva imitation can make an excellent searching pattern by itself, or an excellent choice to tie on a short tippet behind a Woolly Bugger when you want to troll, explore a lake, and use your flies to try to find its fish. Still, the pupal stage is most important to anglers because larvae are seldom available to trout in concentrated numbers. When trout get selective to midges, it's almost always to pupae or emergers.

Midges pupate in bottom silts, inside a burrow or within a shelter. The pupal transformation usually lasts a few days, longer in

Midge nymph imitations, especially when fished in tandem with larger Woolly Buggers, make excellent searching dressings when you need to troll in order to find trout in the vast expanse of an unexplored lake.

larger species. While the actual transformation takes place, the insect is safe from trout predation. But when it's over, midges risk lots of trouble with trout in order to get to the surface, where they emerge into the reproductive adult stage.

Danger begins when the pupa leaves its burrow or shelter and starts its ascent to the surface. Most are feeble swimmers. How does the midge pupa look to a trout? Pretty small, usually, but an easy target, well worth the trouble. When they're big pupae, toward the north, trout get quite excited about them.

Midge pupae ascend to the surface for emergence in late winter through late fall, but they tend to do it when the weather is favorable for the survival of the fragile adults. I don't have any scientific backup for my belief, but I do think midges prefer to hatch when the surface is not torn by wind, and that the pupae near the bottom have some means to sense when the surface is peaceful and when it's not.

I fished a pond hanging onto the side of a minor mountain, overlooking a vast valley, in New Mexico one wintry March day, with A. K. Best and a cast of fine characters from the Sangre de Cristo Fly Casters club in Santa Fe. Snow lay in patches around the banks of the pond. While we suited up in layers of clothes and neoprene waders, in order to pilot float tubes on the frigid water without freezing, we heard thunder and looked over the edge to see a pair of fighter jets roaring after each other up the valley bottom, far down in the distance below us.

An intermittent wind alternately riffled the surface of the pond, then left it placid, the surface smooth. It took a long time to notice that when the surface was rough, no action would happen. Then the wind would die for a few minutes, the surface would flatten out, and about five minutes later a bunch of rises would erupt all over the pond. We'd catch a trout or at most two on midge pupa patterns. Then the wind would come up, we'd see a few more splashy rises in the wind-riffled surface, and abruptly after that the pond would die.

It took several of these sequences before I began to speculate— I have never been able to confirm it—that midge pupae, holding suspended down below, would see or sense the calmness of the surface and release for the trip to the top. We would have a flurry of action every time the surface got smooth. The reason a few rises would continue after the wind roughened it up again—again I speculate—is that midge pupae already on their way up couldn't just change their minds, reverse their courses, once they'd started the trip toward the surface. They were committed.

When a midge pupa gets to the surface, it bumps against the surface tension. As with mayflies, the formidability of the barrier is in direct relation to the size of the insect. Arbitrarily, I'll say that if a midge is size 14 or larger, it will penetrate the surface film with little trouble, and therefore you'll find fewer cripples during a hatch. If it's size 16 and under, the barrier will be more difficult to break through, and more midges will get stuck and be taken by trout hanging helplessly at the top.

Surface tension becomes more of a barrier when the surface is still, less of a barrier when slight wind ripples and wavelets break it up. On calm days, midges can hang at the surface in great numbers for fatally long periods. On breezy days, they can poke right through and get into the air quickly and on about their reproductive business. In high winds, such as we had that day on the hang-

On a mountain pond in New Mexico, the trout would rise to midges and there would be a brief flurry of fishing activity every time the wind died for a few minutes and the surface calmed a bit. When the wind came up again, the action died down.

ing mountain pond in New Mexico, midges are discouraged from hatching at all except when the wind suddenly dies.

When emergence through the surface film is complete, the adult midge leaves the water and flies to nearby vegetation. It rests there until it is ready to mate, in a day or two. Midges mate in the air, sometimes in vast swarms, with all sorts of species mixed in the swirl.

I walked back toward my tent one desert dusk, after a day spent wade-fishing the shoreline of a vast sun-struck and sage-rimmed lake. There were no machines for a hundred miles, yet I kept hearing a high-pitched whine, a little like an electric motor running at excessively high RPMs somewhere up in the air above me. I was sure I was going crazy, but it kept coming back. Finally I stopped and studied the air with the miniature binoculars I usually wear around my neck when I'm fishing. High up, where I couldn't see them with the naked eye, a vast cloud of midges hovered. They were like a fog of dark, dancing particles in the sunlit sky. The whine I heard was their collective high-speed wingbeats. It was the drone of a mosquito magnified a million times.

Midges lay their eggs in just about every way you could imagine for aquatic insects. Some deposit them on the surface. Others struggle under and deposit them on the bottom. Many deposit their eggs on protruding plants, bridge timbers, and other structures above water, from which the tiny larvae fall to the water after leaving the egg.

Midge adults on the water as singles can be important in some river situations, most notably on slow, meandering streams and rivers with heavy populations of the tiny aquatics, mostly midges and mayflies, that are abundant enough to cause trout to feed selectively on such small bites. I've seen this happen on the Green River, in the tailwater section downstream from Flaming Gorge Dam. Trout there get pestered constantly. During midge hatches, it might be necessary to go to a hackled midge adult dressing, such as the Grizzly Midge or Griffith's Gnat, in size 24 or 26.

More often, midge adults become important, in terms of imitation, only when they gather in clusters and boat the current almost in rafts. This behavior happens most often on moving water, and in my experience, most often on tailwaters in late winter or early spring, in the kind of weather when you're fishing with fingerless wool gloves and sometimes with ice in the guides.

I've experienced these cluster midge situations in February on the Crooked River in Oregon, in March on the Madison River below Bear Trap Canyon in Montana, and in April on a beaver-meadow reach of the Cimarron River in New Mexico. They do happen on other kinds of rivers, at all times of year, but early-season midge cluster hatches on moving but meandering water have been the rule for me.

It's a wonderful thing to witness: dark midges so thick they swirl down tendrils of modest current in waving lines, the lines sort of seething back and forth in contradiction to the currents under their feet, the wings of the insects all whirring, the tiny midges gathering here and there along the length of the line in little balls or larger knots. Trout noses poke up to take down several midges at one time.

If you choose the right size and color fly to represent a cluster of the hatching midges, and send it down the drift line at the moment a trout is positioned to rise again, you're going to get your hands wet and cold handling and releasing a trout. Often, on those kinds of waters, it will be a big one.

Midge Larvae

Natural

The midge larva is the least important stage of the insect to fly fishermen. Though eaten extensively by trout, their habitat is difficult terrain to explore with tiny flies and is crowded with larger organisms that present more promising angling opportunities. Why fish a size 18 midge larva on a 6X tippet fifteen feet deep when you can tow a size 8 dragonfly nymph dressing through the same zone on a stouter tippet, have a better chance of enticing a take, and have a lot better chance of landing a large trout? It's smarter to tie the midge dressing behind the bigger fly and thereby offer trout a choice.

There are, however, lots of midge larvae. Their habitat is everywhere, worldwide, in all waters. Their season is forever and when-

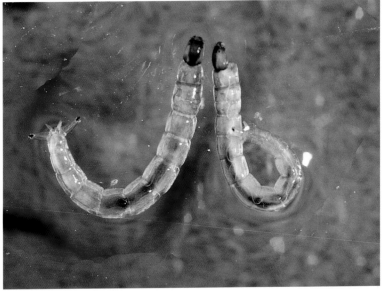

Midge larvae are simple tubes, but with distinct head capsules and lacking any jointed legs.

A tangle of bloodworm midge larvae and their imitations, from a large lake in British Columbia.

ever. So they might be important anytime, anyplace. The most likely place they'll be important is on a northern lake, where they attain greater size, and therefore make more interesting bites for trout.

Recognizing midge larvae is not your easy everyday amateur's chore. Some taxonomic rules can be stated for them: They have well-developed head capsules, which lots of related insect types lack, and they have fleshy prolegs on the first thoracic segment and last abdominal segment, which successfully separates them from a few related groups. The truth is they are simple wormlike tubes, and a few of their close but less important relatives are wormlike tubes, too.

The size of these insects ranges from too small to imitate with a fly tied on any existing hook, up to size 8 northern specimens that trout never pass up if they can get a chance at them. As with earlier groups, however, some common sizes prevail. Average midge larvae are small, from about size 16 down to about size 20. Predominant colors amount to camouflage, ranging from green to dark brown to tan.

One large group of midges lives as larvae on the bottom in waters so deep and so covered with decomposing matter that very little oxygen is available. Midges can be prolific in these conditions. Those that live in them have hemoglobin in their systems and are almost as red as blood. These so-called bloodworms are probably the most important midge larvae, if not for their abundance, then for the brilliance with which they show themselves to trout.

As a pattern style, the Traditional Midge Larva is the simplest and most realistic. It is, like the natural, simply a tube, in this case of yarn or of fur dubbed onto a slightly weighted hook. There's little reason to get any more complicated than that. Start the body down around the hook bend to give it a natural curve. Rib it with your working thread or fine wire to give it the segmented appearance of the natural.

In truth, I don't recommend tying these unless you discover trout taking the naturals selectively. I don't think you will have that happen unless you fish the Kamloops region of British Columbia, in which case a bloodworm tie in sizes 10 and 12 might be very valuable. Even then, most of the trout you take on it might mistake it for a midge pupa, not a midge larva. But it will work, and that's most of what counts.

TRADITIONAL MIDGE LARVA

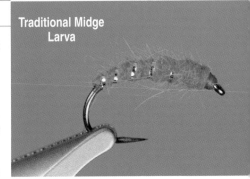

Traditional Midge Larva

Hook	2X or 3X long, or curved scud hook, sizes 8–26.
Thread	Match body color.
Weight	10 to 20 turns fine lead wire.
Rib	Working thread, fine silver wire, or silver Mylar tinsel.
Body	Yarn, or fur or synthetic dubbing to match insect color.

Many other dressings listed in this book should get your meager tying time long before midge larval patterns. Tie these only if you find you need them. I doubt you will. If you desire to have a few in your box, make them bright red, in sizes 14 to 18 in most of the states, 16 up to 10 in the northern states and the Canadian provinces.

Presentation
Midge larvae twist and turn on their dervish courses right near the bottom or in among vegetation. Their body movement is a quick flick-flick, but their forward progress is slow. It might not even be forward. To imitate this kind of swimming, the best you can do is get your fly down deep and fish it with a patient hand-twist retrieve.

Strikes can be subtle and difficult to detect. A strike indicator at the junction of your leader and line can help you catch more trout. Many experts fish midge larvae on long, fine leaders, with a bit of putty weight added to the leader just above the fly, and the strike indicator a distance up the leader that is just short of the depth of the water. The fly is cast out, allowed to sink, and then just left sitting there. A trout comes along, inhales it, keeps on going. The indicator twitches or dips under, and if you're paying attention, you set the hook.

My problem with this kind of fishing is that unless the action has some speed to it, I'm always caught gazing off at the mountains or forest or desert or whatever else is in the view when a fish happens randomly past. If I'm fishing with you, you'll yell, "Hey, Dave, you just had one!" And that's the way it will be all day. At least you'll catch some trout.

Midge Pupae

Natural
Unlike larvae, the importance of midge pupae is far from marginal. The short transitional period of the pupal stage, from the time it leaves its retreat on the bottom or in vegetation until it escapes its shuck and turns into a winged adult at the surface, is the midge's briefest but most important moment to trout, and to us as anglers.

Pupae are known to *stage*—that is, to suspend in great numbers in the same layer of water, usually near the bottom, perhaps waiting for conditions to become perfect up top. Trout cruise through that layer and take these suspended midge pupae at will. During this staging, and during the ascent from the bottom to the surface, midge pupae have no defense against trout, not even much mobility. Near the surface or hanging from the rafters, often in the same kinds of great gatherings found at the staging level, midge pupae are even less able to escape trout.

Like the larvae, midge pupae are distributed worldwide and are found in all water types, though they're most important in stillwaters and in moving waters with less than forceful flows. Midge pupae are important in most spring creeks and tailwaters, and also on flats and fairly slow and smooth runs of many freestone streams.

Midges might emerge at any time of year. They can produce good fishing in the center of winter in lakes that do not ice over. Their emergences might start soon after ice-out on lakes that do freeze. They'll go on all through spring, summer, and even fall. They might be difficult to notice because of their small size, especially in the southern tier of states, and also because the adults are not easy to notice on the water. Like mayflies, their hatches often move into the morning or evening hours in warm weather. If you fish only the center of the day, you might never notice that trout feed on them.

The primary reason the importance of midge pupae is so often overlooked is the habit of trout to feed on them down deep, in their staging areas, and in the mid-depths, on their way to the surface. When trout take midges hanging in the surface film, it's easy to see it happening. At all other times, feeding on midge pupae can go unnoticed unless you manage to get a stomach sample, or catch a volunteer for a throat-pump sample.

On stillwaters, you can employ a depth finder, if you own one, though these brief notes will tell you only that it's beneficial to do that, not how to do it, since I don't. I have fished with the great Brian Chan, British Columbia fish biologist and stillwater expert, and watched him use his depth finder to locate trout. Several things became suddenly clear.

First, it's easy to tell the depth of the water, therefore the depth at which you might successfully fish a midge pupa imitation when trout are feeding on suspended naturals just above the bottom. Sec-

Noted stillwater fly fisherman Brian Chan, of Kamloops, British Columbia, motors out onto a lake while studying the screen of his depth finder, looking for indications of trout cruising and feeding on midges.

ond, if trout are indeed down there and big enough, you'll see them on the screen. That helps find them. Third, when a lake is clouded by an algal bloom, the phytoplankton that causes it extends only fifteen to twenty feet or so down, and the water is clean and clear beneath it. That layer of clear water shows on the screen, beneath the bloom, and tells you that a fly fished between the bloom and the bottom will be seen by cruising trout, even though what you see when you look over the side is an opaque green fog.

If you don't own a depth finder, or are fishing a stream and not a stillwater, the importance of midges can be difficult to gauge, because it's difficult to determine when they are being taken by trout. An important stillwater rule and small moving-water rule is to suspect midge pupae whenever trout are rising but you can't see what they're taking. It's likely to be midges in this almost invisible transitional stage.

Recognition of midge pupae has some of the same elements that makes recognition of midge larvae difficult. It's easy to identify something as looking like a midge pupa, more difficult to confirm the sighting. But again, if it looks like one and behaves like one, you can fish its imitation as if it were one. All this is written to keep me on safe ground with entomologists, for whom I have a great deal of respect.

Entomologists know two things: first, how determined fly fishermen can be to know the exact species of every insect they ever see; and second, how often anglers, and especially angling writers, know with misplaced conviction that an insect is exactly what it isn't. Professional bug folks cringe at our mistakes. Our mistakes arise out of our refusal to accept our limitations and get on with our fishing. We simply can't identify all insects to all levels. Not even professionals can do that.

At its simplest and most useful level, a midge pupa looks like a hunchbacked midge larva. The body is tapered, with a short, two-lobed swimming paddle at the end of the abdomen. The tiny wings and legs and antennae of the adult are all encased in the pupal cuticle, gathered at the thorax of the insect, and lumped together with the head. Whitish plumes of respiratory filaments are usually visible at this head end, looking like a wig of short, white hair above the humped head and thorax.

It's wise to note that if you take your midge pupae from trout stomach samples, their peripheral parts—swimming paddles at the stern and respiratory filaments at the bow—will often be eroded away by stomach acids.

Let me note that I'm not recommending that you kill trout just to study what they've been eating. But I do recommend that you not kill trout to eat without harvesting as well all the information you can about what they've been doing down there in their watery world. Anything you can learn about trout will increase your ability to catch them, whether that information is applied immediately, in the form of an imitation tied to your tippet at once, or becomes a

Midge pupae have their forming wings, legs, and antennae all gathered in a lump at the head end of the insect.

part of your body of knowledge about trout and the world in which they live and is applied over time.

The size range of pupal midges is the same as that for larvae, from too tiny to imitate to some so large they require dressings tied on size 8 and 10 long-shank hooks. The most common range in the states is sizes 16 to 20. But never overlook the larger midges that are common across the northern tier of states, and especially in Canada. These larger midges are the most important insects in many waters where they're abundant.

Almost the entire color spectrum is covered by pupal midges, but the most common are shades of dark brown to black, olive, and blood red. These can easily be ordered into a small selection of black, green, and red patterns so that whenever you encounter midge pupae, you will have a dressing that is near enough to the natural to take trout.

Imitation

The Traditional Midge Pupa is a simple tie that works very well whenever trout are feeding on midges size 14 and smaller. It has a slender body of yarn or dubbing wound on a curved hook, ribbed with gold or silver wire or tinsel. The thorax and head region of the natural are represented with a small knot of the same dubbing, which is left unribbed and rough, or teased out, so that it is thicker than the body.

My most productive variation on this simple style is tied on curved scud hooks in sizes 12 through 20. It has a black fur body ribbed with silver wire in the smallest sizes, silver Mylar tinsel in the larger sizes. The thorax is a few turns of peacock herl. That's all there is to it. It takes a very few minutes to tie up what amounts to a spring supply of them. I fish them on a variety of lowland and mountain lakes, plus some favorite arid-country ponds and big wind-swept lakes. They seem to work equally well wherever I fish them in stillwaters, and often take trout even when midges are not in the mix of the moment, on both stillwaters and streams.

I tie the style in green and red as well and fish those when my collecting reveals trout feeding on naturals in those colors. The combined thorax and head is tied with fur the same color as the body, rather than with peacock herl. Just enough weight is added to the hook shank to get the fly through the surface film and on its way down a foot or two. If more depth is desired, it is better to attain it with a sinking line than with lead on the fly, as an over-weighted fly would not let you fish shallow when you want.

TRADITIONAL MIDGE PUPA

Hook	Curved scud hook, sizes 12–20.
Weight	10 to 15 turns of under-size lead wire.
Thread	Black, olive, or red.
Rib	Silver wire or Mylar tinsel.
Body	Black, green, or red yarn or dubbing.
Thorax/ head	Peacock herl, or green or red dubbing.

Black Traditional Midge Pupa

The dressing as described will take trout in almost all situations. There are, however, many tiers who enjoy adding extra touches to their flies. If you are one of these, you might increase the effectiveness of this midge pupal pattern by adding something to represent the swimmer paddles at one end and the respiratory tufts at the other. Since both are white, there is an easy way to do it. Just peel a sparse hank out of a one-inch piece of white polypro yarn. Weight the fly as usual, and start the thread. Then catch the hank of yarn against the hook along with your tying thread, letting the yarn stick out at bow and stern.

Continue to tie the rest of the fly as you normally would. When finished, clip the yarn at

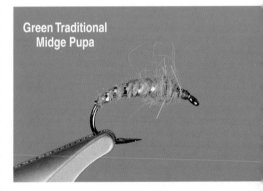

Green Traditional Midge Pupa

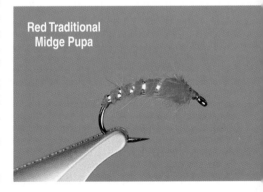

Red Traditional Midge Pupa

Traditional Midge Pupa pattern with yarn added to represent swimmer paddles and respiratory tufts.

both ends to leave short, white tufts at both ends. It's easy to do, even on the tiniest sizes, and it adds a note of realism to the artificial fly. You'll be proud you did it. I usually neglect it, and haven't noticed a difference, but what do I know about trout not caught?

It's wise to have a more realistic imitation in your fly boxes if you fish the northern latitudes, where midges grow larger. Trout are so accustomed to feeding on red and green midge pupae in northern stillwaters that they are susceptible to such a fly pattern even when naturals are not about.

Philip Rowley, in his *Fly Patterns for Stillwaters* (Frank Amato Publications, 2000), lists a specific and imitative style for his favorite Kamloops, British Columbia, region lakes. Not surprisingly, the fly was originated by Phil's friend and fishing partner Brian Chan.

CHAN'S RED BUTT
CHIRONOMID PUPA

Chan's Red Butt
Chironomid

Hook	2X or 3X long, sizes 10-16.
Thread	Dark brown.
Butt	Bright red floss.
Rib	Narrow gold Mylar tinsel.
Body	Pheasant center tail herl.
Wing case	Pheasant center tail fibers.
Thorax	Peacock herl.
Gills	White Antron, polypro yarn, or Sparkle Yarn.

This same style tied with a green floss butt and body would arm you to imitate the two most common colors seen in the large midges that hatch up north: blood red and green.

A final fly style for midge pupae represents the naturals in the surface, half in and half out of their shucks. When trout take midges in the surface film, they're feeding on emergers far more often than on winged adults. The Palomino style, originated by Brett Smith, has a long tail of New Dub to remind trout about the hanging shuck of the midge pupa, and a wing case of white or light gray Z-lon fibers that looks like the half-emerged wings of an adult.

When midges emerge, they hang at about a 45-degree angle to the surface and look somewhat sticklike. The thorax of the pupa breaks through the film, and the wings of the adult begin to emerge. The adult slowly extracts itself, in the end standing on the cast shuck as if it were a raft awash in the water. Trout key on this helpless phase at times and often focus their surface feeding on this precise moment when the natural is half in and half out of the water.

The best three colors are black, olive, and red. I fish emergers most often in black on my own waters, but you need to collect on your own waters and notice what the trout might be seeing. Sizes are tiny, 16 to 22. The Palomino is not designed for those large northern midges, but it does very well over the average run of them on most stillwaters. It also fishes well when trout feed on emerging midges in spring creeks and tailwaters.

PALOMINO

Black Palomino

Hook	Curved scud hook, sizes 16–22.
Thread	Black, olive, or red.
Tail	Black, olive, or red New Dub.
Wing case	Light gray Z-lon.
Body	Black, olive, or red fur.

The wing case is tied in at the bend of the hook, pulled forward over the body, and clipped long, leaving about the length of the wing case itself sticking out over the front of the hook eye. This is called antennae in some descriptions of the fly; it might imitate the antennae of male midges but more likely looks to trout like the emerging wings of the natural insect.

I like the Palomino style because it's excellent as an emerging pupa, when fished in the film, but it can also be pulled under and fished as a submerged pupa on a very slow hand-twist retrieve. This probably violates the intentions of its originator, but I've had very good luck fishing the fly both ways. I usually do it on a single cast.

If I've made my presentation to a cruising trout, and the fish has failed to take the fly for some reason of its own, or has altered its path without seeing the fly, I'll let the Palomino sit for some reasonable time, hoping for the same trout to return or another to show up. But if nothing happens, I get restless after a while. That's when I like to give the line a tug to pull the fly under, and then begin creeping it back toward me. I catch a lot of trout on this style. If the truth were forced out of me, I'd admit that I catch more than half of them on the retrieve.

The Klinkhamer Special, originated by Hans van Klinken, is designed to float in the surface film while suspending the body of the fly at an angle beneath it. It's a nearly ideal imitation of the posture of a natural midge pupa hanging at the surface, waiting for its moment to emerge through it. This parachute style dressing can be tied with a wide variety of body and wingpost materials. My favorite is no more than an addition of the parachute post and hackle to my favorite Black Traditional Midge Pupa.

KLINKHAMER SPECIAL

Hook	Curved scud hook, size 12–20.
Thread	Black 8/0.
Wingpost	White polypro yarn or CDC.
Rib	3X tippet material.
Body	Black rabbit-fur dubbing.
Hackle	Grizzly.
Thorax	Peacock herl.

Klinkhamer Special

In my own fishing, this has been the most useful color, but the same style fly can be used in tan, red, or olive, depending on the color midges you find hatching on the lake or pond you're fishing.

Presentation

To fish midge pupa patterns effectively, you must first find the level at which trout are feeding on the naturals. Most often, this will be either a foot or two off the bottom or about the same distance beneath the surface. Less often, trout will feed on them in the middle portion of the water column, somewhere between the bottom and the top, and on very visible occasions when the naturals are suspended in the surface film. Presentation of pupae generally gives you a choice between fishing them deep and almost still or fishing them shallow and almost without movement.

If you're fishing midges from anything but the shore, it will at least help, and at times be necessary, to anchor both ends of whatever you're using—boat, float tube, or pontoon craft. That allows you to cast from a stationary platform. If one end of your transportation is swinging in the wind, it will alternately drag your fly along at an unrealistic speed as the wind blows you away from the fly, then cause you to lose touch with it entirely as the wind blows you back toward it.

To fish deep, you can use a standard-length leader, eight to ten feet, and a line with the appropriate sink rate for the depth you must attain. Usually you'll need an extra-fast-sinking line or even high-density line. I carry a set of shooting tapers in different sink rates when I'm fishing stillwaters, in order to be able to select the correct one for the water depth I want to fish.

The countdown method is used to get the fly to the proper depth. Start by counting fifteen seconds, then initiating a very slow hand-twist retrieve. If that doesn't touch weeds, bottom, or a fish, count twenty seconds and repeat the process. Sometimes you'll end up with a count of more than sixty seconds. Whatever it takes, get the fly near the bottom before beginning your retrieve, even if the takes you get are nearer the surface. As Philip states it in his book, "It is easy to think the fish are cruising near the surface but don't fall into this trap. Remember that the trout follows the fly up from the depths."

Another method for fishing a midge pupa deep calls for a floating fly line and very long leader, from fifteen to twenty-five feet, most of it fine tippet. I avoid these extremes, preferring different rigging, but several years ago Rick Hafele returned from a trip to the Kamloops area, shaking his head. He told me leaders more than twenty feet long, with tiny midge pupal patterns at their ends, were the only way he and his partner caught any fish on the trip. And they caught some wallopers, up to five and six pounds.

With such long leaders, you must use weighted flies, and even add a bit of putty weight to the leader a foot or two above the fly. Even with the weight, countdown times can be between thirty seconds and almost forever, or so it seems. Once you've managed to get the fly down to where you want it, you should keep it fishing there as long as possible on each cast. Use the very slowest hand-twist retrieve, just enough to keep in touch with the fly so you'll be able to feel takes.

A more effective method for probing depths beyond fifteen feet is derived from nymph-and-indicator fishing as it's done on streams and rivers. I recently fished the method with Brian Chan on his home lake near Kamloops. Fishing was slow as a result of water drawdowns in the lake, which was dammed for irrigation, but the few trout we caught would not have been taken any other way.

Brian is expert with a depth finder and used what its screen told him, in addition to his long experience on the lake, to find the areas most likely to be productive. We were rarely able to locate more than one or two cruising trout in any one location, but Brian anchored over them, hoping others were moving in and out of the same water.

When you fish midge pupal patterns,
anchor both ends of your boat to keep it
from swinging in even the slightest breeze.

The first step then was to find the exact depth of the water. Brian did this by clipping his hemostat, used for releasing trout, to the end of his leader, dropping it over the side, letting it sink. When it struck bottom, that told him the length of leader he needed and the precise place to put his suspending strike indicator, a foot or two short of that.

The leader was almost all 4X or 5X tippet; trout down deep don't seem to be astonishingly leader shy. The fly was tied to the tip with a loop knot, to give it freedom of movement, and a bit of putty weight was molded to the leader a foot above it. The indicator was placed to suspend the fly two feet off the bottom. That was it. The cast was made with a very open loop, and with all that leader, it was awkward at best. It felt good to get the fly fifty feet away from the double-anchored boat, but in truth, it doesn't matter much how far you can cast. According to Brian, you could as well drop your fly right over the side, though I'm not sure you'd be fly-fishing if you did.

The fly was given all the time it required to sink. No retrieve was made. The wind was allowed to push the line, when there was a wind, and whatever waves were present, if there were any, gave the fly a slight up-and-down action far down below. That was considered beneficial.

The key to the method is to keep your eye on the indicator. Signs of a take, relayed all the way up that long leader, are more often subtle twitches than a total submergence. By the time news reaches you, the trout is getting rid of that irritating bit of steel and floss, fur, or feathers, if it hasn't already accomplished it. If you react slowly, the trout will almost always be gone. But don't set the hook brutally. If you pull sharply one way while the stung trout abruptly heads the other, you'll instantly be separated from each other. With trout the size of Kamloops rainbows, that can be disappointing.

If you fail to find fish, shorten the distance between the fly and the indicator, a couple of feet at a time, until you get strikes or feel it's time to move the boat. Give the place a chance, half an hour to an hour, but don't sit at one anchorage for hours waiting for something to happen, especially if you are not using a depth finder. It's always best to explore stillwaters by moving around, because trout tend to hang out in pods. If you do find fish, then repeat what you did on the previous cast. You've likely found more than one fish, and you've also discovered the right depth and retrieve.

To fish midge pupae a foot or two beneath the surface, rig with a floating line and leader in the ten- to twelve-foot range. The tippet itself should be no heavier than 4X, with 5X or 6X being better choices in most midge situations. At times fragile 7X tippets will be needed to fool the fish. Make your cast, give your fly some seconds to sink, usually ten to twenty, then begin that same slow retrieve.

Floating line and long, fine leader are my favorite rigging for some home ponds out in the Oregon desert. Trout are often seen working intermittently on invisibles, which might be midge adults or emergers in the surface film. When this is going on, I rig with my favorite pupa, the traditional tie in black with the peacock herl thorax, on a size 16 or 18 lightly weighted hook, and fish it about two feet deep on a very slow hand-twist retrieve.

I was taking some broad-shouldered two- to four-pound trout with this fly and method last spring, on one of these ponds, while my wife, standing next to me and apparantly doing exactly the same thing with the same rigging, was busy catching nothing. It was naturally quite frustrating for her. After I'd caught enough trout to make me realize I was about to be in big trouble, I stopped fishing long enough to watch her fish out a cast. In her eagerness to catch up with me, she was practically galloping her fly.

It took a while to convince her that the fly should be almost stopped. Suddenly she was into trout, and I was able to go back to my own happiness. Most often on stillwaters, the slower the retrieve, the faster the fishing.

The final method for fishing a sunk midge pupae, hanging it up near the surface, has its attendant problems. It's difficult to hang the fly in or near the film without either getting it stuck on the surface itself or letting it sink too deep, below fish that have their attention focused upward. One way around this is to dress your leader with floatant to within a foot or six inches of the fly.

Another way to support your flies up near the ceiling is to tie a substantial dry fly to the end of the tippet. Then tie a midge pupa pattern on a one- to two-foot tippet dangled off the hook bend of

Midge pupae often hang from the surface film for some time before they're able to break through it and emerge.

the dry fly. This will not only keep the pupa up where you want it, but also give you a clear signal when a trout takes it.

If trout are feeding in the surface itself, fish a Palomino by dressing your leader to within six or so inches of it, or by applying dry-fly floatant to the Z-lon wings. Don't dress the entire fly. The idea, though difficult to execute precisely, is to hang the fly from the surface film, with the tail representing the cast shuck of the natural, and the wings in the film representing the wings of the insect beginning to pull out of the pupal shuck.

Fish the surface fly as a dry, without any retrieve. Cast it to rises and let it sit. If no trout comes to it after a minute or so, lift it off and cast to another rise. Refrain, however, from frantically casting it into every set of rise rings you see. Sometimes it's best to just cast it out, let it rest, wait for a trout to come to it.

Because trout feed in pods in lakes and ponds, and on the quiet flats of spring creeks and tailwaters, your best bet is to let cruising trout find the fly, rather than risk frightening all the trout out of the area.

I'll mention here at the end of the midge pupa section a single fly and single method for fishing this stage of the insect on moving water. One changeable spring day, I fished a somewhat slow set of currents on the Madison River, at the lower end of Beartrap Canyon in Montana, with Sylvester Nemes, the soft-hackle guru. He'd just published a book titled *Soft-Hackled Fly Imitations* (self-published, 1991), and I had just written the foreword for it. One of the flies in the book is Syl's Midge, and much of its development took place on the water we fished that day, though not in such terrible weather.

At first it didn't look like we were going to get to fish. A dark cloud loomed over us on the drive from Bozeman. By the time we reached the river, we were enveloped in a snowstorm. We sat in the car with the heater on, talking and laughing—you always laugh a lot when you fish with Sylvester—and wondering what in the world we were doing there. Then the Montana weather, as it does in spring, changed abruptly. The sun came out. Birds sang. Midges hatched. Trout rose.

The insects were tiny and black, coming off in slow tendrils of current right along the shallow edges of the river. I tied on a size 16 Adams dry fly and fished it as the closest thing I owned to a Cluster Midge. A couple of nice trout took it, and I would have been satisfied with them, had Sylvester not waded out about forty feet from shore, turned back to fish a wet fly in toward the shore on a down-and-across swing.

He was constantly into fish.

I'd read his book closely enough to know he was fishing his Syl's Midge, a pupa pattern designed to be fished under hatches of adults, on the assumption that trout rising visibly when midges are hatching are merely the tip of an iceberg of trout feeding more heavily beneath the surface. It turned out to be true that day on the peaceful Beartrap reach of the Madison.

I whined about my own inactivity until Sylvester got tired of it and loaned me a couple of his small flies. I was then able to enjoy some fast action of my own.

Syl's Midge is tied with a peacock herl body and a single turn of gray partridge hackle. That's it. It has been highly effective for me on many occasions when trout appear to be feeding on adult midges in moving water. Perhaps they take it for an adult drowned in the process of emergence.

SYL'S MIDGE

Syl's Midge

Hook	Standard wet fly, sizes 16–18.
Thread	Black.
Body	Peacock herl.
Hackle	Gray partridge.

It's usually most effective to fish traditional midge pupal dressings upstream on moving water, to rising trout, just as if they were dry flies. Because they are so tiny, float flush in the surface film at best, and are taken beneath the surface most often, they're very difficult to follow in the drift. A small yarn strike indicator four to six feet up the leader from the fly greatly increases your ability to notice takes.

Syl's Midge can be fished upstream with the same methods, but the fly is designed to be fished through pods of rising trout on a very slow downstream wet-fly swing. If the current causes a downstream belly in your line and speeds the swing beyond a slight cross-stream swim, mend to slow it down. Sylvester fishes this and most of his other soft-hackle dressings, for which he is famous, with the same constant mends.

Sylvester ties his Syl's Midge in size 16, mostly because it's difficult to find partridge hackles small enough for smaller sizes. For some reason that I'm unable to explain, the fly and method work even when the natural midges are not at all like it in size and color. If that were not true, I might suggest you try size and color variations of it. But I've not done that.

Midge Adults

Natural

Midge adults are a puzzle. They are the most visible stage of the midge, to the angler. When trout rise to feed on midges, to all appearances they take midge adults. Yet close observation of the riseforms will tell you, first, that they are generally just subsurface, and second, that it's seldom a fully emerged adult disappearing in the swirl. Rises that are on the surface are generally to emergers, not to winged adults.

The most important thing to know about midge adults might be that their presence is an excellent indicator of midge pupa activity. But the adult can be important if you consider it just after it has gotten its head and thorax popped through the surface film, and has unsheathed its wings, but still stands on the pupal cuticle. For a short time, the adult remains attached to that cast skin. The result, from the point of view of a trout, is an easy target just sitting there on the surface.

The season of midge hatches is all year long, whenever the water is free of ice. If one were to identify times of greatest impor-

Sylvester Nemes fishing his Syl's Midge along the shallow edges of Montana's Madison River during a midge hatch.

The presence of midge adults is often an indicator for the importance of midge pupae or emergers.

When you see midge adults in the air, and even on the water, it's often an indication that trout are feeding on cripples stuck half in and half out of the pupal shuck.

tance for adult midges, it might be best to relate it to the times of least importance for other aquatic insects. Late spring, early summer, and early fall are times when mayflies, caddisflies, and stoneflies hatch and dominate the field. That leaves gaps in winter, early spring, in the heat of summer, and in late fall. Those conditions—too hot or too cold for other insects—don't stop midges. They keep right on hatching. On warm winter days, they emerge at midday. When it's hot in summer, they emerge in the cool of morning and evening. The condition they'll usually avoid is a high wind, but that is true for other aquatic insects as well.

Midges can take up the slack and become most useful to the angler when other insects are least useful. But they can also hatch in great numbers in spring, early summer, and fall. If they do, trout will turn to them, often with pebble-size minds that are closed to all other insects.

Midge adult distribution is unlimited. Their habitat is all waters. But they are most important in stillwaters and in gently flowing streams. Those are the same kinds of waters where trout key in on small insects rather than just accepting them as something mixed in with a variety of other items passing on the current.

Recognizing midge adults is pleasantly easy, although it depends on capturing a male. If you encounter an emergence of tiny insects, capture a fair-size random sample, at least five or six specimens, to make sure it includes a male. Now look for the one key feature that separates midges from other insects: Male midges have two plumelike antennae on the head. These sensitive instruments pick up the wingbeat frequency of a female of the same species.

A mating swarm of midges, such as the one that I saw high above that desert lake, might contain quite a few separate species, all swirling around together. With his special radar, a male midge can locate and mate with a friendly female rather than risk a figurative slap in the face for wooing the wrong one.

Other features of midges are shared with all species of the order to which they belong. They have two wings rather than four. The hindwings have evolved into a pair of knobs set on stalks, called *halteres*. These are miniature gyroscopes. Without them, the insect would spiral in and crash as quickly as a pilot with vertigo if inserted into a cloud bank.

Midges have no tails. They also have no long piercing proboscis, which separates them from their look-alike and sound-alike close cousins, the dreaded mosquitoes. The key features of midges are the absence of tails, a single pair of wings rather than the two pairs of wings of most insects, and plumelike antennae on the males. If your captured insect has those features, it's a midge adult, whether it's small or large.

The size variation of adult midges is from 28 up to 8. The most common and useful sizes fall in the 16 to 22 range on most trout waters, but in some northern lakes, trout at times get chances at the largest of them. Colors range almost from black to white, with nearly all the stops covered in between. But the most common, and therefore most important, colors are dark gray, pale and delicate green, and red. Some seem almost translucent.

Imitation

The hackled Traditional Midge is the first fly to consider when you encounter trout feeding selectively on adult midges. It's a very easy tie, a necessary attribute when you work with tiny hooks. It does a fine job of catching the salient features of the natural, which are the dimples made on the water by the feet of the adult midge and the cast shuck of the pupa still attached to it. The hackle collar does the one, the hackle-fiber tail the other.

Useful sizes range from 12 to 28, but I suggest carrying them from 16 to 22 until trout request something outside that limited supply. The single most useful color is the Grizzly Midge, or Adams Midge, with its smoke of gray hackle that causes it to look approximately like most midges. Again, size, form, and finally color are the salient aspects of flies, and they're important in that order.

Often if you get the size of a midge dressing correct, nothing else matters. When you're looking at the small end of the range, a miss of a single size can be very significant. I've fished the Flaming Gorge tailwater on the Green River in Utah during heavy midge hatches. They were size 26. That's the size my fly had to be, no larger and obviously not smaller. Once I got the size right, I was able to fool very selective trout on both Grizzly Midges and Griffith's Gnats, and it's likely that other dressings would have worked as well, so long as they were tied on size 26 hooks.

TRADITIONAL MIDGE

Hook	Standard dry fly, 1X fine, sizes 12–28.
Thread	Match body color.
Tail	Black, grizzly, ginger, brown, or olive-dyed hackle fibers.
Body	Black, gray, creamish tan, red, or olive dubbing (use thread for the body in the smallest sizes).
Hackle	Black, grizzly, ginger, brown, or olive.

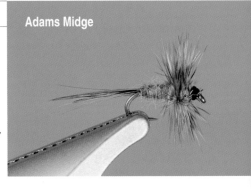

Adams Midge

Griffith's Gnat

The Adams Midge calls for a mix of grizzly and brown for tail and hackle collar, with a muskrat fur body. It's an excellent tie, because the mix of colors causes the fly to look even more mottled, but I confess I sometimes simplify it by omitting the brown hackle. If you have time—I prefer to keep my time weighted more heavily to fly fishing, less heavily to fly tying—then I highly recommend tying it with both grizzly and brown hackles.

One of the best dressing styles for adult midges strikes back to the emerging phase. It represents, in a tangled sort of way, the adult together with the cast shuck of the natural. It is highly impressionistic, making it difficult, from the angler's point of view outside of the water, to understand why fish accept it more readily than they do an exact imitation of an adult midge. From the trout's view, beneath the water, it gives the right combination of dimples in the surface film to represent an adult midge standing on that raft of the cast pupal shuck.

The style is the Griffith's Gnat. It is a strikingly simple tie, no more than a body of peacock herl with a grizzly hackle wound the length of it. The midges on which trout feed do not need to be olive in order for the peacock herl body to work. The size of the fly and the impression it makes on the water seem more important to trout than the correct color.

The Griffith's Gnat can also be tied with a slender fur body, or in the smallest sizes just wound with whatever color thread you'd like, to match any color midge you encounter. It can also be tied with tails added at the stern or with oversize hackle. That might give it the impression, on the water, of a cluster of midges. Trout often focus on groups of adults, ignoring singles, during midge hatches.

My own favorite floating dressing for midge hatches is a Cluster Midge, which is nothing more than a simplified Adams with an added hackle palmered over the body. I tie and fish it in sizes 14 to 18. It works well during hatches of midges that are size 16 down to almost invisible. The idea is to represent a bunch of midges gathered together. So I fish the fly two or three sizes larger than the prevailing insect.

I first fished this fly on the Cimarron River in New Mexico, in company with a fine bunch of folks from the Sangre de Cristo Flycasters in Santa Fe. The stretch of the river we fished was meandering and meadowish, with beaver dams backing up or at least slowing the flow in places. Tiny, dark midges were hatching so heavily that they seethed on the surface almost like tendrils of mist. Exact imitations fooled none of the fish that held in the gentle flows and rose patiently to sip from the lines of naturals.

A defeat on an Oregon tailwater during similar activity had prompted me to tie a brushy version of the Grizzly Midge when I got home. I hadn't had a chance to try it. I chose one far oversize for the midges on the Cimarron, tied it on, almost at once began to have fish on. A rain- and windstorm gusted down the canyon not long later, stamped out the hatch, so I was unable to confirm the qualities of the fly that day. But I've used it during midge hatches consistently ever since, and it's always worked well so long as midges are hatching heavily enough that they're gathering into clusters.

CLUSTER MIDGE

Hook	Standard dry fly, 1X fine, sizes 14–18.
Thread	Black.
Wings	Hen grizzly hackle tips.
Tail	Grizzly hackle fibers.
Body hackle	Undersized grizzly.
Body	Muskrat fur.
Hackle collar	Grizzly.

Cluster Midge

I've tied and used the same style fly in light ginger over the years but have found it far less useful than the listed dressing. The most common naturals I've encountered in these stream situations—and I almost always find the cluster imitation useful on moving water in late winter and early spring—are gray to black. Even when the naturals are not the approximate color of the fly, I've found it works. You might try variations of the style if you find midges of very different colors hatching and trout refuse this dressing.

Presentation
Midge adult dressings should be fished dead drift on streams, allowing the fly to arrive quietly and unstirring to rising trout. One recent spring day, on a Montana spring creek, I had to deal with trout rising to invisibles about seventy feet from the deepest position into which I could wade. There was no way for me to tell what was going on way out there.

The trout worked in a pod. I don't know how many fish were in it, but their rises were an almost constant disturbance of the surface in an area about ten feet around. This patch of disturbed water moved upstream about fifty feet, disappeared for a while, reappeared about fifty feet downstream, and began working across my front again, way out there where I would have difficulty presenting a fly with any sort of grace.

As I usually do in such puzzling situations, I frantically tried half a dozen dry flies and nymphs. Blue-winged olives had been hatching downstream, and I had to give them the first shot. But

When midges hatch on water as smooth as some stretches of Montana's Bighorn River, you must go to tiny flies and fragile tippets in order to fool trout feeding on them.

they provided me with no success. I began to suspect midges just because I could see no BWOs, and anything larger than midges would have been visible even from such a distance.

I switched to a Griffith's Gnat in size 20, dressed it lightly with floatant, cast it about ten feet in front of the lead trout in the pod. At that distance, I could not drop the fly accurately on the nose of the trout without the probability that I'd frighten them all. The fly landed at the end of a leader that was coiled on the surface. Though that was an accident, because of my poor casting at that range, it turned out to be perfect. As the patient current coaxed the fly downstream toward the rising bunch of trout, the leader slowly straightened out. The fly would have achieved a very long, free float had the trout allowed it.

I saw a swirl where I thought my fly should be. It was one rise among many, and I didn't know for sure if it was at my fly. I raised the rod gently, testing for weight at the other end. There was nothing gentle about the reaction. A large trout thrashed on the surface, dove for the weeds, and broke me off in an instant. The 6X leader failed to hold the trout, but I knew 5X wouldn't have fooled it. It was the famous catch-22 of fishing tiny flies over large trout: A tippet fine enough to fool them is not strong enough to hold them.

I stuck with 6X and lost three more of the tiny dressings before I finally brought a plump sixteen-inch rainbow to the net. "If I could handle this one on 6X," I wondered as I released it, "how big are the ones I'm losing?" I never did find out. I'd finally put the pod down.

On lakes, the best way to present any adult midge pattern is dead still. Cast it out and let it sit. Try to read the progression of rises to determine where a trout is headed. Drop the fly in front of it. Let it come to the fly.

If you have trouble seeing your dry, whether you're fishing moving water or still, tie a small yarn strike indicator into the leader four to six feet from the fly. It will relay news about takes.

CRANEFLIES

Craneflies are not midges. But they are in the same aquatic insect order and for that reason will be covered briefly here. In the old sense of the word *midge,* meaning any small fly, these large, lumbering creatures are anything but midges.

Cranefly larvae are juicy bites to trout, but they're not often available except during very heavy flows.

The importance of craneflies is not great. Many are terrestrial or only semiaquatic; their larvae live in damp soil, often inhabiting stream and lake boundary areas, or even your back lawn. The larvae of aquatic species spend most of their time deep in the gravel and sand of the bottom, where trout cannot get at them in normal conditions. After a heavy rain, when the river has gotten so violent it's torn itself up, lots of cranefly larvae get washed out where trout can get them. But who wants to fish when the water is *that* angry?

Craneflies pupate in damp soil alongside streams. Again, trout have difficulty taking them there and are unlikely to be found selective for cranefly pupae until they learn to use their fins as gardening trowels.

Adult craneflies are a different story. They hang out near streams, in damp places. They like rotten logs, dripping soil banks, crevices in rocks. Coolness and moisture are their favorite things.

When a soft summer rain sweeps through and dampens dry foliage, craneflies come out and dance above the currents of pools and riffles. They are ungainly, with long legs, heavy bodies, and wings that seem inadequate for their size.

They often go tumbling down to the water. They struggle on the surface, then lift off again if their struggles are not interrupted by trout. Sometimes they whir right across the surface, their long legs dangling to it or almost to it, their wings a blur. I suspect this is the way trout see them most often, though on occasion one is seen lying spent on the surface, usually in shallow backwaters. My guess is that spent adults are seen only where trout can't get to them, because the ones trout can get to are quickly converted to groceries. Craneflies make big and juicy bites.

Trout take splashy pokes at craneflies skimming over the surface. Sometimes they get them. More often they don't. But they

Adult craneflies are ungainly insects that can stir up frightful rises. Note the knobbed stalks, called halteres, in place of the second pair of wings. These are common to midges and mosquitoes as well.

come up eagerly and quickly to natural cranefly adults, and they can be brought up the same way to bushy dry flies fished with the same erratic behavior.

The most interesting pattern style tied to represent craneflies is Ed Hewitt's old Skater. It's an ungainly thing, like the natural. It is tied with two oversize badger hackles wound on a hook shank, concave sides toward each other. The two hackles are gently worked along the hook shank, toward each other, until their tips meet as points. It's very difficult to get the right hackles to tie the fly, because of the current quest for smaller and finer hackles. The best you'll be able to do is to use the biggest feathers on a badger cape, the kind of feathers you usually discard. But they're not perfect.

Tie the fly with unwaxed thread. That allows you to wind the hackles, then push them along the shank toward each other. Waxed thread won't slide as well. If it's done right, the hackle tips will come together in an almost knife-edged point all around the circumference of the fly, but with the hackles available today, that's very difficult to achieve. Try it anyway; even if it is less than perfect, the Skater will still coax up some trout that will be reluctant to take anything else.

SKATER

Hook	1X short, sizes 14–16.
Thread	Black, unwaxed.
Hackle	Badger.

Skater

This style fly does nothing more than suggest a giant awkward insect skittering across the water. That's the way it should be fished. Drop it lightly to a flat or pool. Let it float freely for a time. If no trout rises to it, lift your rod and whisper the fly across the surface.

This fly and style of fishing have been used, historically, more to mark the lie of a trout than to catch it. The attempted take is so

Biologist Poul Bech dancing a Skater over the surface of a British Columbia trout stream.

splashy and quick that the trout seems to frighten itself. It darts back to its hold, fins all aquiver. But you can mark its lie and fish for it later with a nymph, streamer, or conventional dry fly. That's the traditional story.

My own experience is thin with these flies. I've used them often on small streams, and they draw up exciting rises, but no more consistently than the more common run of small-stream flies such as the Elk Hair Caddis or Royal Wulff, which are easier to fish. But just last season, I fished with fisheries biologist Poul Bech over selective rainbows on the upper reaches of a forested British Columbia river. The stream gradient was gentle in places, forming long glides and pools. An occasional western green drake dun lumbered off the water, and a few craneflies were out and about, seen intermittently by us but possibly more often by the trout. The trout were reluctant to take any of the normal run of Green Drake dry flies, or even searching nymphs.

Poul was familiar with the stream and its bashful trout. He came armed with a small fly box holding several Skaters. I watched him fish them for a while. He would cast at a slight angle across the current, usually downstream though sometimes upstream, over current tongues, over slowly moving flats, tight against banks with overhanging conifer boughs, to any likely holding water. He'd usually give the fly a free float the first time on any line of drift. The next time through, he'd alternate dead-drift with skitters and twitches.

The fly stood on its hackle tips and looked nervous. The trout came up and pounced on it. That was fun to watch. Some would smack the fly, sending spray into the air. Others would sip it down, almost with an audible *blub*. Many would hurl themselves out of the water, take the fly on the way down.

Poul wasn't using the method to locate trout that he could return to catch later on more reasonable flies. Almost all the fish that attacked his fly were hooked well.

I had no Skaters with me on that trip. A few of them, with their fifty-cent-piece diameters, take up a lot of room in a fly box. Poul had only a few, and we were backpacking, so there was no source for more. He gave me two, saying, "That's all you'll get."

They worked. They were a delight to fish. They were soon gone to trout. Whether the result is a hooked fish or a found fish, Skaters make an exciting way to explore a stream on any cool, damp midsummer day.

MOSQUITOES

Mosquitoes are better known to trout fishermen than they are to trout. The reason is fairly simple: Mosquito habitat and trout habitat seldom overlap. Many fly patterns have been designed to imitate these pesky insects, but it's likely that most of them are based on misidentified midges, to which they are closely related.

Mosquito larval habitat is restricted to shallow water with no current. Shallow is inches deep, not feet deep. They prefer puddles, stock-watering troughs, rain gutters, and swamps or marshes with broad reaches of thin standing water. That is not the preferred habitat of trout, nor of trout fishermen.

In high mountain lakes, mosquitoes are considered to be important. Trout do feed around the rims of them, especially in the weeks after ice-out. And some mosquito larvae do flit about in the very shallowest water in bays and backwaters, so they might possibly be important in that restricted environment. But again, what is thought to be a mosquito larva is more likely to be a midge.

The mosquito life cycle is of great interest, though we might wish it were different. The larva creeps around in its shallow-water habitat. It swims with quick contractions of its entire body. It lives on whatever microscopic plant and animal life it can filter out of the water. It depends on the atmosphere for its oxygen, so it hangs, head down, piercing the surface film with spiracles where its tails would be if it had any, which it doesn't. That is why oil spread over water asphyxiates them: It prevents them from penetrating the surface to take oxygen from the air.

Mosquito larvae hang from the surface film and take oxygen from the air, using a spiracle that penetrates the surface. It's rare that their habitat overlaps with trout habitat.

Mosquitoes pupate in open water, trading one end for the other. Pupae depend on spiracles near the head for their air, so they hang from the surface right side up instead of upside down. Other than that, they look a lot like mosquito larvae. Mosquitoes emerge much like midges, poking the thorax through the film, splitting along the back, the adult slowly working its way out into winged life.

The rest of the mosquito life cycle is too familiar. The female mosquito is the only one that bites. She depends on a blood meal for the maturation of a full complement of eggs, though a small number will hatch without it. She gets this blood meal from rodents, deer, you, and me.

If there is an important part of the mosquito life cycle—which I doubt—from the angling point of view, it is those larvae and pupae hanging from the surface. That's when trout can get at them most effectively, if the naturals are in water suitable to trout, which normally they are not.

Most mosquito patterns have been created to match midge pupae mistakenly identified as mosquito larvae. I suggest that the flies you tied for the pupal stage of the midges will solve any mosquito selectivity you might encounter. That is going out on a slight limb, but the purpose of this book is to simplify hatch matching, not complicate it.

It's a minor axiom of this book that if something resembles something else so closely that anglers and trout mistake it for whatever else it looks like, then a pattern that imitates the something else will work fine, and there's no need to create and carry a new one.

Chapter 8

Dragonflies and Damselflies

I got to the lake late. In an hour, it would be night. I grabbed my gear out of the car and hurried down the forested trail to the shore. I hopped onto a favorite floating log, an old waterlogged hemlock with a butt so big I could sit on it comfortably while I strung my rod in the failing light.

The lake was still and lifeless. A couple of bobber-watchers sat forlornly on another floating log across a narrow neck of the lake. Their voices carried softly across the water to me. They were complaining to each other about how bad the fishing had been all day.

Because no fish rose, I spooled a wet-tip line and tied on a size 8 Dark Cahill wet fly. "It's as good as anything," I thought, "and there's nothing to indicate that something else might work better." Wet flies aren't used much in America today, but a generic wet fly still makes an excellent searching dressing whenever you don't have any reason to use something more specific.

I stripped line from the reel and punched a long cast out across the lake. I'd get in some casting practice, if nothing else. The line landed hard but straight. I counted slowly to twenty to give time for the line to tug the fly down toward the shallow, limb-tangled bottom, and for the line's harsh arrival to be forgotten by any fish that might be in the area. Then I began retrieving in short, six-inch strips, with the rod tip held low to the water to reduce slack between the rod and the fly.

On the first cast, there was a surprising sharp rap. I let the line in my left hand slip through my fingers, and the trout took off straight toward the bobber-watchers. It took out all the line I'd cast, then spun the reel and caused it to squawk. The trout came up and flapped end over end in the air. It was a rainbow, but it had the chunky profile of a bass.

Three times the fish became a black silhouette suspended in the evening air out there toward the bait fishermen, closer to them than to me. Then I brought it in, landing it awkwardly in my hand. It nearly broke off; I'd forgotten my net.

The trout was sixteen inches long, and fat far out of any proportion to its length. I rapped it with a stick and laid it on the log. It was a holdover plant in a lake with no stream in which trout could spawn, and I'd been ordered to return with dinner for four.

I cast again out into the stillness, waited awhile before beginning my retrieve, and again got a sharp rap. Another fat trout danced over the lake, then came reluctantly to my hand. I heard the other fishermen talking. I looked over and saw them reeling in their unbobbed bobbers. They stalked off their log, and I heard an angry grinding of gears as their rig bounced away on the old woods road.

I kept the second fish. It was the same size as the first and completed that dinner for four. I released three more trout and lost two on shattered tippets before it was too dark to fish any longer.

I cleaned the two fish there on the log, feeding their entrails to crayfish scuttling in the shallows. But first I sliced the stomachs open and squeezed their copious contents into a pickle-jar lid. I added water, then stirred the stew to separate out the various ingredients, while I examined it all in the beam of a flashlight. There were lots of small items: a miscellany of midges and mayflies and cased caddis too various and too digested to recognize. But each trout stomach contained a half dozen or so large, hourglass-shaped nymphs, dark in color, about size 8.

In those youthful days, I didn't recognize them as dragonfly nymphs. I didn't learn until a long time later that these large and somewhat strange stillwater beasts migrate toward shore for emergence in summer, sometimes in great numbers, and that when doing it they either crawl over the bottom or swim just above it in short, four- to six-inch bursts. I didn't know that at times dragonfly nymphs act just like wet flies fished deep with a stripping retrieve.

Those trout had been busy feeding on dragonfly nymphs on their annual migration toward shore for emergence. I had imitated their size, roughly their shape, approximately their color, and almost exactly their behavior, but all entirely by accident.

DRAGONFLY LIFE CYCLE

Little in the fly-fishing literature that I had read up to that time indicated the importance of dragonflies. Since then, they've been treated with the respect they deserve by those who appreciate stillwaters. Their nymphs inhabit nearly all lakes and ponds, and they also live in the quiet backwaters of some rivers and streams. One group, only occasionally important to fly fishermen, lives and hunts among riffle rocks, but most often in silted and weedy waters, more associated with smallmouth bass than with trout.

Dragonfly adults are prevalent on lakes and ponds but are not often important to anglers. They hold their wings to the sides when at rest, unlike damseflies, which hold their wings straight back.

Dragonflies have two- to three-year life cycles. Their metamorphosis is incomplete, with nymph and adult stages, and no pupal stage between. Everybody knows about dragonfly adults, with their agile scouting flights along shorelines and their fatal patrols out over nearby roads and bordering fields, where they capture smaller insects and often eat them in the air while continuing to hunt.

Dragonfly nymphs are hunters as well, but they are secretive. They creep around in bottom silts or stalk patiently along the stems of aquatic vegetation. They spend most of their time camouflaged in the silt of the bottom or cryptic in the vegetation, waiting to ambush smaller insects and even the fry of trout that later would eat them.

Dragonfly nymphs are fierce. I once put three in an aquarium with about 150 fat scuds, along with some sticks and plants among which they could all hide from each other. I thought the scuds would be enough grub to keep the dragonflies happy until I got a chance to photograph them. But I got involved in a writing project and forgot about them. Two weeks later, I came up for air, looked into the aquarium, and it appeared to be empty of everything. There were no scuds, and no dragonfly nymphs.

"Strange!" I thought. "Where could they have gone?"

I pulled out the vegetation and then the bits of wood I had left for habitat, examining each carefully. Finally I found a single dragonfly nymph clinging to the underside of a piece of rotten wood. It was as fat as a well-fed puppy. That nymph had grown a full hook size in just a couple of weeks. It had consumed every scud, apparently many of them by way of its fellow dragonfly nymphs. I photographed it and released it back to the pond from which I had captured it. Such effective maliciousness deserved its reward.

Dragonfly nymphs have a peculiar adaptation that enhances their ability to express their ferocity. The lower labium, an appendage comparable to our lower jaw, has evolved into a hinged, or elbowed, armlike apparatus. At rest, this extendable labium is held tucked in under the head. When innocent prey, such as a mayfly nymph, midge larva, or trout fry, ambles within reach of the camouflaged predator, this labium fires out like a frog's tongue, grasping the prey and pulling it in. The victim is then eaten alive.

Some dragonfly nymphs, called *silters,* creep around the bottom. They are hairy and entrap silt and debris on their bodies. This serves as camouflage as they half bury themselves in the silt and wait for a luckless insect or scud to pass within reach. Others clamber about in vegetation or on the twigs and limbs of trees fallen into the water. These are called *climbers.* They stalk their prey or wait in ambush for it. These can often be collected by walking along the shoreline and flipping wood debris over. They cling to it without moving, probably wondering what has turned their world upside down.

Dragonfly nymphs can be quite active at times during their two- and three-year life cycles. As they grow, they become sizable attractions to foraging trout. Even after the mature third-year class has emerged for the season, first- and second-year nymphs are still available to fish. This makes imitations useful at all seasons of the stillwater year.

Dragonflies begin to emerge when the sun of late spring warms the water to 60 degrees F and more. Their primary months of emergence are late May, June, and early July. A few continue to emerge in late July, August, and early September. But prime activity, and fish interest, centers on the late-spring and early-summer months.

The nymphs do not hatch out in open water. They migrate to shore or to weed beds, partially submerged logs, or anything else that protrudes from the water. This migratory behavior is of great interest to trout, and should be to you as well if you fish stillwaters at all, because it exposes great numbers of the big nymphs to predation by trout.

When they've reached shore, or some vegetation protruding from the water, dragonfly nymphs wait for evening. Sometimes hundreds of them gather up near shore for emergence in a single evening. Lifting a piece of floating debris from the water can reveal eight or ten clinging together in the same small space.

Emergence takes place at dusk, after dark, or in the early morning. This is a defense against bird predation. The heaviest numbers of nymphs do not leave the water until after dark. Then they crawl out on reeds, bulrushes, or on shore. The nymph gets a good grip with its tarsal claws, the nymphal cuticle splits along the back, and the adult slowly emerges. The wings of the adult unfold and

After emergence, which usually happens at night, the wings of the adult dragonfly must extend and harden before it is able to fly.

straighten as the wing veins are pumped full of fluid. It takes quite some time for this fluid to dry and harden. Until that happens, the wings are not stiff, and the insect is unable to fly.

Dragonfly emergence is a very slow process, taking several minutes to an hour or more. If it happened in daylight blackbirds and robins would hunt the shorelines, picking the helpless new dragonflies like fat berries.

Dragonfly adults form a catching basket with their long front legs, then swoop through the air in their agile flight, capturing and devouring mayflies, midges, and mosquitoes. This third diet item wins them great favor among anglers and other folks. Some townships in New England accomplish mosquito control by releasing thousands of dragonfly nymphs into nearby waters. The nymphs eat mosquito larvae. When they hatch, the adults continue the predation in the air. The result is preferable to killing the mosquito larvae by spreading oil over swamps.

Adult dragonflies mate on lakeside vegetation. You will often see them flying through the air, male and female joined front and back, returning to the water to deposit eggs. The fertilized female returns to the water, where she holds on to floating logs, reeds, or other protruding vegetation and extends her long abdomen to sow her eggs into the material beneath the waterline. The male may accompany the female during this process, grasping her behind the head while she lowers her abdomen under the water.

Trout feed on dragonfly nymphs whenever they get a chance, which is often, but they get only occasional opportunities to take dragonfly adults. It's rare, but the results can be explosive. Because of its rarity, and because I've tried fishing adult dragonflies often with no positive result, no adult dressings are offered here.

That doesn't mean trout don't take the naturals. We've all seen dragonflies hovering over the surface and seen trout leap out, try to knock them down. One in a hundred of us has seen a trout succeed. I haven't.

I fished a remote Andean lake in Chile once—we had to ride horses for miles through dense rain forest to get to the lake—where dragons were thick and trout consistently tried for them. We stood on shore and watched winged dragonflies wandering all over, often just a foot off the water. We saw numerous big splashes erupt under them but saw no successes.

The prescribed flies for the lake were bass poppers. We had none, so we tied on the largest dry salmon fly dressings we had and even braced big cork indicators against the eyes of the hooks. These contraptions, like the dragonflies, drew explosive takes, presumably from trout mistaking them for downed dragonflies. We were asked to exercise catch-and-release, so I'll never know if stomach contents would have revealed selective feeding on dragonfly adults.

I've never seen such a thing in North America, which doesn't mean it doesn't happen. But it's never happened to me.

Dragonfly Nymphs

Natural

Dragonfly nymphs are most important during their late-spring and early-summer migrations toward shore for emergence. But they are also an interesting bite for trout at other times of year. Whenever stillwater trout show no signs that they're feeding selectively, a dragonfly nymph imitation is one of the largest, and therefore best, items with which to tempt them.

It's easy to recognize dragonfly nymphs. They have wide heads, narrow thoraxes, and bulbous abdomens, which give them their peculiar hourglass shape. Their eyes are very large, their antennae short. The hinged and extensible labium is easily seen if the nymph is turned over. This, along with their large size and peculiar shape, makes them difficult to confuse with any other organism.

Their manner of respiration, unique in the underwater world of aquatic insects, gives dragonfly nymphs a strange propulsion system. Their gills are inside that bulbous abdomen. Water is taken in and expelled, much like we breathe air in and out of our lungs. But dragonfly nymphs inhale and exhale water through the anus.

When startled, a dragonfly nymph clamps down and squirts water out the back in a strong stream. The force of the expelled water jets the insect forward a few inches. When this is done repeatedly, it darts along in short bursts, just like a wet fly or nymph retrieved with short strips.

That's why my Dark Cahill wet, which was the approximate size and color of the dragonfly nymphs taken by the trout that day, worked so well on that log-rimmed lake. My retrieve was exactly right to mimic the jetlike swimming of the naturals. And it's probably safe to assume, though hard to confirm, that when dragonfly

Dragonfly nymphs have an hourglass aspect. They breathe through an anal opening, taking water into the abdomen and jetting it back out.

nymphs are chased by trout, they have their afterburners cut in. So trout probably take them most often as they're jetting along.

The size range of dragonfly nymphs is wide, from early instar specimens a quarter inch long up to mature individuals a full two inches long. It's best when imitating them to strike some sort of medium, using dressings tied on long-shank hooks in the range of size 6 down to 10.

The color range is narrower. Like most nymphs, dragonflies rely on camouflage for protection. They will be approximately the color of what they have been living on and around. If it's a tannish brown bottom, they will be tannish brown. If they have been clambering in vegetation, shades of olive will be added to their dominant colors. Green might even become their dominant color. Most dragonfly nymphs I have collected have been dark olive-brown, and an imitation in that color will almost always be effective when trout are feeding on them.

Imitation

My favorite searching fly for stillwaters, when I see no signs that trout are feeding on any particular food form, has become an Olive Woolly Bugger in size 10 or 12. This dressing looks a little like a lot of things that trout eat in the depths of lakes and ponds, but so far as I know, it's not an exact imitation of any of them. Part of its success is likely based on its slight resemblance to dragonfly nymphs.

If I haven't mentioned it and fail to later, my most consistent searching combination for stillwater trout is an Olive Woolly Bugger trailed by a size 14 or 16 black Traditional Midge Pupa on a couple feet of fine tippet. I usually rig it on whatever line will get it down near the bottom on a slow retrieve or at a slow troll. This is my exploring rig, when I'm trying to plumb a stillwater, to figure out where its trout are located and what they might be doing.

If I get any indication that trout are feeding, whether selectively or opportunistically, on dragonfly nymphs, I'll make my Olive Woolly Bugger more imitative for them by pinching off the after half of its marabou tails. That's it. That's my favorite dragonfly nymph imitation.

It's far from an exact imitation, but it gives a good rough impression of the natural, it fools the fish, and it's something I've always got on me.

OLIVE WOOLLY BUGGER

Olive Woolly Bugger

Hook	3X long, sizes 6–12.
Weight	10 to 20 turns of lead wire the diameter of the hook shank.
Thread	Olive.
Tail	Olive marabou, pinched short when fished as a dragonfly nymph.
Body	Olive chenille.
Hackle	Brown hen hackle palmered over body.

The weight gets the fly down and also helps give it a portly appearance. When the back half of the tail is pinched off, the fly lacks the hourglass shape of the natural but still looks a lot like a dragonfly nymph, or so the trout tell me.

A more realistic pattern might be necessary during dragonfly nymph migrations, though in truth I've found that the truncated Woolly Bugger is usually all I need even then. If a more imitative dressing is desired, one of the best I've found is the Lake Dragon, from Ron Cordes and Randall Kaufmann's *Lake Fishing with a Fly* (Frank Amato, 1984). Many complicated ways have been devised to capture the hourglass shape of the natural. This fly is built around one of the easiest.

LAKE DRAGON

Lake Dragon

Hook	3X to 4X long, sizes 6–12.
Eyes	Olive or black monofilament eyes.
Weight	15 to 25 turns of lead wire, flattened.
Rib	Brown yarn.
Body	Olive fur dubbing.
Wing case	Turkey feather section.
Legs	Brown partridge.
Thorax/ head	Olive fur dubbing.

If you don't have monofilament eyes available, you can form your own out of 25- to 50-pound-test Maxima leader. Hold a half-inch section of leader with a pair of needlenose pliers. Heat one end with a cigarette lighter or candle until it melts into a ball. Blow on it to cool and harden it. If it ignites, blow it out. Treat the other end the same way, and you'll have a dumbbell-shaped set of eyes. Tie it in just behind the hook eye.

Wrap the lead weighting wire, then flatten it with the same set of needlenose pliers. Don't squeeze too hard; just knock the lead well out of round, creating an underbody that is oval rather than round.

Make your abdomen with thick, loose dubbing, narrow at the back, fat in the middle, then narrowing again about a quarter of the shank length behind the hook eye. After ribbing it, tease out the sides to give the fly an oval body. Cut a section of turkey feather to shape, tie it in, and wind a partridge hackle in front of it. Gather the hackle to the sides, then dub the thorax over and around the mono eyes.

Presentation

When dragonfly nymphs are migrating, it's best to fish their imitations near shore or over shoals, especially over weed beds, around floating logs, and near emerging fields of cattails and bulrushes. I've read and heard that it's important to fish your imitation in the direction that the naturals are heading: toward shore. I can't confirm this in my own experience, but attempt to fish them by casting out from the shore, and retrieving them back, whenever it is practical.

When the naturals are not migrating, your nymphs should be fished deep, either near the bottom or just above weed beds.

Some friends and I once portaged canoes into a big British Columbia lake. After setting up camp, we cruised in different directions, scouting out the bottom structure. Al Buhr, the famous steelhead fly fisherman, came back and reported he'd located a dropoff, where water about eight feet deep dropped over a rounded shoulder and disappeared into darkness.

The next morning, we anchored our little fleet of canoes in a line a few feet inside the shallow side of that dropoff, and rigged with fast-sinking shooting tapers. We made our casts out over the

Creep a dragonfly nymph imitation near the bottom of a lake or pond, and you're very likely to propel some fat trout into the air.

depths, gave our lines long counts to tug dragonfly nymphs down. Then we crept them back up that shoulder. Action was far from constant, but it was sufficient that we all paddled happily back to have lunch. Some of the Kamloops rainbows we'd caught were close to five pounds.

The creeping hand-twist retrieve, right along the bottom or just above it, is a good place to start when you're imitating dragonfly nymphs. It's good for those forms that nestle into the silt of the bottom, and also good for those that hunt with stealth through the vegetation. If a slow retrieve fails to interest trout, then speed it up.

The most effective stripping retrieve is the same as that used most often with wet flies and streamers. But keep the strips short. Dragonfly nymphs move four to six inches with each jet-propelled burst. Your strips should be no more than the amount of line you can draw in with a twitch of your wrist.

DAMSELFLIES

It was a tiny mountain pond. The sun warmed its shallows. A flock of cedar waxwings, passing north on their spring migration, paused to perch on the limbs of fallen trees. They speared accurately upward, at intervals, to take at the apex of flight the sporadic caddisflies and mayflies and midges that came off all day. There were so few I think they got them all.

No concentrated hatch happened, and no fish broke the surface. I caught a few trout by dredging deep nymphs, but I was a disappointed angler when I stirred the canned stew that was my camp dinner early that evening. Later I went back out and sat on the shore to watch night settle over the pond. I carried my rod, as an angler will, and had it strung with a floating line, as one wishing for evening activity will do. But I had little hope after the long, dismal day.

I had not been sitting long when a bull of a boil erupted to the surface not far from a deadfall in front of me. I rushed down and dropped a dry fly over the rise, but the trout refused to come up again. A few minutes later, there was a similar vigorous boil next to another nearby log. Again I rushed to it, teetering out on the log this time, and dropped a dry fly over it. Nothing rose again.

Rises began to trouble the water more consistently all around me. I cast the dry fly in frustration, not wanting to change flies because I had no idea what to change to, but finally stopped and looked closely enough to notice that the rises were clearly subsurface. That made me wonder what was going on out there. I got onto my hands and knees on the log and peered into the water. Before long I saw a long, whip-slender nymph paddle laboriously by, just a few inches deep.

I scooped the nymph into an aquarium net and examined it closely. Its three willow-leaf tails marked it as a damselfly. The behavior of those trout became abruptly clear. They were boiling for the damsels as the nymphs swam toward shore for an emergence that would start just after dark.

I tied on the nearest thing I had to the damselfly, an Olive Woolly Worm tied on a long-shank hook. I cast it out parallel to the log on which I stood. After letting it sink a few inches, I started it back toward me with a slow hand-twist retrieve. On about the fifth cast, the line tip twitched, I raised the rod, and a rainbow swept up and danced on the surface. I landed it, and three more like it, on the same simple dressing before it became too dark to fish.

The fish were plump and pan-size, not large. Nor did they take that ancient Woolly Worm with any visible eagerness. It was not a very good match for the slender naturals, but it did give me an hour of modestly happy fishing. A better match would have meant more exciting fishing, as I've found out numerous times since.

DAMSELFLY LIFE CYCLE

The damselfly life cycle is similar to that of its close relative, the dragonfly. But it's usually just one year, in some cases two, never the three that is the average for the larger dragonflies.

Damselfly nymphs greatly favor rooted vegetation. They stalk among the submerged stems and leaves that camouflage them so well. They have the same extendable labium possessed by dragonflies, but it is not so stout and powerful, and most slender damselfly nymphs stalk smaller prey.

Damsel nymphs are always found in water shallow enough to allow penetration of adequate sunlight to promote plant growth. They are less prolific in lakes with clean sandy bottoms than in the cluttered kind that harbor lots of little organisms such as mayfly nymphs and midge larvae. Some species live in rivers and streams, but these are more important to smallmouth bass anglers than they are to trout fishermen.

Damselfly nymphs are much less bulky than dragonfly nymphs, though some are almost as long. They reach a length of one and a half inches, but most are an inch or so long, excluding their tails, at maturity. That is a relatively large insect, compared with the average-size bite a trout eats, and fish definitely key on them when they are available in good numbers, as they are when they migrate. But damselfly nymphs are out there, available to trout, almost all season, and trout always seem to have their last meal of damsel in mind. A nymph imitation makes an excellent searching pattern on any stillwater, and your lake and pond fly boxes should be well stocked with them.

Migration for emergence puts damsel nymphs in their greatest peril. They seem to have an instinct for the direction to the nearest protruding vegetation. Once Dick Haward and I observed a spo-

The long, slender aspect and three leaf-shaped caudal gills make damselfly nymphs easy to recognize.

radic migration of damselfly nymphs while fishing Davis Lake, in central Oregon. They came marching from all directions, and all headed unerringly for a small, circular patch of bulrush that stuck up like an island. It was a hundred yards from the shore of the lake and seemed like a much less likely destination than the shoreline itself.

Most damselfly nymphs swim laboriously toward shore, although a few species are capable of bursts of almost minnowlike speed. Few of them have more than feeble means to escape trout. Once they commit to their shoreward journey, leaving the shelter of vegetation, they are at the mercy of cruising and feeding trout. Though you'll sometimes see individuals swimming up near the surface, most of them migrate a few feet down. Feeding on them is more often invisible than it is visible, reflected in takes that you're occasionally able to see as subsurface rises up near the top.

Emergence takes place on floating logs, on the stems of reeds, or at the shoreline itself. As with dragonflies, it most often takes place under the cover of darkness. But it's far from uncommon to see damselfly nymphs crawl out onto mats of vegetation or lily

When damselfly adults first emerge, they are unable to fly. Trout are said to nose among protruding plant stems to knock them into the water, though I haven't seen that happen.

pads and emerge in afternoon, if the day is at all overcast. If you fish stillwaters with fair populations of damselflies and keep your eyes open, you'll see the emergence happen.

Last summer, I was photographing damselfly nymphs and placed a particularly large one into my miniature aquarium. It immediately crawled out, got a grip on the glass, and emerged in bright sunlight. It wasn't happy about it and wanted sunglasses, it told me, but preferred emergence to confinement.

Damselfly adults, like dragonflies, use their legs as a catching basket to capture prey in the air. They usually feed on the smallest organisms, such as gnats, midges, and mosquitoes, though I've seen a damselfly adult capture and consume a fair-size moth.

Damselflies prefer to fly when the sun is bright. If a passing cloud obscures the sun, all those in the air will disappear almost instantly. They will fly in a breeze, but not in a light wind. If a gust hits the lake, they'll take to shore almost at once. The same gust, or brisk wind, will often knock them off their rests. If those perching places are near water, trout know what a wind can provide them in the way of unhappy damselfly adults. When a puff of wind rattles the reeds and knocks damselflies to the water, waiting trout eagerly chase them down before they can escape.

Mating takes place on vegetation or in the air. Damselflies deposit their eggs by sowing them into plant stems, sometimes crawling underwater to accomplish this. They often fly in tandem, a male grasping a female behind the head with claspers on the end of his abdomen. Because they're clumsy when locked together, it is quite common for them to fall to the water in pairs and to be taken by trout as doubles. Once I thought I saw trout selective to paired adult damsels, but I'm still not sure that's what was happening.

More often than I'd like—because I'm seldom prepared for them—I've seen trout selective to single damselfly adults.

Damselfly Nymphs

Natural
Most damselfly nymph migrations take place in spring and early summer, though some continue through the late-summer months, and a few into fall. I have fished migrations on a high-desert lake when an early-May wind struck down off snowbound mountains

and made it almost too cold to fish. More often, they migrate after the sun has had some chance to warm the water, and when water temperatures rise toward 60 degrees F.

A few nymphs might make their emergence move in the morning. More will move in the afternoon, and the migration will usually be strongest in the evening. The importance of an accurate imitation increases with the number of naturals trout see and take. Selectivity always increases as fish turn their attention strongly to a single insect.

Damselfly nymphs are perhaps the easiest of all nymphs to recognize. They have three caudal gills in place of tails. These are leaflike, some slender like willow leaves, others oval like alder leaves. All have tracheal systems branched through them that look like the veins of the leaves they resemble. These tracheal tubes gather oxygen from the flat gills and deliver it to the body cells of the nymph.

Damsels swim with a side-to-side movement that is sinuous, like that of a snake. But in most cases, their progress is slow. This vigorous movement, resulting in little forward motion, makes them one of the most difficult insects to imitate successfully. That is why I was happy taking a fish every few casts that waxwing evening on a Woolly Worm. I'd have been happy to catch that many trout on an exact imitation.

Damselfly nymph migrations are not unlike those of the related dragonflies. But they seem to be concentrated into a tighter time frame. And the nymphs cruise through the mid-depths and up near the surface rather than hugging the bottom. They cause selective feeding more often because of their numbers. They prompt more visible activity because of their nearness to the surface.

Damsels average about an inch long, an inch and a quarter when their tails are added. Some are a bit smaller at maturity. A reasonable size range for imitations can be quite narrow. When considering mature specimens, which are the only kind that migrate to emerge, damselfly nymphs can be imitated on 3X long size 8 and 10 hooks. Flies tied to fish outside migration periods are usually more effective when tied a bit smaller, on size 12, 14, and even 16 long-shank hooks.

The color range is similarly narrow and again reflects the colors of the bottom and the vegetation where they live. Green and dark brownish olive are the two most common colors. Some species are tannish brown, or tannish olive. Some have translucent and beautifully mottled tails. Almost always there is a strong element of green or dark olive in the natural nymphs.

Imitation

I don't recommend relying on an Olive Woolly Worm to fish over trout feeding on damselfly nymphs. The fly is excellent and looks like a lot of things that trout eat in stillwaters. If they're feeding opportunistically, it will fool them even when they're taking damselfly nymphs. But trout feeding selectively will most likely turn away from it unless they're driven by hunger accumulated during winter.

An appropriate Olive Woolly Bugger, with its active marabou tails, can be a different story. I have resorted to thinning out about half of the tails and trimming all but a few hackle fibers sticking out to the sides, up near the head, to make a Woolly Bugger work when trout were focused on damselfly nymphs. It's worth remembering, since it's likely you will have this pattern on you. It makes a better imitation than some of the more rigid flies I've seen created to imitate this insect exactly.

One of the best pattern styles to imitate damsels also incorporates marabou for movement. Polly Rosborough's Green Damsel, from his *Tying and Fishing the Fuzzy Nymphs* (Stackpole, 1978), is tied on a long-shank hook, with green a marabou tail, slender green yarn or dubbing body, and green marabou wing case. The legs of the natural are represented with a few speckled guinea fibers. A single variation of this dressing would have the same materials in olive-brown colors.

I have used this dressing for more years than I care to count, most often in smaller sizes than its originator tied it in. Polly called for size 8 and 10 imitations, to fish during damsel migrations. I tie it in those sizes but fish it more often in sizes 12 and 14 when trout are not focused on these nymphs. It makes an excellent searching pattern, especially in and around weed beds, all spring and summer. It's just about the first fly I reach for when I'm fishing weedy waters and have no idea what to try.

GREEN DAMSEL

Green Damsel

Hook	3X long, sizes 8–14.
Thread	Green.
Tail	Green-dyed marabou.
Body	Green yarn or fur.
Wing case	Green marabou.
Legs	Speckled guinea fibers.

The same pattern style with olive-brown marabou and fur will nearly complete the color spectrum of damselfly nymph dressings. Other colors can be tied if you collect specimens that call for them. The late Polly never weighted his nymphs, though I occasionally do what I call under-weighting them: use eight to ten turns of lead wire one diameter finer than the hook shank, to get the fly started sinking.

There are many more exact imitations to choose from when imitating damselfly nymphs. My favorite among them, mostly because I've had a great amount of success with it, is Henry Hoffman's Chickabou Damsel. Henry, of Super Grizzly hackle fame, is a friend and showed me how to tie this fly in his living room. It depends on the availability of Chickabou, the back and rump patch of the same chicken that provides an excellent cape and saddle. Most fly shops carry it, and all can order it, dyed to the right colors.

The fly is tied on a 3X long hook that is bent up slightly in the front one-third of its length. The eyes are monofilament, the same as those for the Lake Dragon. Soft Chickabou fibers are tied in for the tail, then the same fibers are wound as herl for the body. Chickabou tips are tied to the sides to represent the legs of the natural. Olive dubbing is wrapped over and around the eyes to form the head of the fly. The resulting fly not only looks very much like the real thing, but when it's wet in the water, it also moves a lot like it.

CHICKABOU DAMSEL

Hook	3X long, sizes 10–14 bent up at front third.
Thread	Olive.
Eyes	Olive or amber monofilament eyes.
Tail	Olive Chickabou.
Rib	Brass wire counterwound over body.
Body	Olive Chickabou.
Legs	Olive Chickabou.
Head	Olive fur dubbing.

Chickabou Damsel

This dressing could be weighted lightly, like Polly's Damsel Nymph, to get it started sinking. You could also weight it slightly just behind the eyes. When you pause in your retrieve, it would then dive, as many naturals do when confronted by hungry trout. But don't ever weight it heavily enough to fatten it up or to kill its action. Keep it looking and acting like a natural. Use a sinking-tip or other type of sinking line, rather than excess weight on the shank, to get it down to the depth you want.

At one time, hinged wiggle nymphs were thought to be excellent for damsel imitations, and I still see a few around to this day. But few natural damsels travel at the terrifying speeds it takes to get any wiggle out of a hinged dressing in stillwater. On a more natural slow retrieve, the rear half of the hinged fly simply flops down, and the fly looks like a damselfly with a broken back. Trout might find that acceptable, but I don't.

Presentation

Presentation of damselfly nymph dressings is based on the sinuous swimming motion of the natural. Polly, in his *Fuzzy Nymphs*, recommends fishing his fly on a wet-tip line and "with one-inch, very fast jerks of the rod tip and line." This type of retrieve sets the marabou in motion and imitates the swimming behavior of the nymph.

I would like to add a couple of tactics that have worked for me, almost always with a floating line and long leader around shallow vegetation, but also with a wet-tip or fast-sinking line in deeper water. The first is a very slow and steady hand-twist retrieve that fishes the fly as it might move when it's hunting for prey, just creeping along. This method has been effective for me when trout are working in and around weed beds or gathered in shallows such as coves. Trout almost always encounter at least an occasional damselfly nymph when cruising in such waters. They rarely seem able to resist an imitation, especially in size 12 or 14, if it is fished on a creeping retrieve.

The second tactic that has worked for me, when both Polly's fast retrieve and my slow one fail, is simply no retrieve at all. I can't explain why this works. Perhaps when the natural sees a trout it goes *tharn,* freezing like the rabbits in the old classic *Watership Down.* But that's unlikely. More likely, the nymphs swim a bit, then rest a bit. Trout must see them in this resting phase, and a fly left unretrieved appears to them like an insect dropping slowly down through the water. For whatever reason, they take a damselfly nymph imitation fished on the sit.

The difficulty is in detecting the take. I use a floating line and long leader and watch the line tip closely. Still, I'm sure I get two, three, or even more hits for every one I manage to detect. But I detect enough, using this method, to make it an effective tactic for me during damselfly nymph migrations.

The smartest tactic is to try all sorts of retrieves, sometimes on the same cast. A combination of a few inches of Polly Rosborough's twitching retrieve, a long pause while the fly sinks, then a span of hand-twist retrieve is probably the most effective way to fish these flies. It combines elements of fast movement and resting and slow movement, the same way the natural makes its journey toward shore to emerge. If you find that trout take on only one type of retrieve, of course you'd want to stick to that.

You should also try various depths. If you suspect damselflies are in the mix that trout are eating, try first with a floating line and long leader. Give the fly plenty of time to sink before beginning the retrieve. If no success ensues, switch to a wet-tip line and shorten the leader a bit; you don't want to get the line tip down while the fly remains suspended high in the water column above it. If the wet-tip doesn't get the fly deep enough, switch to a wet-head, full sinking line, or shooting taper, and experiment with countdown times until you hook weed beds, bottom, or trout.

A damselfly nymph retrieved slowly in the shallows and weedy backwaters of any stillwater can create explosive action.

Damselfly nymphs are among the most difficult stages of any aquatic insect to solve with any consistency. But they are also some of the most effective stillwater flies when trout are seeing any of the naturals at all. If you fish lakes and ponds, they'll be very important to you as both searching and imitative dressings.

Damselfly Adults

Natural
The adult of the damsel can be important in limited circumstances. But when it's important, trout are greedy for it. The wise angler will

The adult damselfly has wide eyes and a slender body, and holds its wings back over the abdomen.

This is the view a trout gets of an adult damselfly, from under the water, and it's what you must match to have any success with its imitation.

at least be aware of the possibility and will be armed with flies to take advantage of it.

Damselfly adults are present on all stillwaters, all across the continent. They can be seen hovering and gliding gracefully in the sun, among reed stems and over lily pad flats. They come to rest almost instantly when the sun is obscured. They glide out and fly over the water again as soon as it reappears. Their predominant color is bright blue, though some are tan and others bright red. At times these slender adults hover in such thick clouds that the air takes on a bluish metallic cast when the sun strikes through a swarm just right. It's a beautiful sight.

Damselfly adults are available to trout just after emergence, if they hatch in the afternoon and a wind comes up when they do. The nymphs crawl out on plant stems or pad tops. The adults emerge slowly, and their wings dry over a period of an hour or two. If a wind comes up before they are able to fly, many are blown onto the water. They are helpless there, and trout take them eagerly.

After adult damselflies have achieved their wings, they hang around at the edges of the lake or pond for days and even weeks. They remain cryptic when the weather is anything but warm and almost windless. On blustery days, with alternate sunshine and cloud, they appear and disappear fleetingly. When the wind gusts through reeds while damsel adults are at rest, many of them get tumbled out and onto the surface of the water. Trout take them eagerly.

Some lakes have thick mats of submerged vegetation that rise to the surface in places and have channels and troughs of open water in other places. Trout cruise the open water, looking for damsels that are blown onto the surface or get carelessly close to the edge of it. When they're feeding on damsel adults in such water, and are seeing anything more than an occasional individual, they'll be selective to them. It was on one such bit of water that I thought I saw them selective to pairs of them.

Recognizing damsel adults is not difficult. They have large eyes, long bodies as slender as straws, and clear wings held together, back over the body, when the insect is at rest. Their size is from an inch and a half up to three inches long. The largest of them can be confused with small dragonflies at first glance, but dragonflies hold their wings outspread when at rest.

Imitation

Just a July ago, I arrived at a mosquito-ridden camp in Oregon's Cascade Mountains, on the shore of a fairly large lake that had its dark depths but also had extensive shallows where pondweed beds were thick and often trailed up to form mats on the surface. Blue damselflies patrolled the lake edges, bedeviling the mosquitoes, which instantly found and began to bedevil me. The best place to get away from the biting insects in such a place is out on the water, especially when it's breezy, which it was. So that's where I headed, launching my eight-foot pram.

My first project on any new lake is to make a complete circuit of it, and if it's small enough, to crisscross it in a place or two. Usually I'll tow a tandem of an Olive Woolly Bugger in front of a Black Midge Pupa, on a wet-tip line. That's what I did on this lake. I set off in the afternoon sunshine to row all the way around it. I thereby was able to fish far too shallow along an entire sweep of what turned out to be a very deep side and caught nothing for two hours.

When I made a turn at the upper end of the lake, I found myself stranded in weedy shallows, fishing too deep even after switching to a floating line. All I caught was tangles of plants, so I reeled in and just rowed for a while. After a few hundred yards, I arrived at an area, one hundred feet off shore, where the weed beds were broken by deep fissures and meandering channels, and only trailed up to about half of the patchwork surface.

Rise rings of feeding trout were sprinkled in the open places. Some of the rises were explosive. It was easy to see that damselflies were at the heart of whatever was going on. Swirls of them filled the air above the weeds, and many were making sorties out across the open water, some as singles and many more paired. Whenever the breeze increased, they'd go to rafts of weeds. Some of the smaller weed patches on the surface became almost blue with them.

The splashy rises always came when an increase of the slight wind riffled the water. I guessed that adult damsels were being blown onto the surface, which turned out to be correct. I removed my trolling flies, tied a perfect damselfly look-alike to my tippet, and cast it over the nearest splashy rise. Nothing happened. I cast it to dozens of rises and sometimes let it sit forever. Nothing always happened.

I brought the fly in, held it in my hand gazing at it, and while I did, an adult damselfly landed on my hand right next to it. They looked so alike I thought the natural had landed to check out mating possibilities with the imitation. It flew away after a moment of inspection, and trout weren't fooled by it either. Not until I got that fly back to shore and put it into a small glass water tank with a mirror underneath did I realize what was wrong.

It looked perfect from the top view, but from beneath, it had hackle and a yarn underwing, both designed to float it, but both obstructing the trouts' view of their silhouettes. I placed a dead natural on the surface of the tank next to it, looked at them side by side in the mirror, and they did not seem even remotely alike.

I did solve one of those trout later, when a very scattered hatch of speckle-wing mayfly duns came off in the same water. I cast an imitation over a trout that rose consistently next to a weed patch. I let the fly sit on a set of wind waves that had come up. After a long bout of idleness, sitting in the pram, watching that fly bounce on the waves, my eyes and thoughts both wandered out over the forest and mountains surrounding the lake. They were brought back to the fly by a terrifying splash.

My arm set the hook without any instructions from me. I played the trout out. It was a brookie, about sixteen inches long and well fattened. Oregon Fish and Wildlife had a project going on in that lake to eradicate non-native brook trout, return it to its native rainbows. I decided to help them. The trout was crammed with adult blue damsels.

Since then, I've done my research, tied a sufficient supply of California tier Andy Burk's Blue Adult Damsel, and had a bit of success with it, so I am nearer to a solution, though I'm not sure I'm there yet. I suspect the rest of the answer lies in adding some movement to the fly, rather than just letting it sit, but that belongs to a separate set of experiments, planned for the same lake in July of next season.

You'll find, in any approach to matching hatches, that there are always some searches going on, that your fly boxes are never completely settled for all of the insects. But that's the way it should be.

ANDY BURK'S BLUE ADULT DAMSEL

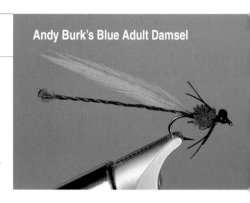

Andy Burk's Blue Adult Damsel

Hook	Standard dry fly, sizes 10–12.
Thread	Blue 3/0 Monocord.
Eyes	Black monofilament nymph eyes.
Abdomen	Blue Z-lon or braided Damsel Body, extended.
Wings	Dun hackle tips.
Thorax	Dark-blue-dyed deer hair, spun and clipped.
Legs	Blue or black 3/0 Monocord.

If you can't find Damsel Body, cut a hank of Z-lon three to four inches long. Grasp each end between forefinger and thumb of each hand. Twist the ends in opposite directions, then move your fingertips together. As you do, the Z-lon will twist into a perfect extended fly body.

If you encounter tan damsels dominant on your waters, you might want a version of the fly that covers that color. It's easy to convert the above blue phase by substituting tan thread, light brown Damsel Body or Z-lon for the body, and tan deer hair for the thorax. With those two versions, you'll have matches for the most common color themes. In truth, you'll rarely need anything but blue.

Presentation

Because naturals are available most frequently on blustery days, imitations are best fished when wind gusts rap reed forests and sweep lily pad flats and the floating surfaces of weed beds. Trout will cruise back in the vegetation and hang out near its edges. Your fly should be presented in pockets among the pads or along the edges of reeds and weed beds. Cruising trout will sometimes be visible. They have even been reported to shoulder in among the stems, deliberately knocking damsel adults into the water so they can feed on them.

A damsel adult imitation fished to
reed edges will often take trout
when naturals are around.

Your imitation should be fished without motion at first. But if it fails to interest trout, give the fly some movement, twitching it, or tug it across the surface a few inches before letting it settle again. I suspect that's where I made the largest part of my mistake on that mosquito-infested lake last season.

I'd invite you to help me work out the rest of the solution, but I know how you hate mosquitoes.

Chapter 9

Water Boatmen and Backswimmers

Water boatmen and backswimmers are members of the same order of insects that includes terrestrial leafhoppers and stinkbugs. The two aquatic groups are important at times to the stillwater trout fisherman. These times are not frequent, but the angler who spends a lot of time on lakes will find trout feeding on them selectively on occasion and will want to carry imitations and know how to present them.

WATER BOATMEN
Hosmer Lake holds Atlantic salmon, transplanted from the East to this mountain lake in the Oregon Cascades, in which they've learned to behave precisely like trout in order to survive. The ski slopes of Mount Bachelor and the snowcaps of the Three Sisters Mountains form a distant and beautiful backdrop for the lake. Vast marshy meadows line much of the shore, where mule deer and herds of elk ghost through mists at dawn, fading from the openings into thick jack-pine forests after nights spent browsing in the meadows.

The edges of the lake are abrupt banks, stalking and casting platforms from which the water drops off to sudden depths of three to six feet. The undercuts beneath the banks are tangles of the groping roots of the marsh grasses that grow on top. These root tangles form perfect havens for myriads of darting little water boatmen. These aquatic oarsmen trade back and forth between the underwater vegetation, on which they browse as peacefully as the deer and

Lakes with shallow vegetation, especially root tangles along undercut banks, will have good populations of water boatmen.

elk up above, and the surface, where they trap air in bubbles tucked under their wings and held along their bodies, before they swim back down to the vegetation to resume feeding.

Hosmer's water is clear. Salmon are visible at long range as they cruise in pods of two and three and more, hunting the shallows of coves and the abrupt banks for aquatic insects. They travel in small pods just as trout do in lakes.

Rick Hafele and I took up casting positions at the apex of a point, with coves indented to either side of us, one warm September morning. We waited like herons for the approaching salmon, which cruised restlessly, most of them right along the undercut banks. We cast all manner of wet flies, streamers, and nymphs in front of the fish, retrieving them in all the ways we knew, from almost stopped to jumping right along. The snobbish Atlantics merely tilted away, sometimes swimming right around the flies, as if they were something distasteful in their way. Every few feet, a passing fish would dart in toward the bank, take something with a quick turn, then return to its cruising.

"What do you think they're taking?" I asked Rick, the aquatic entomologist.

"Don't know," he answered. "But whatever it is, it seems to be clear back under the banks."

Rick laid aside his rod, picked up his ever-present long-handled insect net, and swept it under the bank from which he'd been fishing, swishing it among the exposed marsh roots. The net came up hopping with tiny olive insects. They were a quarter to three-eighths inch long. Their shape was beetlelike, with hard shellbacks and long swimming legs. The kicking of these legs, attempts to swim, caused them to hop up and down in the net.

"What are they?" I asked.

"Water boatmen," Rick told me. "There must be thousands of them feeding among the roots." He plucked a few out of the net and dropped them into the water. They immediately darted downward with brisk disapproving kicks of their oarlike hind legs, and disappeared back under the bank at our feet.

The closest dressings we had to them were fat-bodied Zug Bugs, tied with peacock herl bodies. We pinched the tails and wing cases off these and cast them ahead of the schools of fish that came nosing down the shoreline. As the salmon approached, we gave the flies quick little darts, imparted by twitching the rod tip. Those difficult fish were suddenly foolishly easy, scooting out of their pods to accept the flies with the same quick turning takes with which we had seen them gun down the naturals.

That night, we tied more realistic imitations, setting up our tying kits on a picnic table and tying in the light of a lantern. The next day, these dressings fished just as well as, but not much better than, the abbreviated Zug Bugs.

Correct presentation, rather than exact imitation, turned out to be the key to inducing takes.

Natural

The life cycle of the water boatman gives it a special time of importance to the angler. It's available in its greatest numbers and largest sizes in fall and winter, when other insects have emerged and regressed to their earliest and smallest instars.

Water boatmen undergo incomplete metamorphosis but do not emerge from aquatic nymphs into aerial adults as other insects do.

They grow through five instars after quitting the egg in spring. Each instar is slightly larger than the one preceding it; each has wings that are slightly more mature. There is no clear line between nymph and adult stages, in terms of appearance. In the last instar, the insect's wings are developed fully, and it is capable of flight. But it rarely leaves the water, except for spring dispersal flights, unless urged by diminishing habitat. When a lake or pond dries up, its water boatmen take to the air and find a new place to live. By the time that happens, trout fishing has also dried up and blown away.

Water boatmen overwinter as adults, which means they attain full size in fall. Trout turn to them then because most other aquatic insects are not as abundant, not as available, and not as large. Throughout summer, they might be taken just as frequently, but more seldom selectively, in part because hatches of other insects overshadow them. In fall and early winter, water boatmen are often the biggest and best bite around. Trout learn to focus on them.

Mature water boatmen remain active all winter in some waters, even swimming around under ice, if pockets of air are trapped under it, where they can get oxygen. In other waters they might hibernate, burrowing into the silt of the bottom to await the warmer water of spring.

At mating time, in spring, a certain percentage of the adults get restless and fly off to colonize new waters. The greatest abundance remain where they are, mating, laying their eggs, and dying in the same waters in which they lived their little lives. It's rare, but you'll sometimes see them flying into the water, hitting the surface like big drops of rain. Trout will feed on them out in open water when that happens, away from the banks and from submerged vegetation. Most of the time, trout feed on water boatmen in shallow water, and very often in relation to undercut banks.

A water boatman has scooplike forelegs with which it winnows through the vegetation or along the bottom, shoveling into its mouth a salad of whatever comes along, including midge larvae and other small organisms. It takes its oxygen from the surface in the form of a bubble trapped under its wings and along the body. It replaces this bubble at frequent intervals, swimming to the surface to do so. As a result of this need for surface air, water boatmen are seldom found more than three to four feet deep. Their imitations are important only in shallow water.

Water boatmen legs are specialized: the front pair for scooping food, the middle pair for holding on to vegetation, the hind pair for swimming. You can see the bright bubble of air held along the body for respiration.

Though primarily stillwater insects, water boatmen also inhabit streams wherever the water pools nearly to stillness and vegetation takes root. You can see them scuttling along ahead of your wadered feet in the shallows of almost any stream. They can be thick in backwater weed beds off to the edges of freestone streams. But in moving waters they're most important in spring creeks and tailwaters, where vegetation is able to take root because of stabilized flows.

The main features separating water boatmen from less important aquatic beetles, which have similar shellback wings, are their scooplike forelegs. Water boatmen also have beaklike mouthparts used for probing plant stems and sucking out juices. Beetles lack these. The folds of water boatman wings form a distinct X in the center of the back, which also separates them from aquatic beetles, whose wings meet in a line down the center of the back.

Imitation

Water boatmen vary in size from a quarter to a half inch long. Their imitations should be tied on hooks with 1X long shanks in sizes, 12, 14, and 16, a narrow size range that is easy to encompass with just a few simple ties.

The color range, as with so many aquatic insects, is the same as that of the bottom types and vegetation on which they live. Predominant colors are dark brown and dark mottled olive on the back, distinctly lighter tan or green on the underside. A couple colors of imitations will be adequate to match most of them. The first would have a light olive body and a dark olive shellback, the other a tan body and a dark brown shellback.

The best imitation style is the simple Water Boatman. A turkey quill segment is tied in at the rear of the hook. The body is dubbed of fur, with two pheasant center tail fibers sticking out in the center to represent the swimming legs of the natural. The turkey shellback is pulled over the back to represent the hard wings of the natural.

The body can also be tied of peacock herl, which will be close to the colors of many of the naturals. Peacock has some undefined natural attraction to trout, so such a tie should be the one you carry until you run into specific water boatmen of a different color and feel the need to imitate them.

WATER BOATMAN

Water Boatman

Hook	1X long, sizes 12–16.
Thread	Brown or olive.
Weight	4 to 6 turns lead wire, optional.
Shellback	Brown or dark olive.
Oar legs	Pheasant tail fibers.
Body	Peacock herl, or tan or green dubbing.

The shellback is tied on first.

The body is wound to the center, where the oar legs are tied in across the shank. Then the rest of the body is wrapped, and the shellback pulled over and tied down. I prefer to weight the fly with a few turns of lead wire so it sinks through the surface film quickly, then settles slowly to the level of cruising trout. You can pinch the legs in the center to put a backward bend in them, making them look more natural, but it's far from necessary.

Presentation
Presentation of water boatman imitations is based on the darting swimming of the naturals. You'll usually want to rig with a floating line and ten- to twelve-foot leader, though there will be times when you want to get down three to four feet fairly quickly, and you should then rig with a wet-tip line and a bit shorter leader. The fly should be cast out and allowed to sink at least a few inches. Then it should be retrieved with a staccato twitching of the rod tip, in tiny one-inch jerks, while the line is retrieved very slowly. Occasional pauses will make the retrieve appear more natural.

If you are fishing to visible trout, be sure to cast the fly well ahead of them, in the direction of travel. Try to time it so the fly and the fish arrive at the same place and same depth at the same time. If the trout does not turn aside to take the dropping fly, a few twitches of the rod tip should be imparted to attract attention.

A word of warning: Trout taking water boatmen in clear water can be maddeningly leader-shy. I have seen them swim up to within an inch of an imitation, then turn away. No retrieve or lack of it would change their minds. The only solution was to go down in tippet size until they got interested again.

BACKSWIMMERS
Backswimmers are close relatives to water boatmen, a different aquatic family in the same order of insects. They share many common habits and much common habitat. Like water boatmen, backswimmers are dwellers of lakes and ponds. There are likely to be exceptions, but I have not collected backswimmers from moving water, nor have I read accounts by those who have. But they dart around in just about all stillwaters.

Backswimmers have the same life cycle as water boatmen: They hatch from the egg in spring, grow through five instars during summer and fall, reach maturity in autumn, and overwinter as

Backswimmers spend time hanging in the surface film, waiting for luckless prey to come near enough to attack. Note that the front legs are raptorial, rather than scooplike as on water boatmen.

adults. Mating takes place the following spring. Dispersal flights are common, but the majority of backswimmers deposit their eggs in the same water where they swam away from the egg the previous spring.

Respiration is from surface air. The backswimmer obtains a bubble, takes it underwater, and uses the oxygen out of it. The insect must return to the top to refresh the bubble, though diffusion of oxygen into the bubble, out of the water, lets them stay down longer than the oxygen in the bubble itself would permit. Because of their dependence on surface air, backswimmers are seldom found more than three to four feet deep.

Backswimmers differ from water boatmen in their diet. Rather than winnowing a salad that includes an occasional bit of living protein, they are predators. Their manner of execution is unique. They have beaklike mouthparts like water boatmen, but theirs are used to inject enzymes into luckless prey. The enzymes break down the inner tissue of tadpoles, fish fry, or other insects. The resulting fluid is then sucked up like soda through a straw. All that is left of a backswimmer victim is an empty skin.

Backswimmers hang at the surface, waiting to dart down and attack anything that passes their way. If what passes their way is a feeding trout, they will dart down to escape it with swift swimming strokes. Trout know this and take backswimmers with strong takes that are almost unmistakable when they happen on a stillwater in fall or early spring.

Two characteristics make backswimmers easy to separate from water boatmen. First, they have sharp raptorial claws rather than broad winnowing scoops on their front legs. Second, when swimming, they travel upside down on their backs—thus the name *backswimmer*.

The size range of these topsy-turvy characters is slightly larger than that of water boatmen, on which they often prey. They run from a quarter to about five-eighths inch long. Their imitations should be tied on 1X long size 10, 12, and 14 hooks, with size 12 the most useful.

Their color range is identical to the water boatman's, with one notable exception: one of the most common species, aptly called the pale moon-winged backswimmer. It has translucent white wings and a dark underside, no doubt camouflage against trout when it hangs in the surface and trout must spot it from below, against the sky.

The most effective imitation style for backswimmers is exactly the same as that for water boatmen. I would be arrogant if I gave you a paper pattern and tried to convince you that trout can tell the difference. The same patterns for the two related insect families, tied in almost the same sizes, will work fine. The common color range is even the same, with the addition of the whitish moon-winged backswimmer.

If you desire to imitate the pale species of the insect, I recommend the Prince Nymph. It is far from exact, but it does have white biot wings, and I believe these represent, to trout, the white color of the natural backswimmer. If that's not true, it's at least true that I've had fine luck with a Prince Nymph whenever I've noticed white backswimmers working the water.

PRINCE NYMPH

Prince Nymph

Hook	Standard nymph, sizes 10–14.
Weight	8 to 12 turns lead wire, diameter of the hook shank.
Thread	Black.
Tails	Brown turkey biots, forked.
Rib	Oval gold tinsel.
Body	Peacock herl.
Hackle	Brown hen, undersize, trimmed from top.
Wings	White goose biots.

I've seen backswimmers hunting, stroking through the shallows of mountain ponds as aggressively as feeding trout, and almost as fast. I've also seen trout cruising the same waters, chasing them down. The fish move swiftly and strike hard. Whenever I've noticed such behavior, I've been able to take advantage of it by fishing a size 12 Prince Nymph on a wet-tip line and a fast stripping retrieve.

If the water is clear, it's fun to watch trout attack and pounce on it.

Chapter 10

Alderflies and Hellgrammites

ALDERFLIES

Occasional fish fed back among the bleached deadfalls that rimmed the forested lakeshore. Their rises were sporadic and clearly subsurface. I could not tell what they were taking, but I assumed it was some sort of nymph intercepted as it approached the surface. I cast various mayfly and caddisfly dressings to pockets in the tangles of logs, but nothing came to my flies.

I finally got down on my hands and knees on a large floating log and snooped along like an Airedale. I peered into the water, expecting to find the solution there. But I didn't see a thing.

Suddenly a large, black insect flew in a heavy descending arc and crash landed on the log in front of my nose. I almost barked at it. The insect gathered itself together and scuttled off to a shady and moist crevice near the log's waterline. Another descended but missed the log, plopping instead to the water beside it. This one struggled a second, but its efforts merely succeeded in tearing a hole in the surface film, through which it slowly sank, still struggling. It was about three inches under when a trout speared out, took it, and turned back beneath the log. The boil of the rise burst to the surface after the trout had already turned down.

Who would have thought to look up into the air when the rises were subsurface? Not me. But after seeing that insect and that trout, I knew enough to look up. The sun was bright. It caught and lit an occasional dark, descending form. Insects fell in awkward arcs out of nearby alder trees. Some landed safely on the logs. Others toppled to the surface, sank, and were taken quickly by boiling trout.

The insects were alderflies, dark caddis look-alikes with tent-shaped wings and short, stout bodies. I tied a wet Alder dressing to my tippet, and cast it where a natural had disappeared not far from a nearby floating log. I gave it a few seconds to sink. Then I began a slow, twitching retrieve. A trout speared out, took, and turned down. I waited until the boil broke on the surface, then I pulled the hook home. The trout shot up out of the water on the far side of the log, fought leapingly, and broke me off quickly.

Throughout the afternoon, I hooked a dozen more trout back among the deadfalls, but only landed three of the smallest of them. They were twelve to fourteen inches long. One I lost looked like it would have weighed three pounds.

Natural

Alderflies have been important to anglers since the historical high point of wet-fly fishing in the mid-1800s in Britain. The first dressings tied for them were wets. No doubt dry flies were tied and fished for them during the following decades of dry-fly purism,

Alderfly adults are shaped like caddisflies but have parchmentlike wings that lack the hairs of caddis wings.

likely with a disappointing lack of success, evidenced by the absence of dry alderfly dressings surviving the period. The most effective dressing to this day, now that the alderfly is better understood, is a holdover wet fly from prepurist history.

The importance of the alderfly is still diminished by misunderstanding. Most of the time, it's mistaken for a caddisfly. There would be nothing wrong with that, because they're shaped the same, and therefore the same flies should work for it. But its greater specific gravity—adult alderflies are much heavier than adult caddis—changes the way you must tie and fish its imitations.

Alderflies undergo complete metamorphosis. Their larvae live in lakes, ponds, and sluggish, leaf-packed eddies and backwaters of streams. Their favorite habitat is a silty mat of decomposing leaves, right on the bottom. They are fiercely predaceous, hunting through these leaf packs, killing and eating whatever fails to kill and eat them.

This habit of hunting beneath the surface layer of bottom debris, rather than prowling around on top of it, protects alderfly larvae from predation by trout. Their pupal stage is even less available to fish. The larvae crawl out on land and burrow in the soil or in rotten logs not far from the stillwater or stream. Pupation takes place there, making the pupae less than useful inspirations for imitation.

Alderfly adults emerge from their pupal cocoons in late May, June, or early July. They hang around trees and other vegetation very near the water. Their name comes from their favored habitat. The larvae hunt in fallen packs of alder leaves; the adults hang out on the limbs and leaves of overhanging alder trees.

Alderflies are warmth-loving insects. They remain cryptic in the trees until warmed by the sun. Then their motors rev up, and they begin to fly and crawl around at random. But their randomness always takes them back toward shore, into vegetation overhanging the water, or out on the trunks and branches of floating deadfalls.

Alderfly adults attach their eggs in neat rows to leaves, limbs, or logs above the water. When the larvae hatch from the eggs, they drop to the water and at once take up their hunting lifestyle. This avoidance of water, on the part of adults, would save them from trout if they weren't such awkward fliers. If water gets in the way of where they are going, on their clumsy flights, they land on it as surely as if it were land. Then, because of their high density, they

Rivers flowing through deciduous forests, such as this gentle tailwater in Tennessee, have fishable populations of alderflies. They're more often important in lakes and ponds.

abruptly sink. That's why dry flies don't fool many fish when adult alderflies are on the wing.

Those that survive egg laying continue to bat about on the wing when the air is warm. If they aren't eaten by birds or trout, they die in a few days. The eggs hatch after a week or so, and the larvae drop to the water, where they immediately look for leaf packs and begin hunting for tiny prey organisms, including midge larvae, scuds, mayfly nymphs, and each other.

Alderflies are distributed throughout the United States and Canada, but the greatest and most important populations are found in the East, where leafed deciduous trees dominate over needled conifers. The prime season is the earliest warm months: May, June, and July. But a few eager specimens might be out on warm April days, and a few tail-enders can still be collected in September.

In the alderfly life cycle, the only important stage to the angler is the adult. Alderflies are most important, in my experience, on tree-lined lakes and ponds. But their numbers can be dramatic in streams that are shrouded by alders and other leaf-dropping trees. Often, when a streamside tree is given a brisk shake, a dark cloud of them will fly out and mill around. When this happens, if they are not examined closely, they will almost invariably be mistaken for caddisflies.

Caddisflies and alderflies both have the same tentlike wings, short bodies, and long antennae. The single key difference is the smooth, parchmentlike wings of the alder as opposed to the hairy wings of the caddis.

The size and color ranges of alderfly adults are both narrow. They vary from three-eighths to five-eighths inch in body length. Flies tied on hook sizes 10, 12, and 14 will imitate most common American hatches, though I've fished over them in size 16 on streams in Tennessee. Colors are dark smoky gray to black.

Imitation

One dark dressing covers all the alders you will ever encounter. The dressing is the same wet Alder I tied on when alderflies began dropping into the water around the log on the lake. It is nearly the same dressing used by early British wet-fly anglers one and a half centuries ago. The body is peacock herl, counterwound with gold wire to keep the fragile herl from breaking and unwinding. The hackle is black hen, tied sparse. The wing is dark turkey quill sections, tied wet, sweeping over the back of the fly. It's a very simple but very effective dressing for the sunk alderfly adult, in both still-waters and streams.

ALDER

Alder

Hook	Standard length, sizes 10–16.
Thread	Black.
Rib	Gold wire.
Body	Peacock herl.
Hackle	Black hen.
Wing	Dark turkey quill.

Presentation

The alderfly characteristic of sinking almost immediately on contact with water makes the wet fly a more effective dressing than a dry. Presentation is based on the struggling of the natural, which results in little forward motion. In lakes, the fly should be fished on a long leader and a floating line. After sinking a few inches, it should be retrieved back with short twitches of the rod tip. The retrieve should be slow, with frequent pauses to let the fly merely settle.

You should of course cover fish when they rise visibly, hitting the rise right on the nose, or casting beyond it to bring the fly back through the same area. If no trout are rising visibly, an Alder Wet can still be an effective searching pattern if any adults are out. Cast in the arc of shoreline near tree-lined banks. Allow the fly to sink a foot or more. Retrieve it along logs, over tangles of submerged limbs, and in the difficult pockets among rafts of blowdowns. You might hook and lose more trout than you hook and land, but you'll get lots of action.

HELLGRAMMITES

Hellgrammites are the larval stage of dobsonflies, a bit of naming confusion we are lucky does not happen often among the aquatic insect groups. Imagine the confusion if every family of insects had a separate name for the larval and adult stages. Perhaps it serves us well in this particular case, as the hellgrammite is at least marginally important to anglers, whereas the dobsonfly is rarely worth noting.

The life cycle of the dobsonfly is similar to that of the related alderfly. It begins with a row of eggs attached to a leaf, limb, or bridge timber overhanging water, though a stream, not a stillwater. The larvae quit the egg, drop to the water, and immediately begin hunting for prey. Their heaviest populations occur where they can burrow far into the bottom gravel beneath the streambed, prowling and probing for smaller insects. This habit keeps them pretty much buried, out of the way of trout, for most of their three-year larval life. They are largely nocturnal, another factor that reduces their importance.

Hellgrammites can grow to a length of three inches as they near maturity. This large size gives them what importance they possess. Anything that big will be taken eagerly by trout whenever chances arise. Dressings imitating hellgrammites make excellent searching patterns.

Pupation takes place out of the stream, in nearby soil or decaying wood. The adult dobsonfly emerges and is a great bird of a beast, with a four- to six-inch wingspan. But it's very retiring, flying only a little, and only toward evening. It usually lives just two to three days. And it deposits its eggs on objects overhanging the stream. All of these factors combine to make the importance of dobsonflies a rarity.

Hellgrammites are most important in the Midwest, followed by the East Coast and the West Coast. They are absent or rare in the Rocky Mountain and Great Basin states. They emerge primarily in May, June, and July. But second-year-class larvae are in the stream the year round. So the season of importance could be considered to be the entire angling season, whenever a searching nymph seems to be indicated.

The larvae are characterized by lateral gill filaments projecting from the sides of the abdominal segments, posterior hooks on the last segment, and large biting mandibles on the head, which you had better keep out of reach of your fingers. They're aggressive, and they will bite you.

Hellgrammites are stout bodied, usually dark brown or black, and have lateral gill projections to the sides of the abdominal segments.

Those lateral gills point precisely to imitation with Woolly Worms. Indeed, trout rarely feed selectively on hellgrammites, so a size 4 or 6 Black Woolly Worm, tied on a 4X long hook, heavily weighted, is likely all you will ever need for them. Imitative dressings are often tied for them, but it is doubtful that a trout that snubs a Woolly Worm will then turn around and take a more exact hellgrammite imitation. If trout feed on the bottom, where hellgrammites live, they seldom will be feeding selectively on hellgrammites and passing up everything else.

BLACK WOOLLY WORM

Black Woolly Worm

Hook	3X to 4X long, sizes 4–6.
Weight	15 to 20 turns lead wire the diameter of hook shank.
Thread	Black.
Tail	Red wool yarn, short.
Body	Black chenille.
Hackle	Grizzly, palmered over body.

In truth, a salmon fly imitation such as the Montana Stone (see chapter 6) will fish for hellgrammites. Anglers from the East or Midwest, visiting the West, often hoist big salmon fly nymphs out of the water and declare them hellgrammites. It's not a major mistake. The same imitation will fish for either, and the presentation will be the same as well.

Presentation, based on the behavior of the natural, calls for getting the fly down to the bottom and tumbling it along helplessly there. Hellgrammites have been observed to swim, but it is a feeble attempt. Most of the time, they crawl, moving equally well forward and backward. When dislodged from their rocky habitat, they are simply tumbled by the current.

Your imitation should be fished the same way. Use a floating line, and rig with the indicator and shot method, the same as described for caddis larvae and salmon fly nymphs.

Conclusion

We sat in the grass next to the Henrys Fork of the Snake River, in Idaho, wadered up and waiting for something to happen. It was already well after noon, nothing had hatched yet, and we were past expecting anything to start. It was early June. We had just arrived, driving over from Oregon to fish the green drake hatch. The famous Harriman Ranch stretch of the river, the green drake water downstream from where we sat in the grass idly absorbing the sun, didn't open to fishing until the next day. The river was open where we were, but we were content to wait for the better-known stretch to open. Sitting there with good friends seemed a good enough thing to be doing, so long as no trout were seen to be rising.

Richard Bunse, as usual, spotted the rises first. He is the best dry-fly fisherman I have ever watched drop a fly over rising trout. His eyes are honed to following the drift of a dry and to spotting its subtle disappearance. He can spot rising trout where the average angler would never suspect them. Bunse picked up his rod and waded into the broad but shallow river, headed out toward the rises that only he could see. Rick Hafele, Jim Schollmeyer, and I all stood up and plopped in after him, like a flock of ducklings splashing after a mallard hen.

When we got halfway across the river, the rest of us began to spot the working fish. They came up in a long strip of water that was roughened on the surface where the current reflected boulders on the bottom below. We watched the water for a bit. Soon we began spotting scattered mayfly duns boating the bouncing water. Bunse collected a specimen, and we gathered into a tight circle, butting heads trying to get a better look at the insect at rest in Bunse's palm.

"It's a march brown!" Rick said.

"What's a march brown doing over here?" Jim asked.

"What's a march brown doing hatching in June?" I asked.

"I don't know any of that," Rick answered. "But that's what it is."

We had already fished the march brown hatch in March, in Oregon, when and where it was supposed to happen. All that great early-spring fishing was three months and a thousand miles behind us. We'd all left our march brown boxes at home. All but Bunse.

"What are we going to match the damned thing with?" I asked nobody. Nobody answered. Nobody but Bunse.

Bunse muttered, "A march brown," and waded away. He tied on a fly and soon began happily catching trout. The rest of us paddled off in different directions, but we weren't soon happily catching anything.

One at a time, we drifted surreptitiously back toward Bunse. He is an excellent tier and generous with his flies. Soon we were all strung out downstream from him, fishing that line of rumpled water, all catching fish and quacking to each other in excitement about how good we were.

The dressing Bunse sprinkled around so generously was a size 12 Compara-dun, tied with split tails, a slender brown body, and a tan wing of flared deer hair. It was the kind of pattern that, tied in the right set of sizes and colors, takes trout during mayfly hatches from coast to coast, without regard to the species of the insects.

By thinking *insect shape, pattern style,* and *repeated color themes,* Bunse was able to carry a single box of mayfly dressings that worked wherever he went, from his home waters in Oregon to the Henrys Fork of the Snake in Idaho to New Zealand, where he later fished a hatch of similar insects with the same flies. Because the flies in that box matched mayflies everywhere, he never made the mistake of leaving it at home.

If you think the way Bunse did, you can tie a set of flies that, like his, will take trout no matter where you live, and no matter where you might fish.

Glossary

Abdominal segments. The segments of the insect between its thorax, which carries the legs and wings, and the tails.

Burrowers. Mayfly nymphs that burrow into bottom silts.

Catskill dry. A style of dry fly tied to imitate mayfly duns. Also called *traditional drys*.

Caudal gills. The leaflike tail gills of damselfly nymphs.

Clingers. Mayfly nymphs that live in fast water and cling tightly to stones.

Compara-dun. A style of dry fly tied to imitate mayfly duns.

Compara-spinner. A style of dry fly tied to imitate mayfly spinners.

Complete metamorphosis. An insect life cycle with all three life stages: larva, pupa, and adult.

Crawlers. Mayfly nymphs whose prime means of movement is crawling along the bottom.

Guard hairs. The long hairs in furs, used as tails in certain fly dressings.

Halteres. Knobbed stalks, in place of the second set of wings, on cranefly, midge, and mosquito adults. They are used by the insects as miniature gyroscopes, for stability in flight.

Imitative. A fly pattern that is an exact imitation of a specific insect.

Impressionistic. A fly pattern that represents the impression of an insect rather than an exact imitation of it.

Incomplete metamorphosis. An insect life cycle that does not have an intermediate pupal stage between the nymph and adult.

Instar. The period of growth between the shedding of nymphal or larval skins.

Larva. The immature form of an insect that undergoes complete metamorphosis.

Nymph. The immature form of an insect that undergoes incomplete metamorphosis.

Pupa. Transitional stage between larva and adult in an insect that undergoes complete metamorphosis.

Scuds. Crustaceans, sometimes called freshwater shrimp.

Soft-hackled fly. A style of wingless wet fly tied with hackle from a feather that is soft and that works well in the water.

Swimmers. Mayfly nymphs whose prime movement is by swimming.

Thorax. The segments between the head and abdomen of an insect.

Tracheal system. Respiratory system of tubes that transport oxygen directly to individual cells of an insect.

Wing cases. The small cases on the back of the nymphal insect or sides of the pupal insect stage holding the forming wings; the parts of an artificial fly that represent the wing cases of the natural insect.

Bibliography

Arbona, Fred L., Jr. *Mayflies, the Angler and the Trout*. Tulsa, OK: Winchester Press, 1980.

Atherton, John. *The Fly and the Fish*. New York: Macmillan, 1951.

Caucci, Al, and Bob Nastasi. *Hatches*. New York: Comparahatch Press, 1975.

Cordes, Ron, and Randall Kaufmann. *Lake Fishing with a Fly*. Portland, OR: Frank Amato, 1984.

Hafele, Rick, and Dave Hughes. *The Complete Book of Western Hatches*. Portland, OR: Frank Amato, 1981.

———. *Western Mayfly Hatches*. Portland, OR: Frank Amato, 2004.

Hellekson, Terry. *Popular Fly Patterns*. Salt Lake City: Peregrine Smith, 1977.

Hughes, Dave. *American Fly Tying Manual*. Portland, OR: Frank Amato, 1986.

———. *Essential Trout Flies*. Mechanicsburg, PA: Stackpole Books, 2000.

———. *Fly Fishing Basics*. Mechanicsburg, PA: Stackpole Books, 1994.

———. *Strategies for Stillwater*. Harrisburg, PA: Stackpole Books, 1991.

———. *Trout Flies*. Mechanicsburg, PA: Stackpole Books, 1999.

———. *Wet Flies*. Mechanicsburg, PA: Stackpole Books, 1995.

Jorgensen, Poul. *Modern Fly Dressings for the Practical Angler*. New York: Winchester Press, 1976.

Kaufmann, Randall. *American Nymph Fly Tying Manual*. Portland, OR: Frank Amato, 1975.

LaFontaine, Gary. *Caddisflies*. New York: Winchester Press/Nick Lyons Books, 1981.

Leiser, Eric, and Robert H. Boyle. *Stoneflies for the Angler*. New York: Alfred A. Knopf, 1982.

Merritt, R. W., and D. W. Cummins. *An Introduction to the Aquatic Insects of North America*. 3rd ed. Dubuque, IA: Kendall/Hunt, 1996.

Nemes, Sylvester. *The Soft-Hackled Fly*. Harrisburg, PA: Stackpole Books, 1975.

———. *The Soft-Hackled Fly Addict*. Harrisburg, PA: Stackpole Books, 1993.

———. *Soft-Hackled Fly Imitations*. Bozeman, MT: Self-published, 1991.

Richards, Carl, Doug Swisher, and Fred Arbona, Jr. *Stoneflies*. New York: Winchester Press/Nick Lyons Books, 1980.

Rosborough, E. H. *Tying and Fishing the Fuzzy Nymphs*. Harrisburg, PA: Stackpole Books, 1978.

Schwiebert, Ernest. *Matching the Hatch*. New York: Macmillan, 1955.

———. *Nymphs*. New York: Winchester Press, 1973.

Solomon, Larry, and Eric Leiser. *The Caddis and the Angler*. Harrisburg, PA: Stackpole Books, 1977.

Swisher, Doug, and Carl Richards. *Fly Fishing Strategy*. New York: Crown, 1975.

———. *Selective Trout*. New York: Crown, 1971.

Usinger, Robert L., et al. *Aquatic Insects of California*. Berkeley: University of California Press, 1956.

Wright, Leonard M., Jr. *Fishing the Dry Fly as a Living Insect*. New York: E. P. Dutton, 1972.

Index

Page numbers in italics indicate illustrations.